What Do We Do Now?

A Practical Guide to Estate Administration for Widows, Widowers and Heirs

Robert E. Kass, JD, LLM
Robert H. Downie, MBA

Carob Tree Press
Detroit

Permissions Department
Carob Tree Press, LLC
211 West Fort Street, Suite 1500
Detroit, Michigan 48226-3281
Telephone: 1-877-537-4178 (toll-free)
Fax: 313-983-3325
E-mail: inquiries@carobtreepress.com

This book is available at special quantity discounts when purchased in bulk by corporations, organizations, or groups. For more information, please contact the publisher at the above address or see our Web site, www.carobtreepress.com.

Printed in the United States of America

ISBN 0-9704862-0-0

What People Are Saying
About This Book

"This will be the first reference book I reach for
when I counsel my clients on estate matters!
Amazingly comprehensive, yet easy to read and understand...
The authors have drawn upon decades of experience in
handling estates to cover everything you need to know during
life which will affect your estate, and literally everything your family
and Personal Representative will need to know at and after your death...
An outstanding work by two professionals who are the best in their field."

—**S. Sam Tootalian**, *CPA, Managing Partner*
Purdy, Donovan & Beal, Certified Public Accountants

"This book makes the task of settling an estate less daunting for the layman.
I especially liked the fact that the authors dealt with the real life issues that
come up, specifically how to keep peace in the family! Too often, despite the
best intentions of the deceased, adult children re-enact childhood
scenarios, thereby creating more sadness for all involved."

—**Pola Friedman**, *CFRE, Senior Development Officer*
Hospice of Michigan

"This book is as good as it gets! A thorough yet concise and sensitive
treatment of a difficult subject which will be an invaluable
companion to any family at a most trying time."

—**Lesley Geary**, *Senior Producer*
CNN Television

"An excellent resource for those who have to navigate the labyrinth of
estate administration...sensitive to the emotional concerns of the survivors,
yet practical enough that complicated issues are easily understood by the layperson.
Especially useful are the checklists, the comprehensive Appendix (including
many related Internet sites), as well as the combined expertise of the
authors as they guide you through the system."

——**Howard J. Mankoff**, *CLU, Financial Representative*
Northwestern Mutual Financial Network

Warning and Disclaimer

This book is intended to provide general information regarding the probate, tax, and other laws applicable to administration of a decedent's estate, and to provide suggestions regarding appropriate action which might be taken in various situations. It is not intended as a substitute for legal, tax, accounting, financial, or other professional advice, and you must therefore not consider this book as your professional advisor in book form.

While every effort has been made to provide accurate, comprehensive, current information on the subject matter, we cannot predict the ways in which the laws will change—and they will change—and court decisions, regulations, and administrative rulings will also be issued which may change the outcome in a particular case. In addition, the facts of a particular situation are crucial to the outcome, and the conclusions described in this book might be different with even slight variations of the facts. Please carefully read the preface, "About this Book," for further discussion of these issues.

The estate which you are handling may be very simple, and you may be able to handle it on your own. However, by reading this book you may become aware of areas which challenge your personal skills, and you will acquire the background to know when to call for help, and what kinds of professionals are available to serve on your team.

Neither the authors, nor the law firm with which they are affiliated, nor the publisher shall have any liability or responsibility to any person or entity with respect to any loss or damage caused, or alleged to be caused, directly or indirectly by the information contained in this book.

If you do not wish to be bound by the above, you may return this book, together with your original receipt, to the publisher for a full refund.

About the Authors

ROBERT E. KASS is a tax attorney whose practice is heavily concentrated in the areas of estate planning and administration. An honors graduate of the University of Michigan Law School, he is a recipient of a Fulbright-Swiss University Fellowship to the Graduate Institute of International Studies in Geneva, Switzerland, and earned his Master's Degree in Taxation from New York University. Bob is a member of the Detroit law firm of Barris, Sott, Denn & Driker, PLLC, where he serves as Chairman of the Tax, Estate Planning and Probate Group.

His practice is also heavily involved in charitable and planned giving techniques. He is an active advisor and member of the Planned Giving Professional Advisory Committees of the Jewish Federation of Metropolitan Detroit, Goodwill Industries Foundation, the Michigan Opera Theatre, and Gleaners Community Food Bank. He is also a member of the Legal and Professional Advisory Committee of the Community Foundation for Southeastern Michigan.

A frequent and lively speaker on tax topics, Bob has delivered lectures for the Michigan Association of Certified Public Accountants and the Institute for Continuing Legal Education, and to numerous civic, professional, and religious groups on subjects related to estate planning and wealth preservation. He is also a national speaker and contributing columnist for Women's American ORT, and has appeared on the CNN and CNN/Financial Television networks.

ROBERT H. DOWNIE is the Estate Administrator of the law firm of Barris, Sott, Denn & Driker. In that role he is responsible for all aspects of estate administration, including preparation of estate tax returns, post-death tax planning and analysis, trust funding, and development of income and estate tax saving strategies.

He previously served as a Vice President in the Trust Tax Department of NBD Bank, handling the tax administration of more than 200 decedents' estates and trusts. He has taught Federal Estate and Gift Tax in the Master of Science in Taxation program at Wayne State University in Detroit, and is on the faculty of the Midwest Trust School.

He holds a BA from the University of Michigan and an MBA from Michigan State University. He has also been designated an Enrolled Agent by the Internal Revenue Service and has been admitted to practice before the IRS.

Dedication

To my wife, Sonja, whose support for this project and over the years, in general, is worthy of a Medal of Valor.

To Jeremie, who at age ten insisted that I buy a computer and has kept me one step ahead in the technology game ever since.

To Alissia, whose infinite patience with my skill level and long distance help have been life savers.

To Adena, whose tolerance, understanding and good humor in the midst of it all have helped us make it to the end.

To my Dad, whose weekend rhetorical question during my teen years, "What are you going to do, sleep your life away?" has enabled me to keep plodding, day or night.

And to my Mom, whose family orientation has inspired me to write this book for all families.

Bob

To my parents, whose love for each other and for their family continues to light my way; and to my aunt and uncle, who first piqued my interest in trusts and estates.

Rob

Acknowledgments

A pamphlet becomes a book, and a book becomes a tome. So it is when you want to share your experiences with others. It would not have been possible without close collaboration with my co-author, Robert H. Downie, a consummate professional, dedicated to the task in every way.

Thanks also to Judy Meshefski, Elizabeth Carrie, Annette Welsh, and Timothy Batdorf, part of our Estate Planning and Administration Team at Barris, Sott, Denn & Driker, PLLC, who assisted in so many ways, including tending to other matters while this book worked its way through the final stages.

I also wish to express my thanks to my fellow members at BSD&D, for their continued support of our estate planning and administration practice over the years. It is truly a pleasure to work with people who believe that there is only one way—the right way. Particular thanks to Donald E. Barris, Herbert Sott, David Denn, and Eugene Driker, with whom I have worked closely on numerous estates, large and small, over the past two decades. Their wisdom, creativity, and enthusiasm for the practice of the law have been contagious.

I would also like to express my gratitude to S. Sam Tootalian, of Purdy, Donovan & Beal, Certified Public Accountants, who has provided constant encouragement and advice over the years. His insights have included not only invaluable substantive input on estates, but also on the importance of clear communication of the legal and tax complexities, undoubtedly reflected in the style of this book, including the checklists.

Thanks also go to those who encouraged the preparation of this work: Judge Ira G. Kaufman, former Chief Judge of the Wayne County Probate Court; Doreen Dziepak Benson, retired Public Affairs Specialist of the Social Security Administration; Herbert Kaufman, Funeral Director, Ira Kaufman Chapel, Inc.; Pola Friedman, Development Officer of Hospice of Michigan; Lesley Geary, Senior Producer at CNN Television; and Howard J. Mankoff, CLU, Financial Representative, Northwestern Mutual Financial Network. All of these people took the time to review the draft and offer comments and encouragement, for which I am most appreciative. The responsibility for any errors obviously remains with the authors.

Finally, a word of thanks to the many clients who have entrusted their family's estate planning and administration to our firm, who have permitted us to learn from their experiences, and who have allowed us to share those lessons with the public at large.

R.E.K.

Acknowledgments

I wish to express my gratitude to the members of Barris, Sott, Denn & Driker, PLLC, particularly Robert E. Kass, my co-author, for their ongoing support and encouragement.

It has been my good fortune to have several mentors in my professional career. Thomas W. Clarke became a second father to me during my years at Flint Ink Corporation. Walter V. Marsh, Robert C. Goodwin, and Lyle F. Dahlberg guided me throughout my tenure at NBD Bank and taught me much of what I know about trusts and estates. Robert B. Joslyn, a friend and nationally known estate planning attorney, has provided me with sound advice and wise counsel over the past many years. To all of these individuals, I give my thanks.

Much of estate administration revolves around the Federal Estate Tax return and the audit of the return by the Government. I have had many dealings with the Estate and Gift Tax Group of the Internal Revenue Service, both in the Detroit office and in the Cincinnati Service Center. All of these individuals are true professionals and our relationship has always been one of mutual respect. While I cannot acknowledge all of them by name, I am compelled to mention Albert Sicking, Angelia Reed, and Diane Walker in Cincinnati, and Brian M. Trindell, Jerome B. Sturman, Kenneth M. Grifka, and Norman Benjamin in Detroit.

Special recognition is due to Debbie S. Miller, Co-Director of Midwest Trust School, who took time to review the draft and give me the benefit of her thoughts.

Finally, much credit goes to Nancy A. Downie, my high school sweetheart, my beautiful and loving wife of three decades, and an accomplished estate planning attorney, who graciously shared with me her excellent teaching materials on Generation-Skipping Transfer Tax, and who read the manuscript and provided many helpful comments.

R.H.D.

About Carob Tree Press

A story is told about an old man, in Biblical times, seen planting some seeds.

A young boy was watching him, and asked what he was planting.

"Carob seeds," said the old man. "They will grow into a fine carob tree, which will bear fruit."

"How long will it take for the tree to bear fruit?" asked the boy.

"Seventy years," replied the old man.

"Then why in the world would you want to plant these seeds, since it is clear that you won't live to see the fruit of the tree?"

"When I came onto this Earth there were carob trees," said the old man, "planted by my parents and grandparents. I do this not for myself, but for future generations."

Books published by Carob Tree Press permit the authors to share their knowledge and experience in the areas of estate planning and administration. The authors and publisher also believe that each of us should be charitable, providing financial support to those in need. Therefore, a portion of the net proceeds of sale of Carob Tree Press books is donated to charity.

Carob Tree Icons

To permit the reader to easily identify features and points of particular interest, we have posted the following landmarks along the way:

The Peace Symbol indicates a practical tip to help you keep peace in the family

The Time Symbol indicates time-sensitive action or an important deadline

The Case Study Symbol denotes a case study based either on the authors' experience or court cases

The Internet Resource Symbol indicates a source of further information on the Internet

The Carob Tree Press Symbol reminds you that all Web sites and Internet links referred to in this book may be accessed directly from our Web site: www.carobtreepress.com

"A problem well defined
is a problem half solved."
—Ralph Waldo Emerson

Contents

Preface: About this Book

The material contained in this book is intended as a general guide to issues which must be addressed in settling an estate. It is also intended to provide other valuable information for survivors. It is not intended to be a substitute for a qualified estate planning or probate attorney, a competent accountant, knowledgeable tax or investment counsel, or a trained grief support counselor. While this book will certainly make you more aware of the issues, you should not rely on it in place of professional guidance.

Having this book as a companion can make it easier to understand when and why to seek counsel and support. It should also facilitate dialogue with your professionals, make the process go more smoothly, and help you develop reasonable expectations of what has to be done, by whom, and when. This is probably the first step in avoiding the frustration that often comes with administering an estate.

Why shouldn't you simply rely on the general rules and conclusions contained in this book?

First, general rules may be helpful as a starting point, but they cannot be relied upon for the specific answer in a given situation. Other circumstances may exist which could yield a dramatically different result. An attorney will help uncover the facts and will know their significance.

Second, many aspects of estate administration are subject to local law. Federal law also comes into play in some cases, particularly with regard to the Federal Gift Tax and Estate Tax, but Wills, trusts, and probate are largely governed by the laws of the various states. It would be very difficult if not impossible for any book of this size to address the laws of all fifty states with regard to these topics, and we have not even attempted to do so. For example, some states have community property law, which we have not considered at all in our discussion.

Therefore, where particular state law is relevant we have based our description on the law in effect at the time of this writing in the State of Michigan, where we practice. In some cases we specifically indicate that the conclusion is based on Michigan law, but if the applicable law is not stated then you should assume that Michigan law is the basis for our conclusion.

Also, the law is constantly changing. For example, Michigan probate law was recently totally rewritten, in a comprehensive new statute, the Estates and Protected Individuals Code, or EPIC, which fills a 513-page volume, including reporter's commentary. Court decisions, regulations, and administrative rulings are issued daily, and all of those, together with the applicable statutes, constitute the "law" which will determine the outcome in a particular situation.

The fact that this book has a Michigan focus does not mean that residents of other states will not find this work of interest. Quite the contrary. In many cases an issue will be resolved under another state's law in the same manner as under Michigan law, although you should certainly not assume that it will be. At least you will be sensitive to the issue—such as whether a person must sign his or her own Will or whether someone else can sign it, or whether a "lost" Will can be probated—and you will then have a reason to ask your attorney about the answer in your state.

However, most of this book deals with areas which are not specific to the law of any state, and the checklists, tips, and insights should be helpful to anyone attempting to handle administration of an estate or deal with issues faced by survivors.

Introduction

If you are reading this book, you probably have been named Executor, Personal Representative, or Successor Trustee of the estate of someone who has recently passed away. Or perhaps you are nervously anticipating that painful moment.

Traditional wisdom has it that the person charged with administering a decedent's estate has three duties: Gather all the assets of the deceased; pay the debts, expenses, and taxes, and then distribute whatever is left to the beneficiaries.

If life—and death—were that simple, you would have to read no further.

Unfortunately, even a relatively small estate can involve a fair amount of work to settle. In many cases issues arise which can test the patience of even the most dedicated person who is simply trying to carry out the decedent's wishes.

The purpose of this book is to level the playing field—to give you an even chance to succeed in an area which is probably new to you and which can challenge even the most experienced attorney. We will provide you a detailed road map based on decades of collective experience in planning and administering estates and advising Personal Representatives and Trustees, accountants, bank trust officers, and attorneys who handle estate administration.

Our goal is not to make a lawyer or professional estate administrator out of you. Rather, we believe that nonprofessionals charged with this responsibility must be able to identify the issues in administering an estate. Our main objective is therefore to provide you extensive checklists of issues to consider.

Along the way, we will alert you to the strict time limits for addressing some of these issues. If you fail to act within the time limit—which can be as short as a few days or as long as several months—there can be disastrous consequences.

For example, you could be liable to the IRS for penalties and interest on the decedent's income taxes, or on the estate's income taxes or estate taxes if not paid when due. You could be removed by the Probate Court for failure to fulfill your legal obligations. Or you could be liable to the beneficiaries—yes, even your own family members—for market losses suffered on the estate's stock portfolio.

This book is also for the survivors, those who are left behind to deal with the loss from an emotional point of view. While traditional estate administration focuses on distribution of the property of the decedent, we have started earlier in the process with thoughts concerning preparation for the funeral, whom to notify, how to notify them, and how *not* to notify them. We also touch upon the need for grief support and provide numerous resources for the survivors.

In this new age of the World Wide Web, we are constantly discovering sources of information on the Internet which relate to estate administration, which we also want to share with you. You will be amazed how many Internet resources can lead you to valuable information, shorten your wait, and provide you contact with governmental agencies, organizations, and people who can be of assistance.

To make your life easier, Carob Tree Press will provide links to each of the Web addresses mentioned in this book, so that you can access them from one convenient location:

http://www.carobtreepress.com.

We have posted a reminder icon in the margin each time we have referenced an Internet address.

We will also share insights into other areas of particular interest to those administering an estate:

When should you call for help, whom should you put on your team, how should you locate and select those people, and how should they be compensated?

And how do you keep peace in the family? The expectation of receiving something from an estate not infrequently brings out the worst in people. We cannot counter years of jealousy, sibling rivalries, and greed. However, we can provide you tips on how to anticipate some of the typical problems which arise, how to keep your head and your balance, and how to avoid losing your own assets in a challenge by beneficiaries who allege that you have acted improperly.

To bring the subject full circle, we end with considerations for the financial and estate planning of the survivors. As you work your way through the administration of the estate of the decedent, you will probably realize that your own planning needs some attention. You will appreciate this even more after you have experienced estate administration first hand.

We will point out areas which require your attention sooner rather than later in view of the decedent's passing. If you act wisely you will be able to preserve your inheritance and hopefully increase its value, lighten the burden on those who will one day have to deal with your estate, certainly save them time and avoid frustration, and possibly save taxes and maintain family relations.

Ultimately our goal is to help you through the estate administration process as quickly as possible. You have suffered the loss of a loved one or dear friend. You need closure, not years of work and anxiety. We offer you this guide to help you through your journey, without necessarily taking short cuts, but at least avoiding the proverbial quicksand and the very real minefields which the system has laid for those who are not properly advised.

R.E.K.
R.H.D.

"A journey of a thousand miles
begins with a single step."
—Chinese Proverb

CHAPTER 1

· · · · · · · · · · · ·

GETTING STARTED

Getting Started

How to Use This Book

This book is a guide, not a treatise. Like a map, you can use it to find your way through uncharted territory. It's not necessary to read it cover to cover, word for word. If there is an area which you know is of interest in the estate you're handling, you can flip through the chapters and find the material which interests you, or locate your topic through the table of contents or index.

If Death is Expected

This is not an estate planning book. For the most part, we assume that death has already occurred and that the person either did or did not do proper estate planning.

However, if death has not yet occurred, and if the person involved is able to assist you, it would be extremely worthwhile to review the checklists with that person, who may have information you will soon need. If you don't take this opportunity it could take you days or months to find what that person could direct you to in a moment.

You will have to be the judge of how to approach this subject. Many people, knowing that the end is near, will be greatly relieved to know that they have helped you "put everything in order." It may give them a sense of satisfaction to help you in this task, particularly if there are facts which only they know and can share with you.

You may also have an opportunity to discuss funeral arrangements and review the issues discussed in the next chapter in connection with preparing for the funeral.

If Death Was Unexpected

If death has occurred unexpectedly, you may be overwhelmed with grief, confused, and not sure where to start. You should use this book to organize your thoughts and as a guide to the process upon which you are about to embark.

With this book at your side, you should feel confident that you can deal with whatever challenges the administration of this estate will bring. You will know what to expect, where to go, whom to call, and when.

You're Not Alone

Although the topic "Where to Turn for Help" is addressed in Chapter 10, you should feel free to consider the issues dealt with in that chapter at any time.

In many books of this sort the authors recommend that you seek help from an attorney immediately after the funeral, and some people do that. However, we wanted to give you an idea of some of the areas with which you will be dealing before suggesting that you bring in third parties.

You will certainly be a more educated client if you gather the important documents and consider a number of issues before your first meeting with the attorney.

The Case Studies

Throughout this book we share case studies which are generally based either on our experience in practice, or on court cases. Some are hypothetical cases which commonly occur. The names used in those descriptions are fictional, to protect the confidences of those involved. However, the basic fact situations have actually occurred and could certainly happen again. We hope that you find them helpful in understanding how the legal concepts relate to real life situations.

Take A Deep Breath

Finally, we urge you to resist the temptation to want to rush through the administration of the estate, helter skelter, without proper consideration of the issues and options.

The refrain "I just want to get it all done" is not uncommon in these situations. By reading through these chapters you should gain an appreciation of the tasks which have to be done, and the time it takes to do them.

If you have realistic expectations, of yourself and of those on your team, you will reach your goal in due time, and avoid the anxiety, frustration, and disappointment that comes with failed expectations.

It may seem like some things which ought to be very simple take an inordinate amount of time to accomplish. You may submit documents and they may become lost and have to be resubmitted—not once but possibly twice or more. You may leave voice mail at a company or government agency and never receive a return call.

Always consider your "Plan B" and, when the first method doesn't work, try another. The business world is not a perfect place, and you should consider yourself very fortunate if everything you do in this estate goes like clock work.

Murphy's Law ("Whatever can go wrong, will") seems to prevail. Yet, with proper precautions you can guard against the worst. Consider these measures in self-defense:

❑ Keep copies of whatever you send, whether that be correspondence or important documents such as stocks or bonds.

❑ Send important letters via certified mail, return receipt requested, or use a private overnight courier service.

❑ Buy yourself a daily agenda and use it. Keep notes of important telephone conversations in it. Include what was said and by whom, and that person's direct dial telephone number, if available. You may start out calling one number in a large organization and be transferred through several people to the one who can finally handle your problem. You'll be thankful you kept the number when you have to contact that person again.

❑ If you are contemplating taking a fee for your services, use your agenda to keep track of what you do and the time you spend. You may need this detail to justify your fee to the Probate Court or to defend against a challenge by disgruntled beneficiaries. (See Chapter 20, "Should You Take Fiduciary Fees?")

❑ If someone promises to do something for you, politely ask them when they expect to have it done, and keep a tickler file to follow up a few days after the promised date. Consider writing short letters to confirm what is to be done and by when. Be tactful, but be clear.

With these tips in mind, and this book in hand, you're on your way to successful administration of the estate!

NOTES

"Oh God,
give us serenity to accept what cannot be changed;
courage to change what should be changed;
and wisdom to distinguish the one from the other."
—Reinhold Niebuhr

CHAPTER 2

· · · · · · · · · · ·

FUNERAL ARRANGEMENTS

Funeral Arrangements

The first job of the survivors is to make all the necessary arrangements for the funeral, which can involve a myriad of details which should be addressed as soon as possible. If you are working closely with a funeral director, he or she will guide you through this process. While each family situation will differ, and religion and custom will dictate practice in some cases, you may find the following checklist helpful:

Preliminary Matters

❑   Determine if funeral and/or burial prearrangements have been made by the deceased.

❑   Select the funeral home or funeral director.

❑   Arrange for the release of the body to the funeral home.

❑   If death occurred in another state or country, coordinate transport of the body with your funeral director, who can provide support and invaluable assistance in this process.

❑   Check the Will or other papers of the deceased, and check with other family members, regarding special wishes. For example: Location of burial; possible desire for cremation; nature of memorial service, and who will be pall bearers.

Check the Will Without Delay

It is important to check the Will and other personal papers of the deceased as soon as possible, to determine whether there were any special wishes concerning funeral, burial, or cremation.

Family members may also have this information.

❏ Determine if there are family burial plots. If so, determine which space should be opened for the deceased.

❏ If there are no available family burial plots, determine where burial should take place.

❏ Decide the type of casket to be used.

❏ Decide the type of burial vault or crypt, if any.

❏ Decide what clothing should be used for the deceased. (In some traditions only a burial shroud is used.)

Planning the Service

❏ Determine when and where the funeral or memorial service should take place.

❏ Decide on the type of service. For example, religious, military, or fraternal.

❏ Determine who should speak.

❏ Decide on special readings, if any.

❏ Decide which clergy should officiate.

❏ Decide on honoraria to be paid to clergy and musicians, if any.

❏ Provide information for the eulogy.

❏ If possible, arrange a meeting with the clergy and the family so that the family can share memories which may be incorporated into the eulogy.

❏ Ask the funeral director if a tape recording of the eulogy can be made available.

❏ Decide who will be pall bearers. Discuss this with them and make sure they are agreeable.

❑ Decide which charitable organizations or fund should be suggested to receive memorial contributions.

❑ Decide on flowers. If no flowers are desired, then provide a charitable organization or fund for memorial contributions in lieu of flowers.

❑ Decide on music, if any, for the funeral or memorial service.

Attending to Family

❑ Decide what items, if any, should be brought to the funeral home for the visitation period, or to the family home if there will be a visitation period after the funeral (for example, family photos, videos, and other memorabilia).

❑ Decide on clothing for yourself and children for the funeral.

❑ Make arrangements for young children during the funeral period.

❑ Decide on transportation for family and guests, including airport transportation if needed, and plan funeral car list.

❑ Consider having out-of-town relatives and guests met at the airport.

❑ Arrange lodging for out-of-town relatives and guests.

❑ Make preparations for the funeral luncheon or other meal, and food and refreshments at home for family and guests.

❑ If necessary, make arrangements for help at home, and extra chairs.

❑ Secure the residences of close family members during the visitation and funeral.

Post-Funeral

❏ Obtain the register of those persons who visited or attended the funeral from the funeral home, and send acknowledgment cards if appropriate.

❏ Make a list of callers, floral tributes, those who provided meals and moral support, and charitable contributions, and send thank you cards.

❏ Ask the funeral director to order multiple copies of the death certificate.

❏ Obtain copies of the tape of the eulogy, if ordered.

Death Certificate

Certified copies of the death certificate will be needed for many purposes, including transferring joint property to the surviving joint owner, claiming insurance and other benefits, and filing with the Federal Estate Tax return.

NOTES

"Chronic remorse is a most undesirable sentiment.
If you have behaved badly, repent,
make what amends you can,
and address yourself to the task
of behaving better the next time.
On no account brood over your wrongdoing.
Rolling in the muck is not the best way of getting clean."
—Aldous Huxley

CHAPTER 3

· · · · · · · · · · ·

NOTIFY
KEY
PEOPLE

Notify Key People

Prompt notification of key people is critical. It is important that everyone who should know about the death be provided timely information, so they can attend the funeral or visitation. Late notice or none at all can also come back to haunt you when people are miffed and interpret it as a sign of how you or the decedent felt about them.

If there is no listing available of all the people who should be contacted, you will have to develop one quickly. Enlist the assistance of family members, friends, and the decedent's associates from work if the deceased was working. Divide the list between several people, if necessary, to reduce the burden on any one person.

Don't forget people who live out of town or abroad. They may not be able to come for the funeral, but in some cases they will, and in any event they will appreciate being notified.

Do keep track of your long distance telephone charges. They should be reimbursed by the estate, and if the estate is subject to estate taxes these expenses will be deductible, so Uncle Sam will pay part of the bill. Keep copies of your phone bills and highlight the charges. Also keep track of your time throughout the entire process. (See Chapter 20, "Should You Take Fiduciary Fees?")

Proper notification is also the first step in avoiding family conflicts. If someone who thinks they should have been notified is not, you may hear about it for years. Consider, also, if there are sensitivities in deciding who will contact certain people. "She couldn't take the time to call me herself" may be a refrain you wish to avoid.

In large families, delegate to certain people the responsibility of notifying others within their family. Impress upon your "team" the importance of following up if a person is not reached with the first call. Assure each of your helpers that their calls can be kept brief if they simply provide the necessary information.

Wherever possible, avoid using e-mail or leaving voice mail or messages on an answering machine. Even where the death is expected because of advanced age or a long illness, it can be very shocking to learn of a death in these ways.

In addition, when you leave a message on voice mail or an answering machine you do not know who will pick up the message or if it is received by the right person. It may be accidentally deleted, or may be heard or seen by someone who is ill equipped to deal with the sad news. If accidentally left at a wrong number the message could have devastating consequences.

Following is a checklist of various categories of people who should be contacted in appropriate cases (and not necessarily in this order):

❑   Relatives

❑   Friends

❑   Neighbors

❑   Clergy

❑   Employer

❑   Employees

❑   Household help

❑   Business partners

❑   Employers of relatives taking off work due to the death

❑   Pall bearers

❑   Religious, fraternal, and veterans' organizations

❑   Members of clubs, social, religious, hobby, and study groups

Consider Public Interest

If the deceased had an interesting life, for whatever reason, the local newspaper may want to run a feature-type obituary. Contact the paper and provide them the necessary background.

This type of story can provide an emotional boost to the family, and also act to transmit the values of the deceased to the broader community, via comments of family and friends included in the article.

❑ Unions to which the decedent belonged

❑ Funeral director

❑ Newspapers regarding death notices or possibly an obituary

❑ Cemetery or memorial park

❑ Doctors

❑ Attorney

❑ Accountant

❑ Banker

❑ Stockbroker and/or investment advisor

❑ Life insurance agent

CHAPTER 4

· · · · · · · · · · ·

GRIEF
SUPPORT

Grief Support

Why Grief Support?

The loss of a loved one will affect different people differently, and the ways of dealing with grief will vary from case to case, from person to person. You, the reader, may be the one who is grieving, or you may see that others around you are suffering. In this chapter we will make you aware of the possible need for grief support, and provide some sources of grief support services.

Why should a book on estate administration even touch upon the topic of grief support? This book is not only for Personal Representatives, but also for the survivors. Our goal is to provide some useful advice and tools to help you through the loss, whether on a financial level or on a personal level.

At the same time, a grieving Personal Representative may become frozen, virtually immobilized. Comments may be made such as, "It's too much to deal with," but the real problem will not be the enormity of the administrative task, but the inability to cope with the loss.

Tremendous prejudice may result to the estate, to the survivors, and to other beneficiaries if those responsible for the administration are unable to function. Assets may not be gathered, tax returns may not be timely filed, decisions may not be made, and investments may be allowed to languish. The situation can go on for years.

The first step, therefore, is to realize that there may be a need for grief support, and then to begin thinking about what it is and how to find help.

The Need to Heal

John and Maxine had been married 40 years when John suddenly passed away.

Maxine was first in denial, then became totally confused by all of the financial matters that required her attention. She refused to open mail, pay bills, or deal with the details of administering John's estate.

It was not so much the difficulty of the task as the grief she was suffering. With caring grief support, Maxine eventually adjusted to her situation and was able to go on with her life and attend to all those details which initially seemed so difficult.

Recognizing the Need

Each of us will react differently to a loss, depending on our relationship with the person who has died, our relationships with others, the depth of the loss, and our own physical and emotional makeup.

The effects can range from physical and mental, to emotional and spiritual. For some, grieving can bring with it symptoms not unlike those of depression, which can make it difficult if not impossible to care for oneself.

The person who is grieving may or may not be able to see changes taking place within himself or herself. However, you may see those changes within yourself or in others, and should be sensitive to any of the following:

① Changes in appearance.

② Changes in attitude.

③ Changes in habits or patterns of behavior.

④ Changes in belief systems.

Some First Steps

One of the first steps in grief support is probably to find someone with whom to talk about the loss. Verbalizing your feelings is usually very helpful in moving through the grieving process.

Learning about the grieving process itself can also be helpful. Knowing that there are stages in grieving, that there is "light at the end of the tunnel," can attenuate the overwhelming feelings that accompany a loss. Truly believing that "This, too, will pass" can provide a needed sense of optimism that eventually things will settle down.

Sharing one's feelings often helps the process. Communicating with others who have suffered a similar loss leads to the recognition that your situation is not unique and can be overcome. As you learn about grief—including what grief is—you will also learn answers to the following:

① Is there a time frame for my grieving?

② Are there common stages of grief that everyone passes through?

③ When should I be really concerned about my grief, or the grief that someone else is experiencing?

④ What help can I get, or give to someone else who is grieving?

Grief Support Sources

Grief support groups and services exist within every community. Each of the following will either offer grief support services or be able to provide referrals to other organizations:

❑ Churches, synagogues, and temples.

❑ Hospice organizations.

❑ Funeral homes.

❑ Hospitals.

❑ Community mental health centers.

The Internet has become a source for grief support. To get an idea of the huge number of sites dedicated to grief support, you need only use your Internet search engine to search for the words "grief support." A recent search turned up over 10,000 sites.

Many of the support groups you will find by doing such a search focus on the needs of those who have suffered certain kinds of losses. For example, they may deal with deaths of children, an infant, a twin, death in an airline crash, or from a certain cause. However, many of them provide general educational literature on the grieving process.

Many Web sites also offer the opportunity to exchange views and feelings with others who have suffered a loss, either via e-mail or in chat groups. Grief support professionals recommend these sites be approached with caution, however, as the person leading the online session may or may not be a qualified grief counselor or have mental health care training, and you may not be able to determine that person's background and training in these areas.

In Appendix C ("Grief Support Services") we provide a number of sources of further information on grief support, as well as grief support services. They are both local and national, and the national sources can direct you to local groups and organizations. The Internet sources of grief support services and information can be directly accessed through links created for your convenience at www.carobtreepress.com.

NOTES

"When one door of happiness closes,
another opens; but often we look so long
at the closed door that we do not see
the one which has opened for us."
—Helen Keller

CHAPTER 5

. . . .

GATHER IMPORTANT DOCUMENTS

Gather Important Documents

The Documents Tell the Story

In the great majority of cases, existing documents will be the starting point in administering the estate. While people may say what the decedent "intended," intentions which are not expressed in a written document are generally not sufficient to be legally binding. A written document will generally override what someone says that the decedent wanted.

There are many documents which should be located to properly administer an estate. Family members can help locate these documents. The decedent's attorney or accountant, or business partners, may also be helpful to you in this search.

The following is a checklist of some of the documents which may exist. However, most of these documents will not exist in every case so do not be overly concerned if you do not locate many of them unless you have reason to believe they do exist.

We recommend you make copies and preserve the originals in a safe place. Do not unstaple any documents for copying! A question could be raised about the authenticity of some of the pages. If it is not possible to copy any document without removing the staples or having the document come apart, then do not copy it.

We suggest that these documents be organized in manila folders, which are labeled to indicate the contents of each folder, one type of document in each folder, which are then stored in banker's boxes available at any office supply store. This will make it easier to store and transport the documents, and to retrieve them for future reference.

If you will be handling the administration of the estate on your own, the documents will form the cornerstone of your work. If you retain an attorney to assist you, the attorney will need to carefully review them.

Wills and Trusts

❏   Last Will and Testament and any Codicils (amendments). This includes any document which is not labeled as a Will but is intended as such. A handwritten note may, in certain circumstances, constitute a valid Will. (See Chapter 6, "Who Should Administer the Estate?" regarding what may constitute a Will, and Chapter 15, "To Probate or Not to Probate," regarding what has to be filed with the Probate Court.)

❏   Prior Wills, even though they may have been superseded. (They may be necessary in the event of an attack on what is considered the current Will.)

❏   Side letters with regard to disposition of personal property or other aspects of the estate.

❏   Trust instruments (for example, Revocable Trusts, Irrevocable Trusts, Qualified Personal Residence Trusts, and Irrevocable Life Insurance Trusts) and any amendments. These trusts may have been created by the decedent, or by someone else and the decedent may have been merely a beneficiary or Trustee under these trusts. In some cases amendments may not be labeled as such, so be sure to retain any documents which look like they are intended to amend or modify another document.

❏   Durable Power of Attorney. (Even though the Power of Attorney is not effective after death, it may still be important to show that certain actions by the Attorney in Fact or Agent were authorized, in connection with audit of an estate tax return.)

Filing the Will

Under Michigan law, anyone who is holding a Will of a decedent is required to file it with the Probate Court within a reasonable time after the death, or may be liable for damages, unless there is reasonable cause for not filing it.

This applies even if there is no probate estate.

Not Filing the Will Can Be Costly

A bank held Henry's Will for safekeeping. Henry died and the family closed his checking account at the bank.

Henry's son found an earlier Will, probated the estate, and distributed the assets based on the provisions of the earlier Will.

Henry's brother subsequently discovered that the bank had the later Will, according to which the estate was to be distributed differently than under the earlier Will.

Because it failed to file the Will with the Probate Court as required by law, the bank provided compensation to the beneficiaries under the later Will.

Insurance

❑ Insurance policies and certificates of insurance for all types of insurance. This would include life, health, long-term care, accident, disability, homeowners (including lists of scheduled property), and any other insurance as to which the decedent was either the owner, beneficiary, or premium payor.

❑ Assignments of insurance policies or rights under policies.

❑ Split-Dollar Agreements.

❑ Life insurance beneficiary designations.

❑ Correspondence with insurance companies or insurance agents concerning changes in beneficiaries, policy loans, policy provisions, or other matters.

Bank Accounts and Securities

❑ Bank account statements.

❑ Certificates of deposit.

❑ Savings account passbooks.

❑ Check books and check registers.

❑ Canceled checks for the past six years. (Hold these for safekeeping; do not copy. See the sidebar comment on the following page regarding the importance of canceled checks.)

❑ Brokerage firm statements.

❑ Mutual fund statements.

❑ Annuity statements.

❑ Shares of stock in certificate form.

❑ U.S. Government bonds (for example, savings bonds, and Series HH bonds).

❑ Statements with regard to bonds held in the U.S. Treasury Direct program.

❑ Foreign government bonds.

Real Estate

❑ Deeds to real estate.

❑ Shares in Cooperative Housing Associations.

❑ Real estate tax bills.

❑ Mortgages of real estate.

❑ Title insurance policies; title searches; abstracts of title; title opinions.

❑ Closing papers with regard to purchases and sales of real estate or Cooperative Housing Association shares.

❑ Land contracts.

❑ Real estate leases (business or residential).

❑ Documents with regard to purchase and ownership of vacation time share units, and obligations for payment of ongoing maintenance fees.

❑ Condominium Association or Cooperative Housing Association bylaws.

❑ Cemetery or memorial park certificates of ownership.

Why Keep Canceled Checks?

Canceled checks can be important for many reasons. For example:

They could be requested by the IRS in case of an income tax audit.

They may be needed to prove that the decedent paid off a debt.

They may indicate that gifts were made which should have been reported on a Federal Gift Tax return.

They may also show that monies were considered loans and not gifts, if so indicated on the check.

They may also prove that taxes were paid, even though erroneously credited to the wrong account.

Vehicles, Boats, and Aircraft

❑ Vehicle and boat titles; aircraft registration papers.

❑ Logs of usage of business-related vehicles, boats, and aircraft, which may be needed in the event of an IRS audit.

❑ Vehicle, boat, or aircraft leases.

❑ Financing documents with regard to vehicles, boats, or aircraft.

❑ Insurance polices with regard to vehicles, boats, or aircraft.

Contracts and Obligations

❑ Leases with regard to personal property (for example, equipment, machinery, computers, and telephones).

❑ Cellular phone service contracts.

❑ Internet service provider agreements.

❑ Terms and conditions relating to credit cards, auto club, buying club, and other club and association memberships.

❑ Other contracts.

❑ Promissory notes, either made by the decedent or by someone else in favor of the decedent.

❑ Bank loan documents.

❑ Guarantees, either made by the decedent or by someone else in favor of the decedent.

❑ Frequent flier account information. Frequent flier points may be transferable in the event of death.

❑ Warranty information.

Unexpected Life Insurance

Credit cards and some club and association memberships may provide life insurance coverage in certain cases.

For example, they may provide life insurance benefits to cover the outstanding credit card balance.

They may also pay death benefits in case of accidental death or in other cases.

Hiding Places

While most people will keep their valuables in the bank or broker-age firm, in a safe deposit box, or home safe, some have been known to hide them in rather unusual places.

Attorneys around the country recently exchanged information about where Executors had found assets of decedents who didn't trust the usual places, and mentioned the following:

Kitchen cabinets; under the stairs; in electric wall outlets; in dryer vents; in cold air returns; in the rafters of the basement; taped under the bottom of desk drawers; on the sides of and behind dresser drawers; inside mattresses; inside upholstered furniture; in the refrigerator or freezer; inside a drop ceiling; under loose wall-to-wall carpeting; under carpeting covering an interior stair-way; inside bags, boxes, and books; inside stacks of papers and magazines; behind mirrors and paintings; under loose floorboards inside the main area of the house and in the attic; in secret com-partments behind closets, and inside the hems of drapes.

One attorney has even recommended that you mark off the back-yard with kite string in one foot grids; then hammer a thin steel rod at least two feet down the center of each grid. You may be surprised to find metal boxes of treasure!

If the decedent was a hunter or outdoorsman, check nearby fields and forests for cash boxes hidden in tree trunks and rock crev-ices.

While the proverbial cookie jar has always been a place to stash cash, don't forget what appears to be a mayonnaise jar, which has been emptied of the original contents and painted white in-side, then filled with cash, jewelry or other valuables. It may be sitting at the rear of a pantry shelf, and the expiration date may be many years in the past.

Employee and Retirement Benefits

❑   Employment agreements.

❑   Independent contractor or consulting agreements.

❑   Employee benefits statements, summaries of benefits, and employee benefit plan documents. (These may relate to plans other than retirement plans, such as nonqualified deferred compensation, stock bonus plans, and phantom stock plans.)

❑   Pension, profit sharing, IRA, and 403(b) account statements.

❑   Beneficiary designations.

❑   Work papers and/or schedules with regard to computation of required minimum distributions from qualified retirement plans and IRAs (where the decedent was over age 70-1/2).

❑   Extended benefit payment elections made with regard to qualified retirement plans (the so-called TEFRA Section 242(b)(2) election). (This may have been made prior to 1984, to allow the decedent to take distributions from qualified retirement plans under rules then in effect, rather than be subject to the general rules which are now effective which prescribe that required minimum distributions must start in the year after attaining age 70-1/2.)

Tax Returns and Social Security

❑   Income tax returns of the decedent (Federal, state, and local).

❑   Intangibles Tax returns.

❑   Federal Gift Tax returns.

❑ Foreign tax returns.

❑ Tax returns of any entity (closely held corporation, general or limited partnership, limited liability company, or trust) in which the decedent had an ownership interest.

❑ Social Security earnings statements.

❑ W-2 statements and Forms 1099. (These are particularly important for the year of death, for income tax return preparation. They may also lead to other assets.)

Closely Held Companies

❑ Agreements with regard to entities in which the decedent was an owner (for example, Shareholder Agreements, Buy-Sell Agreements, Partnership Agreements, Limited Partnership Agreements, and Limited Liability Operating Agreements or Governing Agreements).

❑ Stock registers and minute books with regard to closely held corporations.

❑ Documents with regard to any private foundation which the decedent operated. (Corporate minute book, IRS exemption letter, Forms 990-PF filed with the Internal Revenue Service, and filings with state authorities. In Michigan, filings would be made with the Michigan Attorney General, Charitable Trust Division.)

Personal Property

❑ Appraisals of real estate, jewelry, art work, or other personal property which may be found in the files of the decedent. (See Chapter 11, "Inventory the Assets," regarding the possible need for new appraisals.)

Tax Information May Lead to Assets

Tax returns and 1099s may lead to assets of the decedent. In any event, the Personal Representative is responsible for having all required tax returns filed if they were not filed by the decedent, for all years not barred by the statute of limitations.

Is the Vault Sealed On Death?

A surviving joint lessee of a joint safe deposit box has full access to the box. Access in all other circumstances is restricted by law.

Ask the financial institution where the box is located or your attorney what procedures must be followed in your case.

❑ Photos or video tape of personal property which the decedent may have retained for purposes of insurance or identification of various items.

❑ Safe deposit box key; safe deposit box rental billing information. Take note of the location of any safe deposit box and box number.

❑ List of any guns owned by the decedent, including serial numbers, and gun permits. (Guns should be held under lock and key for safekeeping.)

❑ Information with regard to people or companies interested in the decedent's collections, who may be helpful for purposes of appraisal or sale.

Vital Information

❑ Full name and any other names used.

❑ Current address and previous addresses used over the last five years.

❑ Birth certificate, or date and place of birth.

❑ Father's name and birth place.

❑ Mother's maiden name and birth place.

❑ Driver's license.

❑ Social Security card or Social Security number.

❑ Medicare card.

❑ Health insurance card.

❑ Credit cards.

❑ Marriage certificate.

❑ Divorce Judgments; Property Settlement Agreements.

❑ Military service discharge papers.

❑ Naturalization papers.

❑ Latest financial statement.

❑ Frequent flier cards.

❑ Family tree or other genealogical information, or in any event a list of names, addresses, and relationship of closest living relatives (for example, spouse, parents, children, grandchildren, and siblings).

❑ Religious name, if any.

NOTES

"If you're going to do something,
you might as well do it
cheerfully and enthusiastically."
—Lucille Babcock

CHAPTER 6

....

WHO SHOULD ADMINISTER THE ESTATE?

Who Should Administer the Estate?

A Word About Terminology

The term *estate* means different things in different contexts. There is the *probate* estate, which includes only those assets, if any, which were owned in the decedent's *sole name*. There is the *taxable* estate, which includes all assets which are subject to estate tax. Unless otherwise indicated, however, we will use *estate* in a general, non-technical sense to encompass all of the legal and financial affairs of a decedent. We will employ the term *estate administration* to refer to the process by which these affairs are wound up and brought to a proper close.

The estate is administered by one or more *fiduciaries*. A fiduciary may be an individual or an institution such as a bank or trust company. A fiduciary who is responsible for the probate estate is known variously as a *Personal Representative, Executor, Executrix, Administrator, or Administratrix*. A fiduciary who is responsible for any trust of the decedent is called a *Trustee*.

As you will see below, an individual has no legal authority to act in estate matters solely by virtue of being the surviving spouse, child, or other close relative of the decedent.

Is There a Valid Will or Trust?

Since the person who will administer the estate is usually named in the Will or trust instrument, if these documents have been located you should first determine if they are valid.

Normally, the most recent Will and any Codicils thereto are valid if they have been executed in accordance with the formalities required by state law in the state where the decedent lived when they were executed. The same is true of the most recent trust instrument and any amendments.

Generally, the decedent's attorney should be able to identify the most recent Will and trust instrument and account for all Codicils and amendments which may have been executed. This is not always foolproof, however, as the decedent may have used more than one attorney. Other professional advisors such as the decedent's trust officer, accountant, or insurance agent may be able to provide clues. Family members may have recollections which might prove helpful.

If a copy of a Will is found but the original Will cannot be located, you should proceed with caution and with the assistance of a competent estate planning attorney. It is possible that the original was simply lost. But it is also possible that the decedent destroyed it with the intention of revoking it. Depending on which scenario is assumed, there could be different fiduciaries, different beneficiaries, and different property rights.

If you have found documents which you believe to be valid, bear in mind that your determination is not conclusive. The documents are subject to challenge by any person who has an interest in the decedent's estate.

Requirements

To make a Will, under Michigan law a person must be 18 years or older and of sound mind.

The Will must either be signed by that person, called the *testator*, or by someone else in the testator's conscious presence and at the testator's direction. In other words, the testator himself does not have to sign it.

In addition, it must be signed by at least two individuals, each of whom signed within a reasonable time after witnessing either (a) the actual signing of the Will by the testator, or (b) the testator's acknowledgment of his signature or acknowledgment of the Will.

If the Will contains certain acknowledgment language specified in the statute, it is considered *self-proved*, which will create a presumption that it is legally valid.

The mere fact that one or more of the witnesses are also beneficiaries of the Will does not invalidate the Will, nor does it

---

The Will May Not Matter

Before delving too deeply into potential issues regarding a Will, try to determine the value of property owned by the decedent in his sole name or that will be payable to the estate. This is the only property that will be distributed under the Will.

If there is little or no such property, the Will may well be moot.

In Her Own Hand

Aunt Emily wrote her Will on a 5x7 card in her own handwriting before going on a trip.

When she later passed away, that Will was admitted to probate as a valid, holographic Will.

automatically invalidate bequests made to the witness under the Will.

In some cases, a document other than a formally drawn Will may be valid as a Will. In Michigan, a writing in which the material portions are in the decedent's handwriting and which is signed and dated by the decedent is valid. It is known as a *holographic* Will. Other writings may also be valid if it can be established, by clear and convincing evidence, that the decedent intended the writing to constitute his Will.

There are fewer formalities required for a trust than a Will. No particular number of witnesses is required for a trust to be valid, nor must it be notarized.

Issues

The following issues can apply to both Wills and trusts. If you feel any of them apply to your situation, review the matter with your attorney:

❑   Do you have any reason to believe that the document may be a forgery? The fact that the document leaves the estate to people whom you did not expect to receive it may surprise you, or offend you, but is certainly not conclusive. In appropriate cases, your attorney will recommend that a handwriting expert be retained to determine the authenticity of the document. (See Appendix A for information on handwriting experts.)

❑   What was the decedent's state of mind at the time the instrument was executed? Was the decedent legally competent? Was the decedent influenced by alcohol or drugs? Evidence of competency or lack thereof may be obtained from interviews with those who knew the decedent, including friends and family members, doctors, and nurses, as well as from hospital and nursing home medical records.

❑   Is there any indication that the decedent may have been subject to undue influence in the making of the Will or trust? You should discuss your concerns with your attorney, who will assist you in gathering evidence to prove or refute undue influence, as appropriate.

The Probate Court will look for a number of factors in determining whether there was undue influence, no single factor being determinative. Those factors might include the following:

①   Was the signer very old or mentally weak?

②   Was there a change from a prior disposition of the property?

③   Are there benefits flowing to a nonrelative?

④   Was the beneficiary involved in having the person sign the new document?

⑤   Were the people who would be the "natural objects" of the signer's bounty disinherited?

⑥   Was there constant association and supervision by the beneficiary, as when the beneficiary lives with or cares for the signer?

⑦   Was there a lack of opportunity for others to visit the signer?

❑   Examine the Will and all Codicils and any trust instrument and all amendments for possible irregularities, such as removal of staples, different kinds of paper, different type styles, words stricken out, or words inserted.

One May Be Competent to Execute a Will But Not a Trust

The standard of competency for execution of a Will is lower than for execution of a trust:

To execute a valid Will a person must only know the approximate size of his estate and who are the "natural objects of his bounty," i.e., the people to whom he would normally want to leave it.

By comparison, a trust is a contract. To enter into a valid contract a person cannot be under any legal disability and must understand the legal effect of the instrument and the effect that it has upon the legal rights of the person to his or her property.

The Typical Situation

A decedent today might have both a Will and a revocable trust.

The Will would appoint a Personal Representative. The revocable trust, which becomes irrevocable on the death of the decedent, would name a Successor Trustee.

The Will would provide that any assets in the probate estate pour over to the trust, and are distributed in accordance with the terms of the trust.

If all of the assets of the decedent were transferred to the trust during lifetime, there may be no probate estate at all.

❑ If the original of a Will or Codicil cannot be located, should a copy be offered for probate? Under Michigan law, if the contents of the Will are known a petition may be filed to probate the estate on the basis of a lost Will.

If There is a Will or Trust

If there is a Will, one or more Personal Representatives are usually nominated in the document. Alternates are often named in the event the primary nominees are deceased or decline to serve. If a probate estate will be necessary, the nominated Personal Representatives should ask the Probate Court to admit the Will to probate and appoint them Personal Representatives. (See Chapter 15, "To Probate or Not to Probate.")

You have no authority to act in estate matters by virtue of being *nominated* as a Personal Representative in the Will. You may not act in your official capacity until you are *appointed* by the Probate Court. Further, your authority extends only to the probate estate. Many times, the decedent will have arranged his affairs so that the bulk of his property is held jointly or in one or more trusts, leaving little or nothing in a probate estate.

If there is a trust of which the decedent was Trustee, the trust agreement will usually designate one or more Successor Trustees to serve after the death of the decedent. If you are the designated Successor Trustee, you should notify the holders of the assets in the trust that the decedent Trustee has died and that you are the successor. A bank or trust company may be the Successor Trustee or Successor Co-Trustee with you and perhaps others.

❑ As a general rule, do not enter into any agreements on behalf of the probate estate until you have been appointed Personal Representative by the Probate Court. However, to get matters started you may consult an attorney and sign a retainer agreement with the attorney as nominated Personal Representative.

❑　If a bank or trust company has been named Personal Representative or Personal Co-Representative, or Successor Trustee or Successor Co-Trustee, request the assignment of an administrative officer. From that point onward you will have a contact person to either take over administration of the estate or handle it with you.

If There is No Will or Trust

If the decedent left no Will, and if there is any property in the decedent's sole name, one or more Personal Representatives must be appointed to administer this property under the laws of *intestate succession*. An *intestate* estate is one in which the decedent died without a Will.

One or more family members should petition the Probate Court to appoint one or more Personal Representatives. (See Chapter 15, "To Probate or Not to Probate.") Under Michigan law, persons seeking appointment as Personal Representative in an intestate estate have priority in the following order:

① The decedent's surviving spouse.

② Other heirs of the decedent.

③ After 42 days after the decedent's death, the nominee of a creditor if the court finds the nominee suitable.

④ The state or county public administrator (under certain circumstances).

If there is no trust of which the decedent was Trustee, then there is no concern with Successor Trustees.

Do You Really Want the Job?

You must appreciate that administering an estate of any size except the smallest is a major undertaking. It will probably require significant work on your part, may last for two years or even longer, and can put you at odds with members of your own family.

"Anyone can steer the ship when the sea is calm."

—Pubilius Syrus

To get a sense of what is involved, take a few minutes to scan the remaining chapters of this book. You will find that you will be responsible for dealing with attorneys and other professionals, determining who is legally entitled to the estate, inventorying and valuing assets and liabilities, providing full information (including periodic accounts) to beneficiaries, complying in some cases with the requirements of the Probate Court, managing assets, settling claims, assisting in the preparation and filing of tax returns, division and distribution of assets and funding of trusts, and a host of other related and miscellaneous matters.

Your Fiduciary Duties

A Personal Representative or Trustee has a fiduciary relationship to the beneficiaries.

You must be aware that as a fiduciary (one holding a position of great trust), you will not be allowed to handle the estate as you wish, as if the property were your own. Rather, you will have a number of duties or standards of behavior imposed by statute or common law, including:

Duty to Exercise Reasonable Care, Skill, and Prudence: You must use your best efforts in the conduct of fiduciary affairs.

Duty of Loyalty: You may be unable to serve if you have a conflict of interest. You may not engage in acts of self-dealing.

Duty Not to Commingle: You must keep the property of the estate or trust separate from your own.

Duty to Preserve and Protect Fiduciary Property: You must act to prevent loss to fiduciary assets.

Duty to Make Property Productive: You must see that fiduciary assets are invested.

Duty Not to Delegate: You are not relieved of responsibility by delegation of your responsibilities to others. In Michigan, you may delegate investment and management functions *only* if you exercise reasonable care, skill, and caution in selecting an agent and establishing the scope and terms of the delegation. You must also periodically review the agent's actions in order to monitor the agent's performance and compliance with the terms of the delegation.

Duty to Deal Impartially with Beneficiaries: You must act impartially in managing and investing fiduciary assets.

Duty to Keep and Render Accounts: You must keep records and account to the beneficiaries of the estate or trust.

Duty to Furnish Information: You must keep the beneficiaries of the estate or trust informed.

Duty to Pay Income: You must pay the income of the estate or trust to those who are entitled to receive it.

You will be responsible to the beneficiaries for meeting these obligations and for the proper administration of the estate or trust. We will discuss some of the above duties further in the context of the particular task to be performed.

Regardless of how conscientiously you think you are performing your job as fiduciary, there are no assurances that the beneficiaries will find your performance acceptable.

You may be questioned, challenged, and even sued. If the Probate Court finds that you did not properly perform your duties, and the estate suffered losses as a result, you may be required to *personally* repay the amount of the losses to the estate. (This is referred to as being *surcharged* by the court). You could even be removed and someone else appointed in your place. All of this could be emotionally very upsetting.

Making the Decision

You have the right to decline to serve, regardless of your relationship to the decedent. However, you should not decline merely because you lack expertise in legal and financial matters. If a bank or trust company will be serving as a co-fiduciary with you, it should handle the technical details. Your role will then be to represent the family and participate in the discussion and resolution of any major issues that may arise.

If the decedent did not provide for a bank or trust company to act as co-fiduciary, it may be possible to *add* one if you wish. Banks and trust companies have the staff and expertise to assist in even the most complex estates.

If the estate is too small to merit a corporate co-fiduciary, or if you wish to minimize fees, with competent professional assistance you will likely be able to administer the estate or trust without serious difficulty, notwithstanding your technical limitations. (See Chapter 10, "Where to Turn for Help.")

However, if you do not have considerable energy, interest, time, and patience, you should consider stepping aside. You should also consider declining if you live in a distant state, if you travel frequently, or if there is a particularly contentious family situation. Finally, if multiple fiduciaries have been named and it is agreed that having less than all of them serve would be more efficient, some of them can decline to serve.

Before you back away from this responsibility consider carefully who may take your place, whether that person can meet the challenge, and whether there are ways that you could fulfill your obligations by enlisting the help of others.

If You Do Decline

If you are named in the Will as Personal Representative, or have priority for appointment in an intestate estate, or are named as a Successor Trustee, and decide you do not want the responsibility, you have several choices:

① You can simply decline to serve and let someone else with priority serve. Generally whoever is named your successor in the Will or trust instrument will be next in line to serve. In an intestate estate someone else with priority may be appointed.

There may also be a procedure in the document indicating how your successor will be chosen. For example, a trust agreement may indicate that if there is no successor willing and able to serve, the person named may be entitled to select a successor, or the beneficiaries may select one.

② If you have priority to serve as Personal Representative and decline to serve, rather than simply allow your named successor to serve, you may nominate a

Was It An Honor?

Sally was honored when she learned that her late aunt had named her Trustee of her trust. But when she talked to her attorney and learned all she would have to do, she changed her mind, declined to serve, and let her named Successor Trustee serve.

qualified person to act as Personal Representative. If two or more people have priority, any who do not renounce their right to serve must agree in nominating another to act for them.

③ You could try to reach an agreement with the beneficiaries as to who will serve and have that validated by the Probate Court.

Dealing with Multiple Fiduciaries

The Will or trust instrument may, and often does, nominate more than one fiduciary. As indicated above, some of those nominated may decline to serve. However, if two or more fiduciaries accept appointment, there is an obvious need for cooperation. One fiduciary cannot act independently of the other.

Under Michigan law, in the case of a probate estate, the concurrence of all Personal Representatives is required. In the case of a trust, two Trustees must act jointly. Unless the trust agreement provides otherwise, three or more Trustees may act by majority decision.

If there is both an estate and a trust, it is not uncommon for each to have different fiduciaries. The decedent may have named his spouse as Personal Representative, but provided for a bank to serve as Successor Trustee of his trust. Once again, there is clearly a need for cooperation between the different fiduciaries.

Objections to the Appointment

If you are unhappy with one or more of the nominated fiduciaries, you should immediately seek the advice of an attorney. It may be possible to get the nominee to decline to serve.

It is often better to have the attorney approach the nominee than to attempt it yourself, especially if the nominee is a family member.

If the person does not agree to decline to serve, objections may be made to the appointment in a formal Probate Court proceeding. This will be a rare occurrence. The attorney and

those with knowledge of the circumstances will have to persuade the judge that the person should not serve. Each case turns on its own facts, but the following might justify not appointing someone with priority:

① If there is a history of acrimonious relations between that person and some or all of the other beneficiaries, so that having that person serve will give rise to continued disputes.

② If that person is involved in a dispute concerning estate assets which creates a conflict of interest. For example, if the decedent created joint property with rights of survivorship with the person seeking appointment, and there are reasons to believe that the joint property should be an estate asset, but the person refuses to pursue that position on behalf of the estate.

③ If that person has a criminal record indicating that he or she should not be trusted with estate administration.

If an objection is made to the appointment of a Personal Representative, the court may appoint anyone with priority, but in certain circumstances may appoint someone else. For example:

① If the estate is large enough to meet exemptions and costs of administration but not large enough to pay anticipated unsecured claims, creditors may petition to appoint *any* qualified person.

② If a person who is left something under the Will (a *devisee*) or an heir who appears to have a substantial interest in the estate objects to the appointment of a person whose priority is not determined by the Will, the court may appoint someone else. The person appointed would generally have to be acceptable to the

"You can't have a family fuss without the whole town knowing about it."

—Proverb

devisees and heirs whose interests in the estate appear to be worth in total more than one-half the probable distributable value. If there is no person acceptable to these people, then the court may appoint *any* suitable person.

Removing a Fiduciary

Once a fiduciary has been appointed, removal is more difficult. An action must be brought in Probate Court. Grounds for removal would include a breach of one or more of the duties of a fiduciary. (See above, "Your Fiduciary Duties.")

As a general rule, repeated, flagrant breaches of these duties would be required for removal, although each case turns on its own facts, which should be discussed with an attorney.

While removal is a possibility, it is also possible that the Probate Court might not remove the fiduciary if the breach of duty was done innocently and if it is promptly corrected. However, ignorance of the law is no excuse.

If an order of removal is obtained, there is generally a transition period, which may be relatively long, involving inventories and accounts by the old and new fiduciaries, as well as the physical transfer of the assets.

Not All Property is Subject to Control by a Fiduciary

A Personal Representative has authority over property in the probate estate. A Trustee is responsible for property in the trust. However, joint property and any property with a named beneficiary, such as life insurance, annuities, IRAs, and retirement plan benefits, pass by operation of law and no fiduciary is involved, unless the estate or trust is a beneficiary.

It is therefore possible that major assets pass outside the Will, to persons not even named in the Will, or in proportions totally different than indicated in the Will. It is also possible that no assets at all pass under the Will.

Related Appointments: Guardian and Conservator

If the decedent left orphaned minor children, a Guardian will have to be appointed for them. This must be done through the Probate Court. The decedent's Will may nominate a guardian. Also, under Michigan law the appointment of a Guardian may be made in any written document signed by the parent and attested by at least two witnesses.

If a minor child has or is to receive a significant amount of money or other property in the child's own name, as a result of the decedent's death, a Conservator should be appointed for the child's property. The appointment is made through the Probate Court and the Conservator must account to the court. The decedent's Will may nominate a Conservator.

CHAPTER 7

. . . .

SOCIAL
SECURITY
BENEFITS

Social Security Benefits

Most of us probably think of Social Security in terms of *retirement benefits* we will receive after a lifetime of work. However, a portion of our Social Security taxes in fact go toward insurance for survivors. If the decedent has worked and paid into Social Security, survivors benefits may be payable to certain family members. These include widows, widowers, divorced widows and widowers, children, and dependent parents.

In this chapter we describe how those benefits are earned, who may receive survivors benefits, the amount of those benefits, and what you will need to make a claim. We also provide contact information and further resources. This information is based on Social Security Administration Publication No. 05-10084 (July 1999).

We'll refer to the decedent as the *deceased worker*, and to the surviving spouse (or surviving divorced spouse) as *you*.

Steps to be Taken Immediately

After the death of a person receiving Social Security retirement benefits, you or some other family member or other person responsible for the deceased worker's affairs should do the following as soon as possible:

❏ Notify the Social Security Administration of the death by calling their toll-free number, 1-800-772-1213. Call between 7:00 a.m. and 7:00 p.m. on business days to speak with a service representative or make an appointment. The lines are busiest early in the week and early in the month, so try to call at other times.

Call first thing in the morning or late afternoon to avoid busy signals. Have the deceased worker's Social Security number at hand. If you are deaf or hard of hearing, you can call Social Security's toll-free TTY number, 1-800-325-0778, during the same times.

❑ If monthly Social Security benefits were being paid by direct deposit to the deceased worker's bank account, you should notify the bank or other financial institution of the death. Request the bank or other institution to return to Social Security as soon as possible any funds received for the month of death and later. Those are overpayments to which the estate is not entitled.

❑ If Social Security benefits were being paid by check, don't cash any checks received for the month in which the death occurred or thereafter. You should promptly return the checks to Social Security. If you do that by mail, keep copies of the checks and your correspondence. However, it is preferable to return the check in person and obtain a receipt.

How Survivors Benefits Accumulate

If the decedent earned enough Social Security *credits*, certain family members may be eligible for Social Security survivors benefits. A worker can earn up to four credits per year.

The number of credits necessary to permit survivors to claim benefits depends on the age of the decedent at the time of death. A younger person would need less credits than an older person for family members to be eligible for survivors benefits. However, no one needs more than 40 credits, or 10 years of work, to be eligible for Social Security benefits.

In some circumstances, lower numbers of credits are sufficient: Benefits can be paid to children and to the surviving spouse who is caring for the children, even though the deceased worker did not have the number of credits normally required. These

The **Social Security Administration** maintains an excellent Web site from which you can obtain the publications referred to in this chapter, and many others:

http://www.ssa.gov

Your local bank branch is experienced in what has to be done with Social Security when a deposit holder dies.

Take a certified copy of the death certificate and meet with a bank customer service representative. He or she will do what is necessary to reverse any direct deposit and return any overpayment to Social Security.

family members can receive benefits even if the deceased worker only had credit for one and one-half years of work in the three years immediately prior to death.

Who is Eligible for Survivors Benefits?

The following is a very brief overview of eligibility. You will find it most useful to discuss your particular situation with a Social Security representative.

Social Security survivor benefits may be payable to the following categories of family members:

Widow or Widower

Full benefits are payable at age 65 or older, if the widow or widower was born before 1938, or reduced benefits may be payable as early as age 60. The age for receiving full benefits gradually increases for people born after 1937 until it reaches age 67 for people born in 1960 and later.

A disabled widow or widower may receive benefits at age 50-60.

The surviving spouse's benefits may be reduced if he or she also receives a pension from employment where Social Security taxes were not withheld. Further information on this reduction is available in Social Security Publication No. 05-100007 ("Government Pension Offset").

A widow or widower may be entitled to benefits at any age if he or she takes care of the decedent's child who is under age 16 or who is disabled and receives benefits.

Unmarried Children

Unmarried children under age 18 (or up to age 19 if they are full-time students in elementary or secondary school) may be entitled to benefits. Also, children of the decedent may be eligible for benefits, regardless of age, if they were disabled before age 22 and remain disabled. Under certain circumstances, benefits can also be paid to stepchildren, grandchildren, or adopted children. Discuss these situations with a Social Security representative.

Dependent Parents

Dependent parents age 62 or older may also be eligible for benefits.

Special One-Time Death Benefit

The surviving spouse or minor children of the deceased worker may be eligible for a special one-time death benefit of $255, if the deceased worker has enough work credits.

This amount is payable to the surviving spouse if he or she was living with the deceased worker at the time of death, or if they were living apart the amount may still be payable if the surviving spouse was receiving Social Security benefits on the deceased worker's earnings record.

If there is no surviving spouse, the amount may be payable to a child who was eligible for benefits on the deceased worker's earnings record in the month of death.

Benefits Available for Surviving Divorced Spouses

If the deceased worker was divorced, the former husband or wife should be able to receive benefits as a widow or widower if the marriage lasted 10 years or more. However, the length-of-marriage rule will not apply if the former spouse is caring for a child of the deceased worker under age 16 or disabled and who is also receiving benefits on the deceased worker's Social Security record. The child must be the natural child of the former spouse, or legally adopted by the former spouse.

Any benefits paid to a surviving former spouse who is age 60 or older (50-60 if disabled) will not affect the benefit rates for other survivors who may be receiving benefits.

Applying for Benefits

How a survivor should apply for survivors benefits depends on whether the survivor is receiving other benefits from Social Security.

Survivors Not Already Receiving Social Security

A survivor who is not already getting Social Security benefits should apply for survivors benefits promptly because, in certain cases, benefits will not be retroactive. You may apply by calling Social Security or at any Social Security office. Local offices are listed in your telephone directory in the Government Offices section.

Certain information and documents will be required to process the application. While it will be helpful if you have everything at the time of application, don't delay just because you're missing something. Social Security will work with you, get the process started, and you can provide the missing documents later. You will need either original documents or copies certified by the agency that issued them.

The information you will need includes the following:

❑ Proof of death (either a death certificate or proof of death from the funeral home).

❑ Social Security numbers of the deceased worker and the survivor.

❑ The survivor's birth certificate.

❑ Marriage certificate, if the survivor is a widow or widower.

❑ Divorce papers, if the survivor is applying as a surviving divorced spouse.

❑ Dependent children's Social Security numbers, if available.

❑ The deceased worker's W-2 forms or Federal self-employment tax return for the most recent year.

❑ The name of the bank or other financial institution and account number to which the benefits can be directly deposited.

Survivors Already Receiving Benefits

If the survivor is already receiving benefits as a wife or husband on the deceased worker's record at the time of death, report the death to Social Security and they will change the payments to survivors benefits. They will contact you if they need further information.

If the survivor is receiving benefits on his or her own work record, it will be necessary to complete an application for survivors benefits. It may be possible to obtain increased benefits as a widow or widower. Ask about this when you call or visit the Social Security office. The deceased spouse's death certificate will be necessary to process the claim.

Benefits for any children will automatically be changed to survivors benefits after the death is reported to Social Security. They will contact you if they need more information.

What is the Amount of Benefits?

The amount of the benefits that family members can expect to receive from Social Security will depend on the deceased worker's average lifetime earnings: The higher the earnings, the higher the benefits.

The amount of the benefits is a percentage of the deceased worker's basic Social Security benefit, based on age and the type of benefit for which the worker was eligible. Here are some typical percentages:

Widow or widower, age 65 or older: 100%
Widow or widower, age 60-64: approximately 71-94%
Widow, any age, with a child under age 16: 75%
Children: 75%.

Contact a Social Security representative to discuss the amount of benefits in your specific situation.

Are There Maximum Benefits Payable to a Family?

There is a maximum amount of Social Security benefits that can be paid to a survivor and members of the family each month. The limit varies, but as a general rule will be about 150-180% of the deceased worker's benefit rate. If the sum of the benefits payable to the family members exceeds the limit, benefits will be reduced.

Retirement Benefits for Widows and Widowers

If a widow or widower (including a divorced widow or widower) is receiving benefits, it is possible to switch over to his or her own retirement benefit as early as age 62. The person must be eligible and his or her retirement rate must be higher than the widow or widower rate. It may even be possible for a widow or widower to begin receiving one benefit at a reduced rate and then switch to the other benefit at an unreduced rate at age 65.

The rules are complicated and vary depending on the situation, so the best thing to do is discuss the matter with a Social Security representative.

Effect of Survivor's Earnings on Benefits

Social Security survivors benefits may be reduced if your earnings exceed certain limits. Those limits vary over time. To find out what the limits are this year and how the earnings above those limits reduce your Social Security benefits, contact Social Security and request Publication No. 05-10069 ("How Work Affects Your Benefits").

There is no earnings limit once you reach age 65. Also, the survivor's earnings will reduce only survivors benefits; they will not reduce the benefits of other family members.

What if the Survivor Remarries?

As a general rule, you cannot receive survivors benefits if you remarry. However, remarriage after age 60 (age 50 if disabled) will not prevent benefit payments on your former spouse's record. Also, at age 62 or older, you may get benefits on the record of your new spouse if they are higher.

Dealing with Social Security

The Social Security Administration has made every effort to streamline the process by use of toll-free telephone numbers and offices located across the nation. They also have a Web site from which you can download important information, including the publications mentioned in this chapter. (See reference on page 7-3.)

If you ask someone to contact Social Security on your behalf, you should know that your personal information is involved, and there are issues of confidentiality with which Social Security is concerned. If someone else is calling on your behalf, it is best that you be at the phone with them to give your permission to discuss your situation. If you have someone visit a Social Security office on your behalf, send a written consent in a simple letter. Otherwise, the Social Security representative will be unable to discuss the specifics of your situation with them.

In the case of a minor child, the natural parent or legal guardian can act on the child's behalf in dealing with Social Security with regard to the child's benefits.

Do You Need Help?

In most cases you will be able to satisfactorily process your claim to Social Security benefits on your own.

However, if you have serious concerns about how your claim is being handled, you may want to consult an attorney specializing in Social Security matters. Ask the attorney assisting with estate administration or your local bar association for a referral.

NOTES

"In 1999, the Trustees of Social Security reported the Trust Funds will have sufficient assets to pay full benefits until the year 2034— another *35 years*. Beyond 2034, Social Security can pay nearly three-quarters of benefits as promised under current law.

"While that gives the American people time to debate the issues and then modify the system, the sooner adjustments are made, the smaller they will have to be. And, those most affected will have longer to prepare for the changes...."

—From an Overview of Social Security Issues
and Challenges provided on the AARP Web site,
http://www.aarp.org/focus/ssecure/part_2/issues.htm

CHAPTER 8

. . . .

VETERAN'S BENEFITS

The **Department of Veteran's Affairs** Web site is located at http://www.va.gov

The full text of the VA manual, "Federal Benefits for Veterans and Dependents," may be downloaded from http://www.va.gov/About_VA/index.htm

The VA has a one-stop service inquiry page: http://www.va.gov/customer/consumer.asp

This provides information on where to get forms, whom to contact on specific issues, and answers to frequently asked questions on veteran's benefits.

Veteran's Benefits

Survivors of veterans may be entitled to various burial-related benefits. Survivors' benefits are also available, but in relatively limited circumstances. In this chapter we provide a general overview of benefits available, eligibility, and sources of further information and assistance in filing applications for benefits.

For the most part, veteran's benefits are not paid automatically, but only upon filing a claim. Claims must generally be filed within two years after permanent burial or cremation.

The following information is based upon the Department of Veterans Affairs (VA) manual, "Federal Benefits for Veterans and Their Dependents" (2000 Edition), a copy of which may be obtained from the VA or downloaded on the Internet. See the sidebar and Appendix A for additional resources. You may also call VA toll-free at 1-800-827-1000 to discuss benefits.

Burial Flag

A United States flag is available for most veterans. The flag may be given to the next of kin or friend of the decedent. Reservists entitled to retired pay are also eligible to receive a burial flag.

When burial is in a national, state, or post cemetery a burial flag will be provided. When burial is in a private cemetery, burial flags may be obtained from VA regional offices, national cemeteries, and most U.S. Post Offices by completing VA Form 2008, **Application for United States Flag for Burial Purposes**, and submitting it with a copy of the veteran's discharge papers at any of these locations.

If the decedent was a veteran, your funeral director may be able to assist you in obtaining a burial flag.

Reimbursement of Burial Expenses

Federal Benefits

VA will pay a burial allowance up to $1,500 if the veteran's death is service connected. In some instances, VA will also pay the cost of transporting the remains of a service disabled veteran to the national cemetery nearest the home of the decedent that has available grave sites. In such cases, the person who bore the veteran's burial expense may claim reimbursement from VA.

VA will pay a $300 burial and funeral expense allowance for veterans who, at the time of death, were entitled to receive pension or compensation or would have been entitled to compensation but for receipt of military retirement pay. Eligibility also may be established when death occurs in a VA facility, a nursing home under VA contract, or a state nursing home. Additional costs of transportation of the remains may be paid.

There is no time limit for filing reimbursement claims of service connected deaths. In other deaths, claims must be filed within two years after permanent burial or cremation.

VA will pay a $150 plot allowance when a veteran is not buried in a cemetery that is under U.S. Government jurisdiction under any of the following circumstances:

① The veteran was discharged from active duty because of disability incurred or aggravated in the line of duty;

② The veteran was in receipt of compensation or pension or would have been except for receiving military retired pay; or

③ The veteran died in a VA facility.

The $150 plot allowance may be paid to the state if a veteran is buried without charge for the cost of a plot or interment is in a state-owned cemetery reserved solely for veteran burials. Burial expenses paid by the decedent's employer or a state agency will not be reimbursed.

State Benefits

Many states provide benefits to veterans. To find out more about what is available from a particular state, go to the following Web address:

http://www.va.gov/partners/stateoffice/index.htm

There you will find a map of the United States, and by clicking on a particular state you will be directed to a Web page which generally describes services provided and benefits available, along with contact information.

County Benefits

Additional burial-related benefits may be available through the Veterans Affairs office in the county of residence. You should determine if these benefits are available by contacting the county office.

County offices in the Metropolitan Detroit area are listed in Appendix A. Those offices may handle not only county benefits, but VA benefits as well. Personnel in these offices are very experienced and knowledgeable. In addition, various veterans organizations have service officers who will provide assistance with benefits. Contact information is available at the VA Web site indicated under "State Benefits" above.

Survivors' Benefits

Veterans' survivors are provided benefits in relatively limited circumstances. These are administered by the Veterans Benefits Administration (VBA), part of the U.S. Department of Veterans Affairs. The rules are relatively detailed and are subject to change. The following information was obtained from the VBA web site. Additional contact information may be found in Appendix A.

Dependency and Indemnity Compensation

Dependency and Indemnity Compensation (DIC) payments may be available for surviving spouses who have not remarried, unmarried children under 18, helpless children, those

The **Veterans Benefit Administration** Web site is located at:

http://www.vba.va.gov

between 18 and 23 if attending a VA-approved school, and low-income parents of deceased service members or veterans.

Eligibility

To be eligible, the death must not have been the result of willful misconduct and must have resulted from one of the following:

① A disease or injury incurred or aggravated while on active duty or active duty for training;

② An injury incurred or aggravated in line of duty while on inactive duty training; or

③ A disability compensable by VA.

If a spouse remarries, eligibility for benefits may be restored if the marriage is terminated later by death or divorce.

DIC payments also may be authorized for survivors of veterans who were totally service-connected disabled at time of death, but whose deaths were not the result of their service-connected disability. The survivor may qualify if :

① The veteran was continuously rated totally disabled for a period of ten or more years immediately preceding death; or

② The veteran was so rated for a period of at least five years from the date of military discharge.

Payments under this provision are subject to offset by the amount received from judicial proceedings brought on account of the veteran's death. The discharge must have been under conditions other than dishonorable.

DIC Payments to Surviving Spouse

Benefits are payable to surviving spouses of veterans who died after January 1, 1993. The current rate is $881 per month.

DIC Payments to Parents and Children

The monthly payment for parents of deceased veterans depends upon their income. There are additional DIC payments for dependent children. A child may be eligible if there is no surviving spouse, and the child is unmarried and under age 18, or if the child is between the age of 18 and 23 and attending school.

Special Allowances

Surviving spouses and parents receiving DIC may be granted a special allowance to pay for aid and attendance by another person if they are patients in a nursing home or require the regular assistance of another person.

Surviving spouses receiving DIC may be granted a special allowance if they are permanently house bound.

Survivors Benefit Plan (SBP)

DIC payments are affected by the receipt of SBP benefits. Consult a benefits counselor at the VA Regional Office that serves your area for more details.

How to Apply

Obtain a copy of VA Form 21-534, **Application for Dependency and Indemnity Compensation, Death Pension and Accrued Benefits by a Surviving Spouse or Child (Including Death Compensation if Applicable)**, from the VA or the forms Web site. Fill in the required information and mail the form to the VA Regional Office that serves your area.

Your VA benefits will generally relate back to the date the VA receives your application for benefits. Your date of application is therefore important to you, and you should apply as soon as possible, even if you do not have all the required supporting evidence or documents. You can complete your file later.

The following supporting evidence and/or documents should be submitted with your application, if available:

❑ **Dependency Documents**: Original or a copy of birth and marriage certificates and copies of divorce/death records terminating all prior marriages for veteran and spouse. Parents applying for DIC should furnish the original or a copy of the veteran's birth certificate.

❑ **Military Discharge**: DD Form 214 (Copy 4 - Member Copy). Those applicants who have a copy of their DD-214 are encouraged to provide a copy with their claim to expedite processing. Otherwise, the VA will attempt to obtain verification from the service department. Copies of missing DD Forms 214 may be obtained from the National Personnel Records Center in St. Louis, Missouri through the National Archives and Records Administration (NARA) web site.

❑ **Certification of Death**: Copy of the veteran's death certificate.

The **National Archives and Records Administration (NARA)** Web site is located at:

http://www.nara.gov

The **NARA National Personnel Records Center** Web site is located at:

http://www.nara.gov/regional/stlouis.html

Most veteran's benefits are available only if the decedent had a service-connected disability.

If the decedent was retired from the military, including the reserves, additional information regarding Survivors Benefit Plan (SPB) and other military survivor benefits may be obtained from the Personnel or Finance Command of the military department in which the decedent served, or sometimes from a local reserve center. Also see the additional resources in Appendix A.

NOTES

"I wouldn't take a million dollars for
the experience I had in the service,
but I wouldn't go through it again
for a million dollars."
—A Veteran

CHAPTER 9

· · · · · · · · · · ·

LIFE INSURANCE

Life Insurance

What Life Insurance Is In Effect?

Sometimes it is very easy to locate all of the life insurance policies and certificates of group insurance on the life of a decedent; in other cases you will have to do some detective work or find someone to help you. In this chapter we provide you tips on how to discover whether there is life insurance, including information on a company which will contact over 1,700 insurance companies on your behalf. We also address important questions to consider before submitting a claim for benefits.

Your first source of information about life insurance on the decedent will probably be the family. Then consider the following to identify all life insurance, including policies which appear to have lapsed:

❑ Contact the life insurance agent of the decedent.

❑ Contact the decedent's attorney, accountant, trust officer, and financial planner, any of whom may have background information on insurance on the decedent's life.

❑ Contact the decedent's employer. Insurance may have been provided as an employee benefit.

❑ If the decedent was a business owner, contact the person responsible for paying the company's bills and determine if the company was paying for life insurance, which may be payable to the company or to others.

❑ Review any estate planning files of the decedent for checklists and other documents which may contain life insurance information.

No Claim, No Benefits

Life insurance provides important cash benefits, which can be used for numerous purposes:

To support minor children, pay educational expenses, improve a beneficiary's life style, supplement retirement income for survivors, or pay estate taxes.

It may also provide needed cash to replace the income of the decedent and allow the family to maintain the home and avoid worries about how to support themselves.

However, the insurance company cannot pay benefits unless a claim is made.

This chapter provides many ways of locating life insurance.

All of these are unnecessary if there is a complete, up-to-date listing of insurance policies, including company name, policy number, amount of death benefit, and location of the policy.

This listing should be prepared as part of everyone's estate planning.

❑ Review the check register and canceled checks of the decedent for the past three years. They may provide clues as to what insurance companies received premium payments, and may also include policy numbers.

❑ Review any divorce documents for evidence of obligations to maintain life insurance.

❑ Review any trusts created by the decedent, particularly irrevocable trusts, which may own insurance on the decedent's life.

❑ Review credit card agreements for life insurance which may exist to pay off the credit card balance. If in doubt, call the credit card company.

❑ Review mortgage payment stubs and mortgage closing papers for insurance (*private mortgage insurance* or PMI) which may pay off the mortgage balance. If in doubt, call the mortgage company.

❑ Review any consumer loan documentation (e.g., auto and boat loans) for insurance intended to pay off the loan balance in the event of death. If in doubt call the bank or finance company which made the loan.

❑ Contact clubs and associations in which the decedent was a member to determine if membership included any life insurance benefits.

❑ If you believe that there was insurance, but cannot locate any specifics, you may want to enlist the services of a company which will contact insurance companies on your behalf. You may also want to do this as part of your due diligence if you are unfamiliar with the decedent's affairs and want to make sure that you have not overlooked possible insurance on his or her life.

LIFE BENEFITS, INC. is a company which offers to contact over 1,700 United States life insurance companies to determine whether life insurance is in force on an insured, for a modest fee.

See their Web site: http://www.lifesearch.net

See Appendix A for further information.

A Double Indemnity Tale

Lloyd, who had a history of heart problems, died in a single-vehicle car crash. The insurance company took the position that the cause of death was a heart attack, not accidental death.

Lloyd's daughter, Maya, asserted a claim for accidental death benefits, which were double the normal policy death benefits. An autopsy was inconclusive as to whether the death was caused by a heart attack or the car crash.

Maya hired an attorney, and the insurance company ultimately paid the accidental death benefits.

Before Claiming Benefits...

Don't rush to file claims for life insurance benefits. Contact each insurance company, on a preliminary basis, to determine what benefits are payable and who are the beneficiaries. Prior to filing the actual claim, review the information in this section to see if there are issues which could affect whether benefits are due, the amount of those benefits, and the proper beneficiaries.

❑ Determine if any premium payments were overdue at the date of death and if those premiums should be paid immediately to prevent lapse.

❑ Examine the circumstances of death to determine if accidental death benefits may be claimed.

❑ Determine if any policy was recently issued on the life of the decedent, so that the incontestability period has not yet run. This is often two years. If circumstances suggest that the insurance company may refuse to pay benefits, contact an attorney to evaluate whether options are available to avoid this defense.

❑ If the life insurance is owned by a partnership or corporation in which the decedent was a partner or stockholder, determine to whom the benefits should be paid. They may be payable to the company, a named beneficiary, the estate, or a co-owner as part of a buyout of the decedent's interest in the company.

❑ Determine if any beneficiary wants to *disclaim* all or any portion of the benefits to which he or she may be entitled. A *disclaimer* is, in effect, a refusal to accept the benefits. This would generally allow the disclaimed amount to pass to the person who would take the benefits if the beneficiary predeceased the insured. (See discussion of disclaimers in Chapter 13,

"Who Shares in the Estate," and Chapter 19, "The Tax Man Cometh.")

If the disclaimer is executed in compliance with Internal Revenue Code rules governing qualified disclaimers, the benefits will be deemed to pass directly to the contingent beneficiary and will not constitute a taxable gift from the beneficiary.

Most importantly, if the beneficiary intends to make a qualified disclaimer of benefits, the beneficiary may not first receive the benefits and then turn them back. In addition, strict time limits must be observed for a qualified disclaimer. Though life insurance benefits may not be considered part of your responsibility as fiduciary of the estate, if you are involved in making the claims you or your attorney should advise the beneficiary about the possibility of a disclaimer before submitting a claim for benefits.

❑ Determine if a change of beneficiary should be given effect, or if the position should be taken that it is ineffective. Reasons why it might be ineffective might include failure to sign the form or to file it with the insurance company, or lack of competence at the time of signing the change of beneficiary form.

❑ If a prior spouse is named as a beneficiary, review divorce decrees and property settlement agreements to determine if the prior spouse is entitled to retain policy proceeds payable to him or her. In some cases the proceeds will have been intended only to secure a balance due under a divorce decree, the insurance may not have been reduced over time as initially contemplated, and the amount due under the divorce decree may already have been paid in full. In other cases, an old beneficiary designation may have been unintentionally left in place and may have been automatically voided by operation of law at the time of the divorce.

The Beneficiary Change That Wasn't

Chester, newly divorced, submitted a form changing the beneficiary on his life insurance from his former wife, Rose, to his father. However, he forgot to sign the form on the signature line, although two witnesses did sign it.

After Chester died, Rose claimed the purported change was ineffective. Under applicable state law, divorce did not automatically void a prior beneficiary designation in favor of an ex-spouse.

The father's attorney argued that the attempted change should be effective because the rules applicable to the policy did not require signature in any particular place on the form, and that Chester had printed his name on the form with the intent to sign it.

The two beneficiaries reached a settlement.

Who Do You Trust?

Carl purchased insurance on his life, which he intended to be used for his children's education. He named his brother, Dwight, as the beneficiary, and advised family members, including Dwight, of the purpose for the insurance.

Carl died several years later, and Dwight made a claim to the proceeds, as the named beneficiary of the policy.

The children also made a claim to the insurance, on the theory that it was intended for their educational expenses, and that Dwight was merely to receive the proceeds for their benefit.

In these circumstances a court could impose a *constructive trust* on the insurance proceeds, and require that they be used for the children's education.

❑ If the decedent was a party to a prenuptial or postnuptial agreement, separation agreement, or divorce decree under which the decedent was entitled to insurance proceeds on the life of the other party, determine if the estate will be entitled to those benefits.

❑ Consider if the facts support a claim that the person named in the beneficiary designation was not intended by the owner of the policy to be the true beneficial owner of the insurance proceeds. In appropriate cases, it may be possible for a court to impose a *constructive trust* on those benefits, and deem that they are to be held for the benefit of someone else.

Claim Life Insurance Benefits

After you determine what insurance is in effect, who are the proper beneficiaries, that there is no desire on the part of a beneficiary to disclaim benefits, and that the beneficiaries do not desire to make the claim themselves:

❑ Obtain and complete the necessary forms on all life insurance on the life of the decedent.

❑ Make copies of all policies, including the application, any beneficiary designations, and assignments of the policies, before submitting the policies for payment.

❑ If there are any outstanding policy loans, consider whether they should be repaid rather than deducted from the death benefits, if that will result in an increased amount of benefits under the settlement options.

❑ Submit claims for death proceeds, preferably by certified mail, return receipt requested.

❑ Request that payment be made in a lump sum or under any other method of payment which is available and which the beneficiary desires.

❑   Insurance companies will sometimes insist on opening a checking account for the beneficiary with the death benefits rather than providing a check for the lump sum proceeds. If a lump sum is desired, request a check for the total benefits. If you forget to ask for a check for the total benefits, or if the checking account is opened in spite of your request, then write a check on that account for the full balance and deposit the check to the desired account.

❑   Request each insurance company to provide U.S. Treasury Form 712 with regard to each policy, as well as copies of any assignments of the policies. Form 712 is necessary to prepare the Federal Estate Tax return. The assignments may be needed to show that the insurance was transferred by the decedent more than three years prior to death, and thus excludable from the gross estate for Federal Estate Tax purposes.

Other Issues Related to Life Insurance

❑   If the insurance proceeds are significantly less than what was expected, consult an attorney. Provide the attorney all the information and documents which cause you to believe there should be more insurance. Ask the attorney to thoroughly review the situation.

❑   Consider with the beneficiary of a large amount of insurance proceeds how those proceeds should be invested. (See Chapter 23, "Financial & Estate Planning for the Survivors.")

❑   If there is insurance on the lives of others, payable to the decedent, consider if it is necessary to change the beneficiary on such insurance.

❑ If there is insurance in effect which was intended to protect the decedent, consider if that insurance should remain in effect. Such insurance may be on the life of the surviving spouse, other family members, or business associates. In some cases that insurance should be retained, for the benefit of others, but in some cases it will be just as well to dispose of it by terminating the policy or in some other manner.

❑ Consider if new insurance should be obtained on the surviving spouse, to provide liquidity to pay estate taxes at the time of that spouse's later death.

❑ If the decedent owned life insurance on the lives of others, consider what should be done with that insurance. There will be cases where it is appropriate to cash it in, let it lapse, distribute the policies to the beneficiaries of the estate, or take other action.

❑ Life insurance proceeds will generally be payable to named beneficiaries without regard to claims of creditors of the decedent. However, if the insurance is payable to the estate, the proceeds will be subject to claims. (See Chapter 17, "Dealing with Creditors.")

CHAPTER 10

. . . .

WHERE TO TURN FOR HELP

Where to Turn for Help

Should You Go It Alone?

The administration of estates is inherently complex. It encompasses elements of law, taxation, accounting, asset management, and other disciplines. It is a rare individual who possesses a level of knowledge in each of these areas sufficient to handle an estate, from beginning to end, without help.

In some cases, the estate may appear to be small and the administration may seem "simple." Appearances can be deceptive. Within a seemingly "simple" estate there can be any number of issues having to do with property rights, valuation, taxation, and the creation and funding of trusts or other entities. Those responsible are subject to personal liability for mistakes or missteps. Ignorance of these issues is not an acceptable excuse.

You may be tempted to try to "get by" on your own. You may be concerned about fees. You may be reluctant to involve outsiders in what you believe are private family matters. Nevertheless, we urge you to seek professional assistance.

In this chapter we review the types of help you should consider, how to locate the right people for your estate, and how they are generally compensated. Finding the right people can make your job much easier and can actually save the estate money that might be lost if mistakes are made or opportunities missed.

People Who Can Help

Attorneys

The administration of an estate is, first and foremost, a legal matter. It is therefore essential that you have competent legal advice.

We recommend that you have an initial consultation with an attorney who practices in the area of probate, trust, and estate planning and administration. Since this is a highly specialized area of law, you should seek an attorney with a primary focus in this area.

Where do you find such an attorney? Following is a checklist of steps you might consider.

❑ If the decedent had an attorney, you may want to start with this individual since he or she will be most familiar with the decedent's affairs.

❑ If the decedent's attorney does not feel comfortable handling all aspects of the estate, he or she may want to locate another attorney to assist and act as co-counsel in certain areas which require particular expertise.

❑ If the decedent did not have an estate planning attorney or if you do not wish to work with that person, then you should look for one. Most major law firms have such individuals and there are smaller firms and sole practitioners with expertise in this area.

❑ You may ask for referrals from the trust department of your bank or from your state or local bar associations.

❑ Recommendations from your own attorney, accountant, financial advisor, or insurance agent may also be helpful.

The **Martindale-Hubbell Law Directory** is available on the Internet:

http://www.martindale.com

You can use their Lawyer Locator function to search for attorneys by location and area of practice. Search for "Probate, Trusts, and Estates" attorneys.

This will generally provide you basic background on attorneys who devote a substantial portion of their practice to probate and estates.

You should cross-match these attorneys with referrals you receive. Then interview those who seem to have the necessary background, to find a proper match for your needs.

❑ You can find biographical information on many attorneys in the Martindale-Hubbell Law Directory, which is available in many libraries and on the Internet, or on the Web site for the attorney or firm.

❑ Do not hesitate to ask the attorney to summarize his or her experience in probate, trust, and estate planning and administration. If the attorney admits that he or she only occasionally handles estate administration and has no one else in the firm who is active in this area, seek another firm.

❑ Try to determine whether you will need assistance in Probate Court matters, in estate tax return preparation, or general administration. The attorney should be able to assess your needs at the first interview. Seek to match your needs with the attorney's skills.

For example, if you anticipate a Will contest, you need a litigator, an attorney who tries cases. If you do not have a probate estate, but have thorny estate tax issues, seek someone who has that background even if he or she never gets to Probate Court.

❑ Since tax is an integral part of estate administration, if the estate is large enough to involve estate taxes you should inquire if the attorney has advanced training in this area, such as a Master of Laws (LLM) degree in taxation.

❑ You should also ask to meet the associate attorney or legal assistant who will be working on the estate. It is important to you that the firm have administrative staff to handle administrative matters for the estate, since the hourly rate for administration should be less than for highly qualified attorneys. You do not want your attorney to be handling every detail of administration.

❑ If you are satisfied with the *competence* of the attorney, you should give some thought to the *chemistry* of the relationship:

① Do you feel that you will be comfortable working with this firm?

② Do you sense that the people you met will be responsive?

③ Did you understand what they were saying to you or did they talk over your head?

④ Were they patient if you asked for additional explanation?

The attorney will ask that you bring various documents to the initial consultation. He or she will review these documents and ask you questions to determine what must be done to administer the estate and the issues that will be involved.

The attorney will then discuss with you the steps that must be taken and any areas of special concern.

You can then decide if you want to engage the attorney to advise you, if you want to consult with another attorney, or if you believe you can handle the estate without the assistance of an attorney. Ultimately, you yourself will have to assess the qualifications of an estate attorney to whom you are referred, unless your own attorney is assisting you in locating an attorney to help with the administration of the estate.

If you decide to engage the attorney, there should be a discussion of which tasks you or other family members will perform and which tasks will be handled by the attorney's office. The attorney may have an estate administration checklist to review for this purpose, or you may want to use this book as a guide.

The attorney should discuss the fee arrangement after reviewing the types of work which will have to be done to administer the estate. Fees will generally be charged on an hourly basis, but the attorney should be able to give you at least a rough estimate of total fees and expenses and advise you whether fees

Who is the Client?

The client of an attorney is the person who engages or hires the attorney. In an estate, the Personal Representative, Trustee, or other fiduciary engages the attorney, and the attorney represents the fiduciary, not the estate as such or the beneficiaries.

If you are a beneficiary or family member but are not the fiduciary, you are not the client, and the attorney is not representing you, even though you may have participated in meetings with or receive correspondence from the attorney.

If you feel your interests are not being properly addressed by the attorney, you should first discuss the matter with the fiduciary. If this does not result in a satisfactory resolution of your concerns, you should consider retaining separate counsel to represent you.

will be billed monthly or at certain stages in the administration. Any estimate will obviously be based on certain assumptions as to what work will have to be done, and if the scope of the work increases significantly you should expect that the actual fees will be higher.

In any event, make it clear that you would like to receive detailed billing statements, with a description of the work done, date, by whom it was done, and hours. This will help you evaluate the services and also the progress that is being made. This is desirable from the attorney's perspective as well, because it will help you appreciate the myriad of details being addressed and what it takes to accomplish seemingly simple tasks.

Also ask about the possibility of a fixed fee, which can sometimes be arranged if the work to be done is very predictable. You should recognize, however, that estate administration often takes twists and turns, and that it is usually difficult for an attorney to agree to a fixed fee.

The attorney should then confirm the proposal or agreement in an engagement letter.

Accountants

You may be required to file a variety of tax returns, for the decedent and for the estate. (See Chapter 19, "The Tax Man Cometh.") If there is a probate estate or a trust, you will have to provide accounts to the beneficiaries. If the decedent had an IRA or was a participant in a qualified retirement plan, you may need a computation of the required minimum distribution from the IRA or plan for the year of death and future years.

Virtually all estate planning attorneys are able to prepare the Federal Estate Tax return, and state estate or inheritance tax returns. Some attorneys will also prepare fiduciary and individual income tax returns, prepare accounts, and calculate IRA and retirement plan distributions. Other attorneys will ask that you engage an accountant to provide these services.

Individual income tax returns for the decedent, or for the decedent and surviving spouse, are probably best done by the decedent's regular tax preparer because of that person's familiarity with the decedent's income and deductions. The decedent's regular tax preparer may also be able to compute required minimum distributions from IRAs and retirement plans.

However, if fiduciary income tax returns and accounts will be required—and they *will* be required if there is a probate estate or a trust—you should engage an accountant who is experienced in these specialized areas. Your attorney should be able to recommend several accountants who are qualified to do this work.

Before engaging an accountant, you should inquire about the experience of the accountant and any staff members who will be working on your behalf. You should confirm what work is to be done, what information you will have to provide, when you will have to provide it, and when the work will be completed. You should also reach an agreement on the fee arrangement. In some cases, there will be a flat fee for each return or other work product. In other cases, fees may be charged on an hourly basis. All of this should be memorialized in an engagement letter.

The accountant should be brought into the picture early because there are typically several income tax issues to be considered, and the sooner these are addressed the better.

Bookkeeping Services

You may be able to handle details of bill paying, check writing, and balancing the checkbook for the estate account yourself, or you may prefer to have those types of services performed by someone else.

These services do not require an accountant, though the accountant may have staff who can provide bookkeeping services for you. You can also seek an outside bookkeeping service based on recommendations from your accountant, your attorney, or friends.

In any event you must keep impeccable records on behalf of the estate. Do not simply continue to use the decedent's accounts, nor should you commingle or mix monies of the estate with your own. If you inadvertently deposit estate funds to your own account, or pay an estate expense from your own funds, correct the error as soon as you discover it and write a memo to document what happened.

Financial Advisors: Stockbrokers, Financial Planners, and Investment Advisors

If there are marketable securities, such as stocks, bonds, and mutual funds, you must see that they are properly managed. (See Chapter 16, "Protect and Preserve Estate Assets.") Alleged mismanagement of investments is a major area of liability exposure for fiduciaries. Unless you have extensive experience in this area, you should seek a competent financial advisor.

We use the term *financial advisor* to include the entire spectrum of professionals who offer services related to the management of investments. This includes, but is not limited to, stockbrokers, financial planners, and investment advisors.

The services that are available from financial advisors range from general advice to specific recommendations to full portfolio management. Therefore, you must first decide on the level of assistance you desire or, to say it differently, the degree of involvement the financial advisor is to have. You should then look for someone who is capable of providing the services you want.

You should consider using the decedent's stockbroker or financial advisor. However, do not feel obligated to do so if you have reservations about his or her ability to meet your needs. Your attorney will probably know of several financial advisors and will likely be familiar with the investment style and performance of each.

If significant assets are involved, you should interview several financial advisors and make a decision based not only on past performance, but also on accessibility and the "chemistry" of the relationship. You may not be a financial wizard yourself, but the financial advisor should not talk down to you. All your questions should be answered completely and politely.

Before committing to a financial advisor, you should have a clear understanding of the services he or she proposes to provide, the fees, and any restrictions or limitations on the advisor's authority.

If the advisor is to have full portfolio management responsibility, you should ask for materials which show the advisor's performance in managing portfolios of similar size and complexity. Results should be shown for the past one-year, three-year, five-year, and ten-year periods, and should include comparisons to industry benchmarks such as the Dow Jones Industrial Average and the Standard & Poors 500 Stock Index.

You should also have some idea of what the prospective portfolio manager has in mind. If, for example, the intention is to immediately sell everything and start over, you should know this up front and not have it come as a surprise when you see the activity on the account statement. You should also be aware that your job as a fiduciary is not necessarily to maximize returns, but to preserve the estate for the period of administration.

Finally, be sure you understand how the financial advisor will be compensated. Various arrangements are possible, sometimes involving fees based on a percentage of the assets, sometimes commissions, and sometimes a combination of the two. You should shop the quoted rates to see if they are competitive. If they are not, you may be able to negotiate a reduction. Be wary of a compensation structure that is weighted too heavily toward commissions, as this could result in excessive buying and selling, a practice known as *churning*.

The entire agreement should be set forth in one or more letters or forms which you will be asked to sign. You should have your attorney review them before you sign.

If significant assets are involved, you should bring a financial advisor on board as soon as possible. The financial markets can be extremely volatile. Allowing investments to go for more than a couple of weeks without someone "minding the store" can result in serious losses.

Getting Out of the Middle

Mildred was appointed Trustee of her late brother's trust. However, after a short time she realized that the attitude and demands of the beneficiaries (her adult nephews) would make her job difficult.

As Trustee she would have to make discretionary decisions with regard to distributions of principal and income. Her nephews were already starting to ask for distributions, and she found it difficult to say "no." However, she knew that the distributions probably should not be made in the amounts and for the reasons requested.

Mildred decided to resign as Trustee, and allow a bank to take over as Successor Trustee. Rather than abdicating her responsibility, she felt this was the best way to keep out of the middle and have an independent third party make the right decisions.

Banks and Trust Companies

If you have a bank or trust company serving along with you as a co-fiduciary, that institution should assign an officer who is experienced in estate administration. That person will, in turn, be supported by specialists in tax, fiduciary accounting, asset valuation, and investment management.

If a bank or trust company is not presently serving, you may wish to add one as co-fiduciary in order to secure the full range of services that such an institution can provide. However, this may require going to Probate Court to change or *reform* the Will or trust.

If you do not want the bank or trust company to have a fiduciary role, you can engage the institution in an *agency* capacity. All of the institution's resources will be available to you, but the institution will serve as your agent and will be subject to your direction.

As an alternative, you can hire a bank or trust company to be *custodian* of the assets of the estate. The institution can either manage the assets or provide investment recommendations to you. If you do not need investment counseling, the institution can simply hold the assets in safekeeping, collect the income, and maintain transaction records. Fees will vary depending on the role which the bank or trust company assumes.

Banks and trust companies acting as fiduciaries typically charge for estate administration services based on a percentage of the assets in the estate or trust. There may be additional fees for account maintenance, for tax return preparation, and for certain other services.

Your attorney should be able to refer you to several banks or trust companies with which he or she is familiar.

Appraisers and Valuation Services

Valuation may be important in connection with an estate tax return, possible sale of an asset, or in connection with distributions. In those cases it is generally not sufficient to estimate values yourself.

An appraiser may be needed to value personal property if there are unusual items, antiques, art work, jewelry, or collectibles. An appraiser may also be required for real estate. If the decedent owned a closely held business or an interest in such a business, a qualified appraiser is a must.

Your attorney can recommend one or more appraisers who are qualified to appraise the type of property in question.

The appraiser may charge a fee based on the time required to complete the appraisal, but for some types of appraisals will be able to quote a fixed fee.

Listed securities will be easier to value, but date-of-death values and alternate values are required for estate tax purposes. Those values do not correspond exactly to the values shown on the brokerage statements. Valuation services provide values for listed securities based on the proper valuation method, based on *mean market* prices, and will also provide any accrued dividends and interest, as required for tax purposes.

The attorney can put you in contact with one or more of these services. However, if the attorney is handling preparation of the estate tax return he or she will probably determine how to value listed securities and obtain the necessary valuations for you.

A valuation service will charge a few dollars for each value provided. You can look up and compute these values yourself, if you have retained the *Wall Street Journal* for the dates required. However, if many securities are involved it is well worth the modest fee to obtain the information from one of the valuation services.

Estate Liquidators

Estate liquidators will typically come to the decedent's residence, set up the house for an estate sale, fix the prices, and hold the sale. Because they know the values of these objects, they may be able to get more than you thought the items were worth. They may arrange for articles not sold to be donated to charity or otherwise disposed of. They may also offer to buy whatever is left for a fixed price.

A Worthwhile Appraisal

Michael was Trustee of his uncle's estate, which included a residence which his uncle left to him and which Michael did not intend to sell.

Initially he hesitated to get an appraisal, thinking it would be too costly. He was surprised to find that in his area a formal residential appraisal only cost $250-$500.

He got the appraisal, and the value of the residence was much less than he had thought. The IRS approved the valuation of the residence at the appraised value for Federal Estate Tax purposes.

In addition to the convenience they offer, estate liquidators spare you the emotional stress of selling the decedent's personal property to strangers, who may denigrate the items in an effort to buy them for less.

Your attorney may be able to recommend one or more estate liquidators. If not, you should be able to find one through the Yellow Pages of the decedent's telephone directory, through ads for estate sales in the local newspaper, or by watching for estate sale signs on the weekend.

Estate liquidators generally charge a commission based on a percentage of the sales proceeds. Check with several to determine the going rate in your area.

Real Estate Brokers

If the decedent left real estate and you have decided to sell the property, a real estate broker can be of assistance. You should look for a broker who is familiar with the real estate market in the area where the property is located.

If the broker is successful in selling the property, he or she will receive an agreed percentage of the sales price as a commission. Ask your attorney what commission is typically charged in your area. Commissions will vary depending on whether commercial or residential property is involved, and may also vary depending on the value of the property.

If you have obtained some prospective buyers yourself, make sure that a special arrangement is made with the broker to either exclude those buyers from the commission arrangement, or for a reduced commission. Your attorney should be able to assist you in working through the details of a listing agreement with the broker.

A real estate broker can also help if you are not selling the property but wish to know its approximate value. For a nominal fee, or perhaps on a complimentary basis, the broker can provide you with a *market analysis* and a range of prices within which the property might sell. (Note, however, that this is not the same as, or equivalent to, an appraisal by a qualified appraiser.)

Specialty Purchasers of Esoteric Items

If the decedent left a rare violin, an original letter written by George Washington, or a collection of stamps, coins, guns, or Civil War artifacts, to mention a few examples, you may have to educate yourself in marketing that type of item in order to obtain the best price. You should expect that a sale to a dealer will be for substantially less than what you might obtain from an individual buyer, if you could find one.

You may want to use a dealer's offer as a base price, on which you should try to improve. Your attorney may know of a dealer who would be interested in the item in question, or you may be able to locate one through the Yellow Pages or on the Internet. If the decedent belonged to an organization or club of collectors, ask those people for suggestions as to how to sell these items.

Fees in Perspective

As this book illustrates, and anyone who has ever administered an estate can tell you, there are many things to be done in all but the very smallest estate.

The professionals you engage to perform or assist with these tasks are just that—professionals. They have invested a great deal of time and money to earn advanced degrees, professional certifications, and state or federal licensure, and they generally pursue continuing professional education to keep their skills up to date.

They have the knowledge and experience to get you successfully through the challenges of estate administration. When viewed in relation to the services they are able to render, their fees are reasonable and necessary.

Indeed, for those who are accustomed to working with professionals, the fees incurred in the administration of an estate will not seem out of line. For the uninitiated, however, the idea of paying thousands of dollars in fees may be deeply disturbing.

Most professionals strive to minimize fees that must be charged by operating as efficiently as possible and by assigning

On Second Thought...

After the first visit to her late husband's attorney, Julia decided not to engage the attorney because of the fees that would be incurred.

Over the next weeks she realized she was unable to do all the work that needed to be done, even with the help of her son, who had his own business to attend to.

She reconsidered and asked the attorney to assist with administration of the estate.

work to staff members with lower billing rates. Most professionals will also advise you of things that you can do yourself.

Any such responsibilities that you can take on will reduce fees, and the resulting savings can be significant. On the other hand, if you have other obligations competing for your time, it may be best to simply let the professionals do their job. If you take on too much, there is a danger that you may not finish your tasks on a timely basis, which can cause further problems and possibly even increase the fees.

Despite all efforts, it is likely that fees will amount to a major expenditure. You must understand and accept this at the outset if you are to see the administration through to a successful conclusion. Consider professional fees an investment to get the job done properly, without mistakes, unnecessary liability on your part, or additional costs for which you could be held personally liable. There is perhaps also some comfort in knowing that professional fees may be deductible for tax purposes.

The Team Approach

It is important that the professionals you employ not "do their own thing" in isolation, but work together as a team. A team approach minimizes duplication of effort and allows for sharing of information and collaborating on decisions.

As but one example, expenses of administering the estate may be deducted either on the Federal Estate Tax return or on the fiduciary income tax return for the estate or trust. The preparers of the different returns should jointly decide how these deductions can be used to greatest overall advantage.

You should see that each member of the team has the names and telephone numbers of the other members. You should also make it clear that they have your permission to exchange information pertaining to the administration of the estate.

Remember that you are the leader of the team. You are the final decision maker and arbiter. In the case of a disagreement, you are the one who must make the call.

CHAPTER 11

....

INVENTORY THE ASSETS

Inventory the Assets

Taking Stock

Before you can administer the estate, you must know exactly what assets the decedent owned or in which he had an interest. General, approximate, or summary knowledge is not sufficient. You must develop a written, itemized list of each and every asset or interest. Such a list is called an *inventory*.

You will have to provide inventories to beneficiaries and possibly to the Probate Court. Inventories will also be used in the preparation of tax returns. It is difficult to overstate the importance of a complete and accurate inventory.

In this chapter, we discuss the steps involved in compiling an inventory and valuing the assets in which the decedent had an interest.

Where to Get the Information

Where do you get the information for the inventory? Most of the decedent's assets will normally be identified in the course of gathering the decedent's important documents. (See Chapter 5, "Gather Important Documents.") Others may be discovered by reviewing the decedent's checking account activity for the year prior to death. Still others may come to light as dividend checks, brokerage account statements, tax bills, premium notices, proxy statements, and other correspondence arrives in the mail. Some assets may only be discovered by contact with the family, the decedent's accountant, attorney, business partners, or employer.

For example, if the decedent loaned money to a family member, and didn't obtain a promissory note, you may only learn about that by talking to the family member or perhaps from other family members. Likewise, the decedent may be entitled to certain benefits from his employment, such as accrued vacation pay, and you may learn about that by contacting his employer. Both the loan receivable and the accrued vacation pay may be assets in which the decedent had an interest, and thus part of the estate.

Assets in Which the Decedent Had An Interest

The assets to be inventoried are not only those which are titled in the decedent's sole name. All assets in which the decedent had any interest, whether outright or in trust, including any joint interest (even if joint with a spouse), must be listed. Any *In Trust For, Payable on Death*, or *Transfer on Death* accounts must also be shown. If the decedent made any transfers in which he retained any type of interest, these may be includible for Federal Estate Tax purposes and should be discussed on a case-by-case basis with your attorney.

Although all assets must be inventoried, it is advisable to make separate inventories for each type of ownership, e.g., assets held in sole name, held jointly, held in the name of a trust, and having a designated beneficiary. This will facilitate notification of beneficiaries, probate filings, periodic accounts, and preparation of tax returns.

The Question of Ownership

For each asset, you must make a positive determination of how it was owned (titled) at the decedent's death. Do not make any assumptions in this regard. You may think that a bank account was in the decedent's name alone when in fact there was a son or daughter who was a joint owner. A husband and wife may have thought that their house was owned jointly when, for whatever reason, it was titled in the husband's sole name.

What is in the Estate?

What is in the "estate" depends on what "estate" you are talking about: The probate estate, the taxable estate for estate tax purposes, or the overall estate which must be administered.

Here we start with the broadest concept, the overall estate. After you have determined absolutely everything in which the decedent had any interest, you can address each item separately and determine if it is necessary to include it in the probate estate or in the taxable estate.

Example: Life insurance, payable to a named beneficiary, may be an asset in which the decedent had an interest, and thus part of the overall estate which must be administered. It may also be included in the taxable estate. However, if the proceeds are payable to a named beneficiary it will not be part of the probate estate.

The Case of the Vanishing Annuity

Making a correct determination of who owns an account may require going beyond the reporting on the brokerage statement and digging into the underlying facts.

In one case Harriet firmly believed she owned an annuity, but it was shown on the brokerage statement of her husband's trust.

When asked about this, the account executive explained: "That's just where we put it to get it on the statement."

Harriet was able to support her position that the annuity was hers, and the necessary correction was made.

For bank accounts, look at the most recent account statement or ask the bank to check the signature card. Do not rely on the names or other information printed on the checks. You may believe that a bank account was owned jointly with someone who had signature authority over the account, but it may actually have been owned only by the decedent and the co-signers may have only been acting under a power of attorney.

If an account is owned jointly with rights of survivorship, ask the surviving tenant if he or she claims ownership in the account or if he or she was joint *for convenience only*, in which case the account should be treated as belonging to the decedent.

For individual securities, look at the actual stock or bond certificate. Do not rely only on notes that may be found in the decedent's records.

For brokerage accounts, check the most recent account statement. If there are any doubts about the correctness of the statement, investigate thoroughly. It is possible that the statement is incorrect. For real estate, if there is any doubt how it is owned based on the records you locate, you should have a title search done by a title company.

Assets to Be Inventoried

The following is a basic checklist of the principal types of assets to be included. Consult your attorney if questions arise about whether an item is part of the estate for various purposes.

❑   Cash (including currency and coin of the United States and foreign countries, as well as collectible coins and currency).

❑   Bank accounts and accrued interest, whether in the decedent's name alone or owned jointly with others.

❑   Securities of any type, whether in certificate form, held in brokerage accounts, mutual funds, or in dividend reinvestment programs, as well as accrued dividends and interest on those securities.

❑   Annuities, even if payable on death to a named beneficiary.

❑   U.S. and foreign government, corporate, or municipal bonds and accrued interest.

❑   Accrued wages, accumulated vacation and sick pay, fringe benefits, and benefits under state worker's compensation laws.

❑   Retirement benefits, including those in employer sponsored plans, self-employed persons' plans and IRAs, even if the benefits are payable to a named beneficiary.

❑   Real estate, whether commercial, investment, or residential, and whether owned solely by the decedent or in joint ownership or partnership with others.

❑   Property in another state or country.

❑   Life insurance, whether on the life of the decedent or owned by the decedent on the life of another.

❑   Motor vehicles and boats.

❑   Personal property, including furniture, household furnishings, jewelry, art work, and collectibles.

❑   Business interests, including partnership and closely held corporate interests.

❑   Debts owed to the decedent.

❑   Lottery winnings, even if not payable until a future date.

❑   Safe deposit box contents.

❑   Interests passing under someone else's Will or trust (for example, the balance under a marital trust, which passes on the decedent's death to someone else).

❑ Rights under pending litigation, even if the amount ultimately to be collected, if any, will not be known until a future date.

❑ Miscellaneous assets, including frequent flier miles.

Valuation

Each asset on the inventory must be valued. Values will be needed for the Federal Estate Tax return, if a return is required to be filed. They will be needed to establish a new basis in the assets for income tax purposes, even if no Federal Estate Tax return is filed. If there is a probate estate, values will be needed for the probate inventory. Finally, values may be needed to equalize distributions to different beneficiaries.

Values are normally determined under the rules set forth in the Internal Revenue Code and Treasury Department Regulations. In this chapter, we address only the most basic and most commonly encountered valuation rules, and there will be exceptions. For example, *alternate values* (see below) are not allowed on a probate inventory.

Each asset must be valued at its fair market value as of the date of the decedent's death. If Federal Estate Tax will be due, the assets should also be valued six months after the decedent's death or, if distributed or sold within the six-month period, on the date of distribution or at their sale price. This so-called *alternate value* may, subject to certain rules, be used for Federal Estate Tax purposes instead of date-of-death values. (See Chapter 19, "The Tax Man Cometh.")

Property is to be valued at its *highest and best use*. To illustrate, if a tract of farm land on the outskirts of an expanding suburb is worth $500,000 if used in agriculture but would fetch $20 million if sold to a condominium developer, then the highest and best use of the property is for the construction of condominiums and its value is $20 million. (In this situation, the property might qualify for special use valuation for Federal Estate Tax purposes. See Chapter 19, "The Tax Man Cometh.")

There are valuation rules for each type of asset. For example, listed securities (stocks and bonds which are listed on an exchange, such as the New York Stock Exchange) must be valued at *mean market value*, which is the average of the high and the low for the day. Interest must be accrued through date of death and shown separately. Dividends are to be shown separately if the date of death was between the record date and the payment date. If the date of death was between the ex-dividend date and the record date, the dividend is not shown separately, but is added to the value of the stock.

In valuing some types of property interests, various premiums and discounts may have to be taken into account. A fractional interest in real estate may be discounted for lack of control and cost of partition. Discounts may also be appropriate if there are transfer restrictions, if the land is not contiguous, or if there are other conditions which would tend to decrease its utility. A business interest may command a premium if it is a controlling interest or represents a swing vote. On the other hand, discounts for lack of control and lack of marketability may be indicated in the case of a minority interest.

Obtaining Values: Who and How?

One of the questions to be decided early in the administration of the estate is who will obtain asset values. You may wish to undertake this task yourself in order to save professional fees. Alternatively, you may prefer to have your attorney or accountant do so. In the latter case, you may be asked to sign a letter authorizing the attorney or accountant to receive this information. Generally the person who is preparing the Federal Estate Tax return will determine how values are obtained and will obtain the necessary valuations.

How asset values are obtained varies with the type of asset. Some of the more common types of assets and method of obtaining values are set forth below.

Fractional Interest Discounts

Jack inherited an undivided one-third interest in lakefront property from his father many years ago. His two siblings inherited the other two-thirds.

When Jack died, his Trustee had the property appraised for $300,000. However, since Jack's one-third interest could not be readily sold to a third party, the appraiser discounted the one-third interest for Federal Estate Tax purposes.

Though fractional interest discounts vary and must be supported by competent appraisal, in that case the appraiser applied a substantial discount and valued the one-third significantly less than $100,000.

Stock Values

Historical stock values may be obtained on the Internet for no charge at:

http://www.chart.yahoo.com/d

Bank and Savings and Loan Accounts

Values for bank or savings and loan accounts and accrued interest may be obtained directly from the financial institution. Write a letter asking for account balances and accrued interest as of the date of death.

Individual Stocks

If securities are held in a brokerage account, it may be possible to obtain mean market values and accrued dividends and interest from the brokerage firm. However, some brokerage firms will provide only closing or month-end values. If the brokerage company is unable to furnish the required values, you will have to get them yourself.

Detailed price information for individual stocks will be found in financial newspapers such as the *Wall Street Journal.* This data includes the high and low for the day, from which you can compute the mean market value. Since newspapers report prices from the prior business day, you should get and keep a copy of a newspaper from the day *after* the decedent's death.

If death occurred over a weekend or on a holiday, it is necessary to average the mean market values for the days which precede and follow the weekend or holiday. You will need copies for the Monday and Tuesday following the weekend or for the two days following the holiday.

Historical price information is also available on the Internet.

Dividend information can be obtained from Standard & Poor's Dividend Record, which can be obtained at many public libraries. Dividends should be shown separately if the date of death was between the record date and the payment date. If the date of death was between the ex-dividend date and the record date, the dividend is not shown separately, but is added to the value of the stock.

Corporate and Government Bonds

Detailed price information is available for corporate and government bonds in the *Wall Street Journal* and other financial newspapers. Pricing is per $100 of face value.

Example: A Ford Motor Company 7.45% bond maturing July 16, 2031 is priced at 95.701. A $10,000 bond is thus valued at $10,000 x 95.701%, or $9,570. However, accrued interest is not included in the price and must be computed.

Tax-Free Municipal Bonds

Values of tax-free municipal bonds are not listed in financial newspapers. Obtain the value, as well as accrued interest, from a stockbroker or a valuation service.

Mutual Funds

The typical *open-end* mutual fund is valued at its *net asset value*, or *NAV*. The NAV at the date of death or alternate valuation date may be obtained from the fund company, from financial newspapers, or on the Internet.

So-called *closed-end* mutual funds, of which there are relatively few, are really not mutual funds but are investment companies whose shares are traded on the stock exchange like stocks. Obtain the value of closed-end funds in the same manner as publicly traded stocks.

Household Effects, Personal Property, and Real Estate

You may determine values for household effects and personal property yourself, if the items are of minimal value, or you may have values determined by an appraiser who specializes in household inventories. However, if there are unusual items, antiques, art work, jewelry, or collectibles, you should have the articles appraised by a qualified appraiser. (See Chapter 10, "Where to Turn for Help.")

Real estate should be appraised by a real estate appraiser who is familiar with the market where the property is located. In cases where the estate is small or a precise value is not needed

> Perhaps the easiest and most economical way to obtain mean market values of stocks and bonds, including ex-dividend adjustments, accrued dividends, or interest, is to order them from a valuation service. (See Chapter 10, "Where to Turn for Help.")

for tax, probate, or determination of property rights, an estimate of the value by a real estate broker or even a value based on the state assessment of the property for real estate tax purposes may suffice. In Michigan, for certain purposes the value of real estate may be estimated at two times the State Equalized Value (SEV) of the property.

If an asset is sold within a reasonable time after death, or if it had been purchased shortly before death, the sale or purchase price may be the best indication of value, assuming the transaction was at arm's length and absent any intervening change in the market. What may be considered a reasonable time depends on all the facts and circumstances. However, a general rule of thumb is that one year is a reasonable time.

Life Insurance

The value of life insurance on the life of the decedent is the amount received by the beneficiary. This amount is reported by the insurance company on Form 712, which you should request from the company. (See Chapter 9, "Life Insurance.")

Note that such insurance is an asset of the estate only if the decedent possessed, at death, one or more *incidents of ownership* over the policy. Incidents of ownership is an expansive concept which you should discuss with your attorney if you feel that insurance proceeds should be excluded from the gross estate because the decedent did not own the policy.

The value of life insurance on the life of another which was owned by the decedent is generally the replacement cost of the policy.

IRAs, Retirement Plans, and Annuities

The value of IRAs, retirement plans, and annuities is the amount payable to the beneficiary or beneficiaries as of the decedent's death. If the beneficiary is to receive a benefit which terminates at his or her death, the value of that benefit as of the decedent's death must be determined on an actuarial basis, taking into account the beneficiary's life expectancy.

Business Interests

If the decedent owned a sole proprietorship, a professional practice, or an interest in one or more partnerships, closely held corporations, or other business entities, you should consult with your attorney and with the business' accountant to determine how the decedent's interest should be valued.

There may be a Buy-Sell Agreement which fixes the amount that is to be paid for the interest. (Such an agreement is controlling for Federal Estate Tax purposes, however, only if it complies with specific provisions of the Internal Revenue Code and Treasury Regulations.) Unless the decedent's interest can be valued by other means, you should obtain an appraisal from a professional appraiser who specializes in the type of business in question.

If there are other types of assets, your attorney can advise you how to obtain values for them.

Valuation and Basis

The *basis* of an asset is its value for determining gain or loss on sale for accounting and income tax purposes. If you sell an asset for $500 and its basis is $300, your gain is $200.

Each asset of the estate that is includible in the decedent's gross estate for Federal Estate Tax purposes receives a new basis equal to its value for Federal Estate Tax purposes. (See Chapter 19, "The Tax Man Cometh.") This is true even if no Federal Estate Tax return is filed. The assets of the estate, in other words, get a step up in basis. If the decedent had purchased stock many years ago at a cost of $100 and that stock is worth $2,000 at his death, its basis "steps up" to $2,000. Therefore, the value you determine for an asset becomes its basis.

If only part of an asset is includible in the gross estate, then only that part receives a step up in basis. If the decedent and his spouse owned their home as tenants by the entireties, only one-half of the value of the home would normally be includible in the decedent's gross estate.

Thus, one-half of the property (which would be deemed to have passed to the spouse from the decedent) would have a basis equal to one-half of the value of the property for Federal Estate Tax purposes. The other one-half of the property (which would be deemed to have belonged to the spouse) would have a basis equal to one-half of the cost of the property, with no step up in basis.

Implications of Valuation

There may be significant implications in using one value as opposed to another for a particular asset.

Lower values will result in lower estate tax and may eliminate estate tax altogether. A low value for something which is actually worth more may also increase the amount of property passing to a particular beneficiary, since the person will receive the item but it may be counted as less of his or her share of the estate. Higher values will cause assets to have a higher basis, which will result in lower income tax on the sale of those assets.

You may be tempted to "skew" valuation in a certain direction to achieve a certain outcome. You may also be subjected to subtle or not-so-subtle pressure from beneficiaries to do so. For many assets, there is a range of values which might be considered reasonable. You cannot be faulted for selecting a value at the upper or lower end of this range, depending on your objective, as long as you can make a case for doing so.

As a fiduciary, however, you are legally obligated to value the assets correctly and fairly. There is a difference between an aggressive position and a blatant valuation misstatement. Such misstatements on the Federal Estate Tax return could result in accuracy-related penalties or even penalties for fraud. You could be compelled to reimburse the estate or trust for these penalties. For these reasons, you should consult with your attorney on all major valuation issues.

Lifetime Gifts

The Federal Transfer Tax system is a unified system that imposes a single tax on the total of taxable gifts made during life and property transferred at death. Therefore, in addition to taking inventory of the decedent's assets, you must determine if the decedent made any taxable gifts during life.

Any such gifts should have been reported on a Federal Gift Tax return. One or more Gift Tax returns may have been found in the course of gathering the decedent's important documents. (See Chapter 5, "Gather Important Documents.") If so, copies of these must be provided to the preparer of the Federal Estate Tax return along with the inventories you compile.

If you are aware of any gifts of money or other property the decedent made to any person which exceeded the amount of the annual gift tax exclusion in any one year (currently $10,000 per donee per year), you should bring this to the attention of your attorney.

These taxable gifts will generally not have to be brought into the estate for administration. However, they may impact computation of the Federal Estate Tax.

Inventory Tips

Preparing a complete inventory of the estate may be a major or minor task, depending on the size and complexity of the estate.

Here are some tips to keep you on track:

✔ Carefully review the decedent's important papers to determine what types of assets may be involved.

✔ Prepare a preliminary listing and approximate values, if known.

✔ Determine whether you will obtain the necessary values or, if not, who will obtain them.

✔ Set target dates for obtaining the values, and periodically check the status and follow up if necessary.

✔ Make sure you understand the implications of valuation of particular assets.

NOTES

"All things are difficult
before they are easy."
—Thomas Fuller, MD

CHAPTER 12

· · · · · · · · · · ·

ARE
THERE
LIABILITIES?

Are There Liabilities?

Y
ou know that you must inventory all of the decedent's assets. You must also catalog the liabilities of the decedent, i.e., amounts owed by the decedent at the time of his death, or obligations for which he was legally liable, though continuing after his death. Hopefully there will be fewer liabilities with which to be concerned, but you must address them nonetheless.

What Are Liabilities?

Liabilities include not only those for which the decedent was solely responsible, but also any obligations for which the decedent was jointly liable with others.

As with the decedent's assets, any major liabilities will normally be identified in the course of gathering the decedent's important documents. (See Chapter 5, "Gather Important Documents.") You will likely learn of others as bills and statements arrive in the mail. You may also be notified after publication of a notice to creditors. (See the discussion of the notice to creditors in Chapter 15, "To Probate or Not to Probate," and see the more detailed discussion in Chapter 17, "Dealing With Creditors.")

"Creditors
have better
memories
than debtors."
—Proverb

As a general rule, you may have to look a little harder for assets than for liabilities. People who feel a debt is owed often make their presence known quite quickly because they want to make sure the debt owed to them is paid. However, beware of false claims. It has happened, probably more than once, that a person fabricated a claim which was not really owing, hoping that the person charged with handling the estate would simply pay it.

By way of example, look for these typical and not so typical liabilities:

Typical Liabilities

❑ Charge account balances, including principal amount of the debt and finance charges.

❑ Income taxes of the decedent.

❑ Real estate taxes.

❑ Utility bills.

❑ Hospital and medical bills.

❑ Ambulance bills.

❑ Amounts owed to care givers.

❑ Principal and interest under mortgages or land contracts payable.

❑ Principal and interest under other loans payable.

❑ Charitable pledges.

❑ Contractual obligations.

❑ Business expenses accrued as of the date of death.

❑ Judgments or pending litigation against the decedent.

❑ Interest and penalties on tax deficiencies.

❑ Claims of a prior spouse, including alimony, child support, and claims under property settlements.

❑ Amounts due at death to professionals, such as attorneys, accountants, and investment managers.

Not So Typical Liabilities

❑ Fees due to the Trustee of a trust the decedent created during his lifetime.

❑ Contingent claims (claims which will not become due until a future event either occurs or does not occur).

Liabilities Can Save Money

When Norman's father died, Norman was very adamant that his father paid all his debts on a current basis, and refused to admit even the possibility of any liabilities.

The estate's attorney managed to convince Norman that he should check his father's papers anyhow, and he found evidence of a significant debt to a friend.

Norman knew his father would have wanted to pay it off, and so he did. At the same time, however, the debt was taken as a liability on the Federal Estate Tax return, and saved the estate significant taxes.

❑ Amounts owed under guarantees made by the decedent.

❑ Claims filed by the state for support of the decedent's child in a state institution.

❑ Claims for repayments of amounts received by the decedent to which the decedent was not legally entitled.

❑ Claims against the decedent for tortious acts committed during his lifetime.

❑ Claims against the decedent for Social Security taxes the decedent did not pay with regard to an employee's wages.

❑ Security deposits which are to be repaid in the future.

Valuing Liabilities

Like assets, the decedent's liabilities must be valued. Generally, this will be a simple matter. Though you may have to distinguish between liabilities accrued at the date of death and liabilities which accrue after death, the amount of the liability will generally be the amount payable.

For example, the liability under a loan is the principal balance due, which can be determined from the records of the lender (such as a bank) or the borrower (the decedent). Accrued interest at the applicable rate, as well as any late payment penalties, can be computed under the terms of the loan. If the loan will continue after the decedent's death, interest will continue to be owed under the note or other instrument evidencing the loan.

Sometimes valuing a liability is more difficult. What is the amount of a liability which will only be payable in the future, perhaps even several years down the road?

What is the amount of a liability which may or may not be owed? The decedent's liability may depend, for example, on whether certain things happen or don't happen. For example, if the decedent promised to pay someone else's debt, under a guaranty, if that person didn't pay, the decedent is liable for that debt only on a *contingent* basis.

Contingent liabilities are important, because they could mature into current liabilities, and they cannot simply be ignored. You must provide actual notice to known creditors, and that includes creditors with contingent claims. See Chapter 17, "Dealing with Creditors."

If you encounter any liability which seems to be out of the ordinary, consult your attorney.

Why Are Liabilities Important?

Liabilities are important to the administration of the estate because they affect how much will ultimately be distributable to the beneficiaries. If the estate has assets valued at $100,000 and liabilities valued at $100,000 there will be potentially no estate to distribute to the beneficiaries after paying all the liabilities.

In other words, as a practical matter, you have to know who is entitled to the estate, and creditors generally—but not always—come before beneficiaries. (See the discussion of the priorities of claims in Chapter 17, "Dealing with Creditors," and the discussion of statutory rights of surviving spouses and other statutory rights in Chapter 18, "Putting the Horror Stories in Perspective.") Certain statutory rights of family members and some creditors have priority over the rights of other creditors.

Next, if the estate is a taxable estate, then liabilities will be important because in most cases they will be deductible in determining the amount of estate taxes due. Though the estate has to pay the liability, it will reduce the amount of estate taxes otherwise payable, so Uncle Sam and your state treasurer may, in effect, be picking up part of the tab. (See Chapter 19, "The Tax Man Cometh.")

What if An Obligation Is Very Old?

Every state has laws generally referred to as the *statute of limitations*. The statute of limitations generally provides that a claim must be pursued within a certain period of time, or the rights to the amount claimed will expire.

Statutes of limitations differ depending on the type of claim. For example, under Michigan law the statute of limitations for bringing a suit under a contract is generally six years. By comparison, an action for medical malpractice which is alleged to have occurred on or after April 1, 1994 may be brought within the longer of two years from the date of the act or omission giving rise to the claim or six months from the date the claimant discovers or should have discovered the existence of the claim. However, a medical malpractice claim under Michigan law may not be brought more than six years after the act or omission giving rise to the claim.

The point is that if a liability is not recent, there may be a way to avoid it under the statute of limitations. Consult your attorney, who can evaluate the facts and determine what statute of limitations is applicable.

What Do I Do About Liabilities?

If the estate will be a taxable estate, you will want to make sure that the person preparing the Federal Estate Tax return knows about all liabilities. In every estate you should address each liability and decide if and when it can be paid.

As a general rule you should not rush to pay any of the decedent's liabilities before determining the total amount of estate assets and liabilities, whether certain claims have higher priority than others, and whether there are any defenses to any of the claims. See Chapter 17, "Dealing With Creditors," for a full discussion of these topics. The present chapter has addressed primarily the need to identify liabilities.

Your attorney can be of great assistance to you in evaluating claims, defending against claims if necessary, and in cutting off your potential personal liability, as fiduciary, for claims.

CHAPTER 13

· · · · · · · · · · ·

WHO SHARES IN THE ESTATE?

Who Shares in the Estate?

Throughout this book we refer to *the beneficiaries*, often assuming that a decision has been made as to who they are. The beneficiaries are the parties who are entitled to share in the estate. To determine who they are should not be rocket science, you think to yourself. Just look in the Will or trust instrument, if there is one, and if not then look at the applicable statute or perhaps a beneficiary designation.

In this chapter we discuss how you determine who will actually share in the estate. The estate, in this context, includes the probate estate, any trusts of the decedent, *In Trust For* accounts, securities registered in *Pay on Death* or *Transfer on Death* form, property which the decedent owned jointly with others with rights of survivorship, insurance on the decedent's life, annuities, IRAs, retirement plans, and trusts created by others of which the decedent was a beneficiary.

In more cases than you would suspect, people who appear to be beneficiaries may not receive what was provided under the documents. In other cases there are no documents and you will need to know what provisions the state has made to distribute property of a decedent who did not make a Will.

Situations in Which a Beneficiary May Lose Out

A beneficiary may be an individual or an organization, such as a charity. The decedent's estate or trust may also be a beneficiary, for example, of a life insurance policy or an IRA.

Just because a beneficiary may appear to be entitled to share in the estate does not mean that the beneficiary will actually receive anything. Following are some examples of facts which could cause an amount not to be payable:

① An insurance company could refuse to pay a claim. This might occur, for example, if the decedent committed suicide during a contestability period, if questions were not answered honestly on the insurance application, if required premiums were not paid, or in some cases if the decedent was not in the same health condition at the time the policy was delivered as when the application was made.

② The beneficiary may not have survived the decedent.

③ Specific property left to a beneficiary may not be in the decedent's possession at death, and the decedent may have clearly indicated that the bequest was to be made only if that property was still owned at death.

④ The estate could be entirely consumed by debts and taxes.

⑤ The decedent may be found to have been incompetent to make a Will, or suffering from an insane delusion when making the Will, so that it is not legally effective.

⑥ The Will or trust instrument may be challenged in Probate Court for lack of authenticity or other reasons. Beneficiary designations on insurance policies, IRAs, and retirement plans may also be challenged.

⑦ The amount provided for the beneficiary may be found to have been satisfied by lifetime gifts.

⑧ The amount payable to the beneficiary may be offset by debts owed to the decedent by the beneficiary.

Equally important, not all those who appear to be beneficiaries will be able to successfully defend their entitlement to share in the estate. Following are some situations in which a beneficiary might be disqualified from taking the share provided for him or her:

A Taxing Experience

Lorraine left her cottage and a small business to her elder son, Leon. She wanted Leon to have the business because he worked there with her.

She left the balance of her estate, principally her splendid residence, to her younger son, Simon. Simon looked forward to living in the residence.

The estate was sizeable, but there were no liquid assets.

There was no tax allocation clause in the Will. Under current Michigan law, estate taxes on the entire estate are therefore payable only out of the residue, which in this case is Simon's share. Simon has to sell the residence to pay the estate taxes.

① A beneficiary may be found to have caused the Will or trust provision to be inserted through undue influence, duress, or other improper means.

② The bequest may be contingent on the beneficiary meeting certain requirements, such as marrying within the faith, or not belonging to a cult, or being the decedent's spouse, and the beneficiary may not meet the particular requirement.

③ A bequest to a charitable organization may be conditioned on the organization meeting certain tax exemption requirements, which it may not satisfy; or it may be required to do something specific with the bequest, which it may not agree to do, or may not be able to do, perhaps within a certain time frame; or the organization may no longer exist in the form originally specified and no successor may be provided.

④ The beneficiary may be disqualified because the beneficiary intentionally killed the decedent.

⑤ Under Michigan law, a surviving spouse may be disqualified from receiving an intestate share if the surviving spouse was willfully absent from the decedent or deserted the decedent for one year or more prior to the death.

Therefore, when making the initial determination of the beneficiaries, you should bear in mind that they are as yet only the *presumptive* beneficiaries.

In this chapter, we explain how these *presumptive* beneficiaries are determined.

If There is a Will or Trust

Where There is a Will

If there is a Will, and the decedent owned property which is subject to the Will, then the beneficiaries of that property are those named in the Will. This may seem obvious, but it is not that simple.

The Will must first be determined to be valid. This is accomplished by a proceeding in Probate Court. (See Chapter 15, "To Probate or Not to Probate.") Until the Will is admitted to probate, it is not the decedent's Will, it is just a purported Will, which may or may not be given legal effect.

The Will may be contested by persons who, for one reason or another, do not want the Will to take effect. It may be found to have been revoked, or invalid for various reasons. If these parties prevail, the Will may be modified or set aside.

If the Will is successfully admitted to probate, the beneficiaries named therein are the legal beneficiaries. Even so, there can be complications:

The Will may provide that personal property is to be distributed according to the terms of a separate writing or memorandum which the decedent may have left, and that property will therefore not be distributed under the Will.

A beneficiary named in the Will may not be living at the testator's death. At common law, the bequest to that beneficiary *lapses*. That is, it becomes void. Michigan and most other states have *anti-lapse statutes* under which the bequest may, under certain circumstances, pass to the deceased beneficiary's descendants.

The Will may direct that a beneficiary is to receive a *specific bequest* of a particular item, such as the decedent's antique desk. However, if the decedent did not own the item at his death, the beneficiary cannot receive it. The decedent may have sold the item, lost it, or given it away during life. This is known as *ademption* and the item is said to have been *adeemed*. In some cases the beneficiary will get something of equal value, but not in all cases.

The Beneficiary Died First

Barry's Will provided for his brother, Kevin, to receive a cash bequest of $50,000.

Kevin died before Barry.

Kevin's two children, Lisa and Amanda, were living at Barry's death.

Under Michigan law, Lisa and Amanda would each receive $25,000. This law is referred to as the "anti-lapse statute."

- The decedent may have already given the item to the beneficiary, an act referred to as *ademption by satisfaction*.
- The Will may provide for two beneficiaries to each receive a cash bequest of $50,000. But if the estate amounts to only $80,000, then each beneficiary can receive only $40,000. This is called *abatement* and each bequest will *abate* or be reduced. The order in which beneficiaries' interests abate is determined by state law. In Michigan, residuary devises abate first, followed by general devises and, finally, by specific devises.
- The decedent may have married after the execution of his or her Will. Likewise, a child may have been born or adopted. Under Michigan law and the laws of many other states, the spouse or child can receive a share of the estate under specified circumstances, even though not provided for under the Will.
- If there is a surviving spouse, the spouse may, under the laws of Michigan and most other states, elect to take under the Will, i.e., to accept what is provided for in the Will, or to take *against* the Will. In the latter case, the spouse can receive a portion of the decedent's property that is fixed by statute. This portion is known as the *elective share, forced share,* or *statutory share*.
- Most states have statutes designed to provide some protection to a surviving spouse, minor children and, in some cases, dependent adult children. In Michigan, a spouse and children are entitled to a homestead allowance, a family allowance, and certain exempt property. Those rights pre-empt whatever is provided under the Will.
- See Chapter 18, "Putting the Horror Stories in Perspective," for a full discussion of the various rights of the surviving spouse and children mentioned above.
- There could be a prenuptial or postnuptial agreement that limits the rights of the surviving spouse.
- If the decedent and a spouse or other beneficiary died in close proximity in time, it must often be decided whether or not the spouse or other beneficiary survived the decedent. This must be determined by reference to the provisions of the Will and rules of survival under state law.
- A beneficiary could be named in the Will whom you do not know or whom you are unable to contact.

There could be a charitable bequest where the exact beneficiary cannot be determined, e.g., a bequest to the "Children's Home," with no indication as to the specific organization which the decedent had in mind.

If the decedent owned no property subject to the Will, the Will generally will not be offered for probate and will be a moot issue.

Where There is a Trust

If there is a trust, and the trust holds property or is to receive property from another source, such as life insurance proceeds or the residue of the decedent's estate, then the beneficiaries of that property are those named in the trust agreement.

As with a Will, there can be complications. Many of the issues discussed above with respect to a Will can also apply to a trust instrument.

A trust does not necessarily terminate at the death of the grantor or settlor (the person who created the trust). The trust may continue, with provisions for distributions to income beneficiaries and ultimate distribution to remainder beneficiaries.

If the trust holds no property, i.e., is *unfunded*, and will not receive any assets as a result of the decedent's death, the trust is a *dry* trust. Notwithstanding the fact that beneficiaries are named, the trust agreement is of no import.

If There is No Will or Trust
Where There is No Will

If there is no Will, and the decedent owned property in his sole name, then the beneficiaries of that property are the decedent's *heirs-at-law* determined under the state's laws governing *intestate succession*.

Many people assume that if the decedent left a surviving spouse, the spouse will be entitled to the entire estate. As you will see, depending on the size of the estate, this may not be the case under Michigan law. In Michigan, the laws of intestate succession provide for the following pattern of distribution, depending on who survives the decedent:

Intestate Share of a Surviving Spouse

The intestate share of a decedent's surviving spouse is one of the following:

① The entire intestate estate if no descendant or parent of the decedent survives the decedent.

② The first $150,000, plus one-half of any balance of the intestate estate, if all of the decedent's surviving descendants are also descendants of the surviving spouse and there is no other descendant of the surviving spouse who survives the decedent.

③ The first $150,000, plus three-quarters of any balance of the intestate estate, if no descendant of the decedent survives the decedent, but a parent of the decedent survives the decedent.

④ The first $150,000, plus one-half of any balance of the intestate estate, if all of the decedent's surviving descendants are also descendants of the surviving spouse and the surviving spouse has one or more surviving descendants who are not descendants of the decedent.

⑤ The first $150,000, plus one-half of any balance of the intestate estate, if one or more, but not all, of the decedent's surviving descendants are not descendants of the surviving spouse.

⑥ The first $100,000, plus one-half of any balance of the intestate estate, if none of the decedent's surviving descendants are descendants of the surviving spouse.

Each dollar amount listed is to be adjusted for changes in the cost of living.

Distribution of Balance of Estate or
Entire Estate if No Surviving Spouse

Any part of the intestate estate that does not pass to the decedent's surviving spouse, or the entire intestate estate if there is no surviving spouse, passes in the following order to the following individuals who survive the decedent:

① The decedent's descendants by representation.

② If there is no surviving descendant, the decedent's parents equally if both survive or to the surviving parent.

③ If there is no surviving descendant or parent, the descendants of the decedent's parents or of either of them by representation.

④ If there is no surviving descendant, parent, or descendant of a parent, but the decedent is survived by one or more grandparents or descendants of grandparents, one-half of the estate passes to the decedent's paternal grandparents equally if both survive, or to the surviving paternal grandparent, or to the descendants of the decedent's paternal grandparents or either of them if both are deceased, the descendants taking by representation; and the other one-half passes to the decedent's maternal relatives in the same manner. If there is no surviving grandparent or descendant of a grandparent on either the paternal or the maternal side, the entire estate passes to the decedent's relatives on the other side in the same manner as the one-half.

There must be a proceeding in Probate Court to determine that the decedent did not leave a valid Will and to determine the identity of the decedent's heirs-at-law.

If the decedent owned no property in his sole name, then intestate succession is not an issue and there is no need to go to Probate Court on the matter.

Where There is No Trust

If there is no trust, then there are no trust beneficiaries. However, the lack of a separate trust instrument or the fact that there are no assets titled in the name of a trust does not necessarily mean that there is no trust. The decedent may have provided for a trust in his Will, i.e., a *testamentary trust*.

Property Passing Outside the Will or Trust

Jointly Owned Property

Property that the decedent owned jointly *with rights of survivorship* automatically becomes the property of the surviving joint tenants. A Will or trust instrument has no impact on this. The only exception is if the property was joint *for convenience only*. In this case, the property will be treated as if it were owned by the decedent in his sole name and it will pass either under the terms of the Will or under the laws of intestacy. (See Chapter 11, "Inventory the Assets.")

Property that the decedent owned jointly with others *as tenants in common* does *not* become the property of the surviving tenants. Instead, the decedent's undivided interest passes under the terms of the Will or under the laws of intestacy.

Beneficiary Designations

Property that has a designated beneficiary or beneficiaries will pass to the beneficiary or beneficiaries named. Again, a Will or trust instrument has no impact on this. Common examples of property that has a named beneficiary are life insurance policies, annuities, IRAs, and retirement plans.

Property Passing Under Someone Else's Will or Trust

The decedent may have been a beneficiary under someone else's Will or trust. The most common example would be one or more trusts established by a predeceased spouse, parent, or grandparent of the decedent. The trust or trusts may

Rights Under Trusts of Another

Gordon's wife, Rachel, died several years before him.

Under her estate plan a marital trust and a family trust were established. Gordon received all the income from the marital trust. Income from the family trust could be paid either to Gordon or to the couple's children.

When Gordon died, both trusts terminated and were distributed, in accordance with their terms, to the children.

have been for the decedent's benefit during the decedent's life. To determine the disposition of the trust or trusts following the decedent's death, it is necessary to consult the governing instrument for the trust.

Other Issues
Disclaimers

Persons who are named to receive property are not bound to accept it. The intended recipient may *renounce* or *disclaim* the property, in whole or in part. In effect, the person is declining property that would otherwise pass to him or her.

There are several reasons why one might want to do so. One common reason is to allow the property to pass to one's children instead. If the requirements under the Internal Revenue Code for a *qualified disclaimer* are met, the distribution to the children will not be treated as a gift from the parent for Gift Tax purposes. In the case of a disclaimer of property passing from a decedent one of these requirements is that any disclaimer must be made within nine months of the decedent's death. (See Chapter 19, "The Tax Man Cometh.")

Will Contests;
Agreements Among Estate Beneficiaries

A Will may be contested in Probate Court, but the result of such an undertaking is uncertain. The court might construe or interpret the Will. The court might set aside the Will and rule that the estate should pass under a prior Will or by intestate succession. It is unlikely, however, that the court will change the dispositive provisions as courts in Michigan and most other jurisdictions are loath to rewrite the decedent's Will.

A better course of action in many cases is for the beneficiaries to come to an agreement on how the estate is to be distributed. In Michigan, subject to the rights of creditors and taxing authorities, beneficiaries may agree to alter the interests, shares, or amounts to which they are entitled under the Will or under the laws of intestacy in any way they provide in a written agree-

Timing of Disclaimers

A qualified disclaimer can permit a beneficiary to allow property to pass to another beneficiary, without creating a taxable gift.

However, disclaimers must be made within certain strict statutory time limits.

Make sure you understand how disclaimers might work in this estate, and that each beneficiary is made aware of the deadline.

Discuss these deadlines with your attorney early in the estate administration process.

ment signed by all who are affected by its provisions.

However, in the absence of a bona fide dispute such an agreement may not be binding upon the IRS, which may consider that a gift has occurred from one beneficiary whose share is decreased to the other beneficiary or beneficiaries whose shares have increased. Depending on how the shares are being shifted, a qualified disclaimer may avoid adverse tax consequences.

Reformation of Trusts; Agreements Among Trust Beneficiaries

If there is evidence that dispositive or other provisions of a trust instrument are incorrect, it is possible to petition the Probate Court to reform the document. Grounds for reformation include fraud, duress, undue influence, and mistake.

An agreement among the trust beneficiaries is also possible. Michigan law allows the Probate Court to approve an interpretation, construction, modification, or other settlement that is agreed upon in writing by all beneficiaries.

Locating Beneficiaries

If beneficiaries cannot be located, you may consider engaging a missing heir search firm to find them. (See Appendix A.)

You should be aware that various firms charge differently for their services. Some will locate heirs at no charge to the estate, but a percentage fee is charged to the heir. Other firms will charge the estate or the heir a flat fee or an hourly fee unrelated to the amount of assets involved.

You can learn a great deal about how these firms work and the relative advantages and disadvantages of each of them by contacting representatives of several firms. You may want to obtain a Probate Court order authorizing engagement of a particular firm and payment of fees for its services.

If the beneficiaries do not turn up or cannot be located in a reasonable time, consult with your attorney about what to do with the property that is distributable to these beneficiaries.

CHAPTER 14

. . . .

KEEP THE BENEFICIARIES INFORMED

Keep the Beneficiaries Informed

Information, Please

Beneficiaries want information. They usually want as much information as they can get, and as soon as possible. To begin to understand the mindset of a beneficiary, you must appreciate that you are merely the "collection agent," and your job is to collect the estate and pass it on to the beneficiaries.

It is *their* money. You may have to deal with a lot of details and thorny issues along the way, lose time from your "day job," have sleepless nights, and turn grey—and you may even be a beneficiary yourself. But as far as the other beneficiaries are concerned, you're working for them!

Some people don't realize this and assume that beneficiaries—particularly beneficiaries who are family members— don't need to be kept informed. Such a person may think:

"I've been given this responsibility by [Mom, Dad, Uncle Al, or whomever] and the beneficiaries should be delighted that I have accepted this tremendous burden and should simply let me get it all done. I'll do what I'm supposed to do and divide up the estate properly at the end."

As you will see, this type of attitude is based on incorrect assumptions, which can actually be hazardous to your emotional well-being and your financial health.

First, if you are the Personal Representative or Trustee, you are *legally obligated* to provide certain information. Under Michigan law, various types of information must be provided to beneficiaries of a probate estate or of a trust, as well as to others, such as creditors and the State Attorney General. Legal implications of violating those obligations vary and should be discussed with your attorney.

Second, as a practical matter, problems with beneficiaries can usually be avoided if you are proactive, anticipate questions, and keep the beneficiaries fully informed at all times.

In this chapter, we first review the statutory requirements and then dispense some practical advice which should help you keep the beneficiaries happy.

You may have a dozen reasons why you honestly feel you don't need to provide information and should be allowed to go about your business of administering the estate without keeping others "in the loop." You may be:

The oldest child;

The only family member with any financial "savvy;"

The closest relative;

The only relative;

The only beneficiary who really knew and cared for the decedent;

The only one who actually visited the decedent in his or her last years;

The only beneficiary in town;

The only beneficiary who doesn't spend his days at the bar;

The beneficiary of the lion's share of the estate; or

The only individual beneficiary, with the rest going to charities.

You may not have been invited to the weddings of the children of the other beneficiaries.

You may not have spoken to the other beneficiaries in years, the last time may have been very unpleasant, and you may not care if you ever speak to them again.

We urge you to review this chapter carefully before you dig in your heels too far. Then have a heart-to-heart talk with your attorney about what you really should do in terms of providing information.

The Best Defense is a Good Offense

Family members expected cousin Bill, who was appointed Personal Representative, to get a lot of grief from cousin Matt, a long-time trouble-maker.

No trouble developed. Why? Because Bill kept everyone informed.

"I've not had a bit of trouble with any of the beneficiaries," Bill said.

"They don't even call me. My strategy is to give them absolutely everything. I give them more than they would ever want to know. And it works!"

Requirements Under Michigan Law

If There is a Probate Estate

The Personal Representative must, within 14 days after appointment, serve interested persons with notice of his or her appointment and duties, and notice regarding any attorney fee agreement which has been made, unless the rights to receive either or both of these notices are waived in writing.

Notice to creditors must be published and actual notice must be given to all known creditors.

Notice must be given to the surviving spouse of the rights of election, allowances, and exempt property.

An inventory of all of the assets of the probate estate must be served on all presumptive distributees.

An account must be provided to all beneficiaries of the probate estate annually and upon completion of the administration.

All of this is explained more fully in Chapter 15, "To Probate or Not to Probate."

If There is a Trust

For a *revocable* trust, within 28 days after accepting the position of Trustee or the death of the person who created the trust (the *grantor* or the *settlor*), whichever is later, the Trustee must inform each interested trust beneficiary of certain things, in writing.

The Trustee must inform each interested trust beneficiary of the trust's existence, of the court in which the trust is registered (if it is registered), of the Trustee's name and address, and of the interested trust beneficiary's right to request and receive both a copy of the trust's terms that describe or affect the interested trust beneficiary's interest and relevant information about the trust property.

The same information must be provided by the Trustee of an *irrevocable* trust within 28 days after acceptance of the trust.

In addition, upon request, the Trustee must provide a beneficiary with a copy of the trust's terms that describe or affect the beneficiary's interest and with relevant information about the trust property.

Unless the trust instrument directs otherwise, the Trustee must provide a statement of account to each current trust beneficiary at least annually and on termination of the trust or a change of the Trustee, and must keep each current trust beneficiary informed of the trust and its administration.

Unless the trust instrument directs otherwise, the Trustee must, on request, provide a statement of account to each interested trust beneficiary who is not also a current trust beneficiary and must keep each of those persons reasonably informed of the trust and its administration.

In the Trustee's discretion, the Trustee may provide a statement of account and other information to any beneficiary.

If there is no probate estate, the Trustee must publish notice to creditors. (The Trustee may also send actual notice to any known creditors. See Chapter 17, "Dealing with Creditors.")

If There are Charitable Beneficiaries

Certain information must be provided to the Michigan Attorney General's Charitable Trust Section for an estate in which the residue is payable to a charitable beneficiary, or for a trust that has specific or residual charitable beneficiaries. Your attorney can tell you what must be done or you can contact:

Assistant Attorney General
Consumer Protection Division
Charitable Trust Section
P. O. Box 30214
Lansing, MI 48909
517-373-1152

Put it in Writing

All important information should be communicated to the beneficiaries in writing. All beneficiaries should receive the same letter, with the same attachments and enclosures. Include a detailed list of whatever is being sent. This will reduce the possibility of misunderstandings and will eliminate any subsequent disagreement over what you did or didn't say, or what was or was not included in the package.

If you are going to use e-mail, keep copies of whatever you send. Either add yourself as a "cc" or "bcc" person and print out the message as it comes back to you, or make a copy of your "sent" e-mail message. However, discuss first with your attorney issues relating to lack of confidentiality of information sent over the Internet.

If you are sending faxes, keep copies of whatever is sent, and consider sending "hard copy" by mail as a general practice. Indicate on each letter or memo you are faxing that a copy is also being sent by mail.

Important letters or packages should be sent by certified mail, return receipt requested, or by overnight courier.

Discuss with your attorney whether he or she should receive copies of whatever you send to beneficiaries or others.

Keep meticulous files. At a minimum, file everything in chronological order. In more complex estates, you should also keep files by topic (e.g., various assets, liabilities, distributions, court filings, and so on). Avoid the tendency to simply jam everything into a file or box, or allow it to pile up on your desk, with the hope that some day you will have time to straighten it all out.

If you keep everything in order as you go, it will be easy. If not, you may never get to it, and some day you will have to find an important note, letter, memo, or other paper and you will spend hours searching for it.

Your First Communication

It is important to win the confidence of the beneficiaries at the very beginning, or you may find yourself on the defensive throughout the administration. With this in mind, beneficiaries should hear from you at the earliest possible date, probably within two weeks of the decedent's death.

You may feel that this is too soon. You may still be involved with post-funeral tasks such as writing acknowledgment notes. You may feel that it is indecent to get into estate business so soon or you may just be inclined to put these matters off. You may find that you have no stomach for administering the estate, or that you are overwhelmed by your responsibilities.

If this is the case, you should— without delay— make arrangements either to step aside or to get help. (See Chapter 6, "Who Should Administer the Estate?" and Chapter 10, "Where to Turn for Help.")

If you choose to serve as a fiduciary, the sooner you begin, the better. As explained above, there are statutory time frames that must be met if there is a probate estate or a trust. Just as importantly, a prompt commencement will be well received by the beneficiaries.

Your first formal communication should be a comprehensive letter, the exact nature of which will vary in each case, but in general at a minimum should:

1. Begin by saying that you are writing in your capacity as Personal Representative and/or Trustee of the decedent, who died on a given date.

2. Describe the decedent's estate planning documents. For example, the decedent may have left a Last Will and Testament of a certain date and/or a trust agreement of a certain date, with Codicils and amendments. Describe each document by name and date, and include copies.

3. Identify the beneficiaries and indicate what each is to receive, whether a specific bequest or percentage of the residue. (Discuss with your attorney how much information should be provided to people receiving specific bequests, i.e., bequests of specific property or fixed dollar amounts.)

4. Enclose a preliminary inventory of assets, stating very clearly that this is preliminary and is subject to change as you learn more.

5. Explain that the estate will be reduced to the extent of debts, expenses, and taxes.

6. Explain that beneficiaries may disclaim (or turn down) all or any portion of what they would otherwise receive, how that would work, and the timing and implications of a disclaimer.

7. If probate will be required, explain what is involved in this process, who the probate beneficiaries are, and what notices and other mailings these beneficiaries can expect to receive.

8. List and discuss the main administrative tasks to be completed and the approximate time frame for each.

9. Explain whether and when the Federal Estate Tax and state estate or inheritance tax returns must be filed and when clearances may be expected.

10. Discuss personal property. If it will be distributed to the beneficiaries, describe when and how this will be done. If it will be sold, describe when and how this will be accomplished.

11. Explain that final distribution cannot be made until all tax clearances have been obtained, although one or more partial distributions *may* be made.

12. Discuss the management of the assets and what actions are planned to preserve and protect the assets, to diversify investments, and to obtain investment advice.

13. State who is entitled to the income earned by the assets during the period of administration.

14. Explain income tax matters, including the fact that taxable income of each beneficiary will be shown on a Form K-1 to be sent to each beneficiary after the end of the year, and that beneficiaries must wait to finalize their personal income taxes until they receive the K-1.

15. Discuss any related entities. (For example, there may have been a trust for the decedent's benefit which will now terminate and pass to other beneficiaries.)

16. State whether or not you intend to charge a fee for your services as Personal Representative and/or Trustee and, if so, the manner in which the fee is to be determined.

17. Provide your contact information (telephone number, fax number, and e-mail address) and solicit questions about the estate.

18. Conclude with assurances that you will provide regular updates as administration of the estate progresses.

The first letter may well be the most difficult that you will have to write, simply because it includes so much information. However, a good, thorough first letter will give the beneficiaries confidence in you. Also, by laying out your timetable, you will forestall inquires from beneficiaries as to when they will receive their shares.

Depending on the size and complexity of the estate, your attorney may prepare a draft of this letter for your review, or you may prepare a draft for the attorney's review. Your attorney should in either case receive a copy of the final letter as sent to the beneficiaries.

If you are the only current beneficiary of the estate, then this letter would not be applicable. If the other beneficiaries are your children, you may decide that so formal a communication is not necessary. In other cases, however, we recommend that a letter of this type be used, although the specific contents will vary in each case.

The statutory requirements must be met in any event. Information regarding a trust must be provided to all *interested* beneficiaries, not just *current* beneficiaries. In other words, the trust agreement may provide that certain persons only receive assets from the trust at a future date, or after the death of someone else, but those people are still interested beneficiaries and should receive a copy of the letter.

Progress Reports

After the first letter, you should provide the beneficiaries regular written progress reports. You should write periodically regarding the following:

❏ Sale of assets. (Enclose a copy of the closing statement or bill of sale, if applicable.)

"Am I Superhuman?"

After reviewing the information required to be provided to beneficiaries, you may wonder if all this is possible within a couple of weeks after the death.

If the death is a complete surprise, then it probably isn't possible.

Just do the best you can, with the recognition that the beneficiaries are waiting and sooner or later the phone will start ringing or you will receive nasty letters from their lawyers.

However, if you know that death is coming you must take advantage of the advance warning to start pulling things together.

❑ Appraisal of assets. (Enclose a copy of the appraisal.)

❑ Significant investment actions.

❑ Annual accounts. (Enclose a copy of the account. Consult with your attorney concerning what the account should contain to maximize its benefit to you as a fiduciary.)

❑ K-1s. (Enclose the K-1 and explain its significance.)

❑ Federal Estate Tax return and state estate or inheritance tax return. (Enclose a copy of the returns.)

❑ Federal and state closing letters. (Enclose a copy.)

Always include a brief summary of what you are currently working on, such as assembling information for the Federal Estate Tax return or for the fiduciary income tax returns. Beneficiaries want to know that you are working to move the administration forward.

Protecting Yourself

You can expect to receive some sort of feedback from the beneficiaries. Ideally, you will get comments to the effect that you are doing a great job. You will appreciate knowing that your hard work has not gone unnoticed.

Unfortunately, this will not always be the case. Some beneficiaries may be critical of your efforts or may be generally hostile to you. If you sense that any beneficiary disagrees with your handling of a matter or with the administration generally, you should take appropriate steps to protect yourself. Discuss with your attorney whether, when, and how you should take any of the steps outlined on the following page.

Checklist

Possible Methods
to Protect the Fiduciary
from Beneficiary Claims

❑ Obtain a **release** for an action you have taken which may give rise to complaints in the future, such as an investment decision.

❑ Obtain **consents** to an action you believe to be proper, but which might negatively impact one or more beneficiaries.

❑ Seek a **Probate Court order** with respect to a particular question or issue. (This can be done even if there is no probate estate.)

❑ File an **account** with the Probate Court, which will include disclosure of the specific action or actions which might otherwise be challenged later, and specifically request approval of those actions in an **order approving the account**.

❑ Enter into a **settlement agreement** with the beneficiaries.

NOTES

"People count up the faults
of those who keep them waiting."
—French Proverb

CHAPTER 15

. . . .

TO
PROBATE OR
NOT TO
PROBATE

To Probate or Not to Probate

Most of us have probably heard stories about what a dreadful experience it is to "go through probate." High expense, assets tied up for years, and lack of privacy are the traditional "evils of probate." The truth is that these alleged "evils" are generally grossly exaggerated and relate to laws and court practices of a bygone era, which have long ago been reformed in many states, including Michigan.

In this chapter, which deals specifically with current Michigan practice, you will learn what it really means to go through probate, when it is necessary, and when it is not. We will review expedited procedures available to small estates, and procedures which typically apply to other estates. We will also provide you samples of most of the basic Michigan probate forms so that you can see what is involved

You may still conclude that probate of any size estate involves administrative work which you would prefer to have handled by your attorney, but at least you will have a better appreciation of what it all really means.

What is Probate?

Probate of a decedent's estate is the court process which determines the validity of a Will, or who the heirs are if there is no Will, allows creditors an opportunity to file their claims, and provides for the remaining assets to be distributed to the rightful takers.

In some cases the Probate Court also supervises the affairs of minors and people who are incapacitated, and appoints Guardians for those people and Conservators for their property, a process which is sometimes referred to as *living probate* and can be quite burdensome.

The Probate Court also deals with other matters. However, our focus here is solely on decedents' estates.

When is Probate Necessary?

If the decedent owned any assets in his or her *sole name*, it is possible that probate proceedings will be required. This is true whether or not the decedent left a Will. A Will itself does not avoid the need for probate.

For example, if the house was left in the name of "William Jones," that would be sole-name property, and to sell his house after his death, or distribute it to his heirs, probate would generally be necessary, regardless of whether William left a Will.

By comparison, if he left his house in joint name with someone else, with rights of survivorship, then probate *of the house* would not be necessary.

For example, William may have put his house in joint name with his daughter during his lifetime. Title to the house would then read as follows: "William Jones and Elizabeth Jones, as joint tenants with rights of survivorship." (Real estate titled jointly with a spouse is called *tenancy by the entirety* instead of joint tenancy, with the same result.)

The house would then pass automatically to the survivor on the death of either William or Elizabeth. No probate of that asset would be required, just the recording of the death certificate of the first to die. However, if there are other probate assets probate would be required of those assets, but not the house.

If the decedent owned sole-name property in another state, it may be necessary to have probate proceedings in that state as well. This is called *ancillary* probate.

What is Not Subject to Probate?

Assets which are not titled in the decedent's sole name, or which have a named beneficiary, are not subject to probate. Examples of non-probate assets include:

❑ Joint property, i.e., property which is held jointly with rights of survivorship (sometimes indicated JTWROS).

Avoiding Probate

A person can avoid probate at his or her death by ensuring that there is no property in the person's sole name.

The person accomplishes this by holding all assets jointly with others, in trust, or in assets which have named beneficiaries, such as life insurance, annuities, or retirement plans.

You may wish to restructure your own finances in this manner. You should do so with care, however, and with the assistance of a competent estate planning attorney.

Make sure that you don't unintentionally change your beneficiaries or their interests. Make sure also that you don't leave yourself open to impoverishment by giving up control of assets.

❑ Property owned by a trust or a Trustee.

❑ Individual Retirement Accounts (IRAs).

❑ Pension, profit sharing, or other retirement plans.

❑ Annuities.

❑ Insurance policies.

❑ Savings bonds with *payable on death* (POD) designations.

❑ Accounts which are held *in trust for* someone else (ITF accounts).

❑ Any other asset payable to a named beneficiary.

None of these assets would generally have to be probated *unless they are payable to the estate.* There may be a specific beneficiary designation which says pay to "the estate" or there may be no beneficiary designated at all and the terms of the contract, for example, may provide for payment to the estate if no beneficiary is named. It is also possible that there is a beneficiary named but that beneficiary is deceased, and there is no other beneficiary named, and in that case the contract may require payment to the estate.

Why the Fuss about Probate?

Probate necessarily involves certain dealings with the Probate Court and this can take time and increase the costs of administering the estate.

Many years ago, the probate process involved payment of heavy fees for court-appointed appraisers, long delay, and filing of the probate inventory with the Probate Court, which resulted in a lack of privacy for the estate. Today in Michigan, and in many other states as well, the probate process can be relatively quick and painless, and involves minimal costs.

However, filings with the Probate Court are still required, which do take some time, and involve some costs, however minor. If you had to do it several times, you would get the hang of it. But for anyone handling a probate estate for the first time, especially without an attorney drafting the papers and telling you what to expect, it can be a bit intimidating and even overwhelming.

For this reason, many people arrange their affairs so that probate will not be necessary upon their death. If the decedent did that, and had only non-probate assets, you're in luck. If not—even if there is only one probate asset—you will probably have the opportunity to find out what probate is all about.

Be patient, keep your sense of humor and your perspective, and hang on. This, too, will end.

The Probate Process

The purpose of probate is to see that claims against the estate are settled, to ensure that state death taxes are paid, and to distribute the decedent's assets to the beneficiaries under the Will or, in the absence of a valid Will, to the decedent's heirs. Remember that when we talk about the estate in this context, we mean the *probate estate*. The probate estate consists *only* of those assets, if any, that the decedent owned in his or her sole name and assets which, for some reason, are payable to the estate.

Probate proceedings take place in the Probate Court for the county where the decedent was domiciled at death. They are governed by state statute, court rules, and the practices of the local Probate Court. In Michigan, those rules can and do vary somewhat from county to county.

There is no requirement that probate administration be handled by an attorney. However, except in the smallest estates, most people would find it difficult, frustrating, and time consuming to attempt this without some degree of professional help.

Probate Court personnel are not allowed to give legal advice and, as a result, can provide only limited assistance. The amount of information you can obtain directly from the court will also vary, depending on the particular court. Larger, busier Probate Courts simply do not have the staff to deal with every inquiry or to provide much information over the telephone.

Furthermore, probate administration does not take place in a vacuum. The appraisal and management of property and the handling of tax matters must be integrated into the process. Consequently, in most cases except the smallest probate estates it is advisable to engage an estate planning attorney to handle or guide you through the probate administration. (See Chapter 10, "Where to Turn for Help.")

Before You Leap...

In limited situations, it may be possible to transfer some sole-name assets without going through the hoops of probate, and you should at least consider this possibility. Here are a few examples:

Family Relationships

In a family relationship, such as where the decedent owned stock in a company with a family member, and the decedent's stock passes to family members, the surviving family members may be perfectly willing to transfer the stock without seeing formal Letters of Authority of a Personal Representative, issued by the Probate Court. If the stock can be transferred without probate proceedings, and if there are no other probate assets, then probate may be dispensed with.

However, if stock is owned in a publicly traded company, New York transfer agents will always require the court appointment of a Personal Representative of the estate. This will require probate. That way, the transfer agent knows that the person instructing the transfer is authorized to do so.

Closely Held Investment Interests

Willingness to make a transfer of a business interest or investment may extend beyond strictly family relationships. For example, if the decedent owned a partnership interest in an investment partnership with other investors, the person in charge of recording transfers of those interests may not insist on having the partnership interest probated.

On the other hand, if the partnership is a very large, publicly traded one, the transfer agent would most certainly be expected to require any partnership interest in the decedent's sole name to be probated.

Decedent with a Living Trust

If the decedent signed a Revocable Living Trust which provides that all of his assets are deemed to be held in the trust, regardless of how they are actually titled, and did not actually transfer title to all of his assets to the trust, that broad language in the trust may, in some cases, help you avoid probate.

In most cases, if a third party is involved, and if the asset is not actually titled in the name of the trust or the decedent as Trustee, the third party will insist on probate.

In some cases, however, you may be able to convince the third party that the language of the trust was sufficient to transfer the asset to the trust, and no probate should be required. This is resolved on a case-by-case basis. If a large institution, such as a bank, brokerage firm, or publicly traded company is involved, it is unlikely the institution will acknowledge the effect of the language in the trust to actually transfer title to the trust. They will insist that the transfer must have been made during the decedent's lifetime on the books of the company.

On the other hand, if personal property is involved, such as jewelry or art work, a better case can be made that the language of the trust should be given effect. If the decedent actually signed an assignment of title to personal property to the trust, then that should suffice, even if the assignment remained in the decedent's files during his lifetime.

Your attorney can help you address your specific fact situation. The worst case is you try to transfer the asset without probate, your efforts are rejected, and you have to probate the asset. In most cases, this is what you should expect.

Remember that the person who allows the transfer, without probate, of an asset which should be probated is taking some risk that the transfer is not authorized. You should understand why your request is denied, then move on, calmly, and embark upon the probate process.

Probate Procedures

Michigan law provides for small estate and affidavit transfer procedures which can be used for estates of less than $15,000, adjusted for inflation. Normal procedures apply to estates over this amount. In the following pages, we provide an overview of the probate process as it applies to both the small estate and the estate which does not qualify as a small estate.

We also provide you references to the official Probate Court form numbers, so you can easily obtain those you need, by number, at the Probate Court or on the Internet. At the end of this chapter we have reproduced the forms used for "small"estates, as well as the other Probate Court forms referenced in this chapter, so that you can see what type of information they require. *Those forms have been reduced in size for printing and may thus not be completed and filed. You will need full-size forms.*

Our explanation is not intended to make you an expert in this arcane area, but rather to give you an appreciation of the steps that must be accomplished in probate administration. Furthermore, the explanation in this chapter is limited to probate procedures *per se.* Matters such as inventorying the assets, protecting and preserving the assets, settling creditor claims, and filing tax returns are covered in other chapters.

Simplified Probate: "Small" Estates
Petition and Order for Assignment

If the total value of property in the decedent's sole name remaining after payment of funeral and burial expenses does not exceed $15,000, as adjusted for cost of living, you may file with the Probate Court a form known as a **Petition and Order for Assignment**, PC 556. You must also present a certified copy of the death certificate and the funeral bill, whether or not it has been paid.

On the form, you list the decedent's assets and the heirs who are entitled to them. You must pay a filing fee (currently $25) and an inventory fee which is computed based on the total value of the assets.

The Probate Court will assign a Probate File Number and complete the last section of the form (Order Assigning Assets), making it an order of the court. You can then obtain certified copies and send one to each holder of the decedent's assets with the request that they make distribution as specified in the order.

Note that under this procedure the decedent's assets are distributed to his or her *heirs*. Those are the people who would be entitled to the decedent's estate, under the law, if there was no Will. The Will, if there is one, is not presented with the form. Therefore, if the decedent left a Will, and the Will has different dispositive provisions, this procedure cannot be used.

Affidavit of Decedent's Successor

If the decedent's probate estate does not exceed $15,000, as adjusted for cost of living, and does not include real property, a person entitled to certain assets of the decedent may claim them by providing the holder of the assets with a copy of the death certificate and a form called an **Affidavit of Decedent's Successor for Delivery of Certain Assets Owned by Decedent**, PC 598.

By law, the holder of the property must then pay or deliver the property to the claimant. More than 28 days must have passed since the decedent's death. This procedure cannot be used if an Application or Petition for the Appointment of a Personal Representative has been granted or is pending, or if a Petition and Order for Assignment (discussed above) has been filed.

The Affidavit is sent directly to the holder of the assets. It is not filed with the Probate Court, nor is it an order of the Probate Court.

As this procedure is new to Michigan law, it is not yet widely understood. Some financial institutions may decline to honor the form, or they may refer it to their legal department for review, which could result in a delay of weeks to months. If you plan to use this procedure, you should be aware that you may encounter some difficulties.

Probate Court Forms

Michigan Probate Court forms are available at any Michigan Probate Court, addresses and telephone numbers of which are listed in Appendix B.

Probate Court forms are also available on the Internet, courtesy of the State Court Administrative Office.

They may be printed from the Web site of ICLE (the Institute of Continuing Legal Education), at:

http://www.icle.org/ michlaw/scao/ courtforms.htm#esttrust

Internet Links To Sources Cited

www.carobtreepress.com

Summary Administration

If the value of the entire probate estate, less liens and encumbrances, does not exceed the homestead allowance, family allowance, exempt property, administration costs and expenses, funeral expenses, and expenses of the decedent's last illness, the Personal Representative, without giving notice to creditors, may immediately distribute the estate and file a **Sworn Closing Statement, Summary Proceeding, Small Estates**, PC 590.

This is considered by some to be a method of closing the estate, since the estate doesn't have to be opened under Summary Administration. See discussion below of closing method #1 under "Close the Probate Estate: Four Methods."

Normal Probate Even If the Estate Isn't Large

In Michigan, the steps in the normal probate process, required for all but the smallest estates, may be summarized as follows:

①   Open the Probate Estate.

②   Provide Required Notices.

③   Prepare the Probate Inventory.

④   Provide Annual Accounts.

⑤   File Notices of Continued Administration.

⑥   Make Distributions to Beneficiaries.

⑦   Close the Probate Estate.

Each of these is explained below in general terms. The explanation, however, is intended only as background information. The precise actions to be taken may vary, depending on the circumstances and local court practice, and each involves a myriad of details which are beyond the scope of this book.

As you read through this discussion, remember that help is available from attorneys who are more familiar with this process than you would ever want to be. Your attorney can obtain the necessary information from you, make recommendations as to the best way to proceed and help you decide, complete the forms, obtain your signature where required, file the forms, send out all the required notices, and assure the successful completion of the probate process.

Remember, also, that even if the Will nominated you as Personal Representative, you cannot act in this capacity until the estate has been opened and you have been appointed by the Probate Court.

① *Open the Probate Estate*

At this point, you are fairly certain that you need to open a probate estate.

You have considered the possibility that assets can be transferred without probate, discussed in the section above entitled "Before You Leap..." You have also considered use of the **Affidavit of Decedent's Successor for Delivery of Certain Assets Owned by Decedent,** PC 598, as explained above.

You should also consider that it may be necessary to *admit the Will*, but it may not be necessary to *appoint a Personal Representative*. These two processes can be separated.

Under Michigan's tax apportionment rules (MCL 700.3920, *et seq.*), non-probate and non-trust property (for example, life insurance, joint property, and annuities) is subject to apportionment unless there is a direction against apportionment *in the Will*.

Being subject to apportionment means that the non-probate assets should be charged with their share of estate taxes. If these assets are *not* subject to apportionment, the people who receive them may not be responsible for estate taxes; they may take the assets free and clear of estate taxes, which will be payable by other beneficiaries of the estate.

If the estate is not large enough to generate estate taxes, then this won't be of concern. (See Chapter 19, "The Tax Man Cometh.")

Opening the Estate

The probate estate must be opened under either Informal or Formal Proceedings.

Under Formal Proceedings, a hearing before a judge is necessary, unless Waivers and Consents have been obtained from all interested persons.

However, in a taxable estate you should ask your attorney whether the Will should be admitted to assure that its direction against tax apportionment will be effective, *even if it is not necessary to appoint a Personal Representative.*

Informal Proceedings

The probate estate can be opened under *Informal* Probate and Appointment Proceedings by filing a dual purpose form, **Application for Informal Probate and/or Appointment of Personal Representative (Testate/Intestate)**, PC 558.

It is possible to file for only *one* of these purposes. For example, a document may give the decedent a power to appoint or designate who will receive certain property, and require that the power be exercised in a Will admitted to probate.

If the sole purpose of probating the Will is to render the power of appointment in the Will effective, application may be made only for informal *probate*. On the other hand, if the sole purpose is to investigate a wrongful death action, application may be made only for informal *appointment*.

The following additional forms must also be filed:

❑ **Testimony of Interested Persons**, PC 565

❑ **Supplemental Testimony of Interested Persons**, PC 566 (if there is a devisee who is not an heir of the testator, such as a trust)

❑ **Register's Statement**, PC 568

❑ **Acceptance of Appointment**, PC 571

❑ **Letters of Authority for Personal Representative**, PC 572

A filing fee (currently $100) must also be paid.

Formal Proceedings

Alternatively, the probate estate can be opened under *Formal* Testacy and Appointment Proceedings by filing a **Petition for Probate and/or Appointment of Personal Representative (Testate/Intestate)**, PC 559.

If *Supervised* Administration is desired, the estate must be opened under *Formal* Testacy and Appointment Proceedings. Supervised Administration will result in Probate Court involvement in every step of the process and may be advisable if disputes or disagreements are anticipated.

The following additional forms must also be filed:

❑   **Waiver/Consent**, PC 561, from each interested person or, if Waivers and Consents cannot be obtained, then **Notice of Hearing**, PC 562

❑   **Testimony of Interested Persons**, PC 565

❑   **Supplemental Testimony of Interested Persons**, PC 566 (if there is a person receiving a bequest under the Will, i.e. a devisee, who is not an heir of the decedent. For example, a trust receiving assets under the Will would be such a person and would require filing of this form.)

❑   **Order of Formal Proceedings**, PC 569

❑   **Acceptance of Appointment**, PC 571

❑   **Letters of Authority for Personal Representative**, PC 572

A filing fee (currently $100) must also be paid.

If a Petition for Formal probate and/or Appointment has been filed, and Waivers and Consents have been obtained from all interested persons, the order may be entered immediately without a hearing. Otherwise:

❑   The Probate Court sets a date and a time for hearing.

❑   The Petitioner must send copies of the Petition, Will, Testimony form(s), and the Notice of Hearing to the interested persons.

❑   A Proof of Service must be filed with the court. This certifies that the required notices and documents have been sent.

❑ If the Petition is unopposed at the time set for hearing, the court may either grant the Petition or conduct a hearing.

Why Use Formal Proceedings?

Is there any reason to open the estate under formal proceedings instead of the simpler informal proceedings? There may be.

First, if the Will is admitted through informal proceedings, there is no statute of limitations on contesting the Will. This means that at some point in the future, even after assets have been distributed and the estate is "closed," someone could challenge the Will.

Second, under informal proceedings, there is no determination of testacy or heirs. This means that there is no formal court order stating who is entitled to share in the estate.

Cautious attorneys therefore advise that in each estate there should be a Probate Court hearing either at the beginning of the probate process, or at the end, for protection on these two important issues.

Finally, informal proceedings may be no "simpler" than formal proceedings. If Waivers and Consents can be obtained from all interested persons in a formal proceeding, the protection of a formal proceeding can be obtained and a hearing can be avoided.

② *Provide Required Notices*

In each type of probate proceeding, whether formal or informal, certain information must be provided.

Notice to Interested Persons

The Personal Representative must, within 14 days after appointment, serve interested persons with:

❑ **Notice of Appointment and Duties of Personal Representative**, PC 573, with copies of:

Provide Required Notices

The Personal Representative must give notice of his or her appointment and duties, as well as arrangements for attorneys' services and fees, to all interested persons.

Notice must also be given to creditors regarding submission of claims and to the surviving spouse regarding the spouse's rights of election and allowances.

❑   Last Will and Testament

❑   **Application for Informal Probate and/or Appointment of Personal Representative (Testate/Intestate),** PC 558, or **Petition for Probate and/or Appointment of Personal Representative (Testate/Intestate),** PC 559

❑   **Testimony of Interested Persons,** PC 565

❑   **Supplemental Testimony of Interested Persons,** PC 566 (if applicable)

❑   **Notice Regarding Attorney Fees,** PC 576. It is *not* necessary to file a copy of the notice or a proof of service with the court. Local court practice may require that a copy of the attorney's fee agreement letter (also called an engagement letter) be sent with the notice.

Notice to Creditors

The Personal Representative must publish a notice notifying creditors of the estate to present their claims within four months after the date of publication or be forever barred. This is done by preparing a **Notice to Creditors, Decedent's Estate,** PC 574.

Courts vary in their procedures for getting this form to the local legal newspaper for publication. The Probate Court will advise you whether they will automatically forward the notice to the newspaper or whether you have to do it.

If there is no Personal Representative, but the decedent had a trust, then the Trustee of the decedent's trust must publish the necessary notice.

The Personal Representative must give actual notice to all known creditors within the four-month period following publication. "Actual notice" means that the notice must be sent to the creditor, not merely published in the legal newspaper.

Notice to Known Creditors, PC 578, must be sent to each creditor of whom the Personal Representative has knowledge, or whose existence is ascertainable from the decedent's records. If actual notice is not given to a known creditor, the creditor will be able to assert a claim against the estate after the expiration of four months from the date of publication of the notice to creditors.

The four-month period is thus a shorter time period for claims which applies only if certain steps are followed. Otherwise, the creditor can assert the claim at any time within the applicable statute of limitations, which could be several years, depending on the nature of the claim.

Also, if the decedent had a trust, the Trustee must be notified of the four-month claims period. This notice must be given within the four-month period. This can be accomplished by sending the Trustee a copy of **Notice to Creditors, Decedent's Estate**, PC 574.

A more detailed treatment of the requirements for giving notice to creditors is found in Chapter 17, "Dealing with Creditors."

Notice to Surviving Spouse

Notice must be given to the surviving spouse within 28 days of the Personal Representative's appointment of the rights of election, allowances, and exempt property. The form used for this purpose is the **Notice to Spouse of Rights of Election and Allowances, Proof of Service, and Election**, PC 581. No notice need be given if the spouse is the Personal Representative or one of the Personal Representatives. For further information, see Chapter 18, "Putting the Horror Stories in Perspective."

③ *Prepare Probate Inventory*

An inventory of all of the assets in the probate estate must be prepared and served on all presumptive distributees (but not to other interested persons, unless they request it) within 91 days of the Personal Representative's appointment. This is done on an **Inventory** form, PC 577.

Prepare Probate Inventory

The Personal Representative must prepare an inventory of all of the assets in the probate estate and provide copies of the inventory to all persons who are expected to receive a distribution from the estate.

The original inventory *may* be filed with the court, but does not have to be, unless the administration is supervised. Proof of Service of the inventory *may* be filed with the court, but does not have to be.

The inventory must be presented to the court for computation of a fee known as the Gross Estate Fee, or sometimes simply as the Inventory Fee. The fee must be paid before closing the estate or within one year after appointment of the Personal Representative, whichever is earlier.

④ *Provide Annual Accounts*

An account must be provided to all beneficiaries of the probate estate annually and upon completion of the administration. The **Account of Fiduciary** form, PC 583 or PC 584, may be used for this purpose. If the estate is supervised, the account must be filed with the court and allowed on Waivers and Consents or after hearing.

⑤ *File Notices of Continued Administration*

Each year, within 28 days after the anniversary of the appointment of the Personal Representative, a **Notice of Continued Administration**, PC 587, must be filed with the court if the probate estate has not yet been closed.

⑥ *Make Distributions to Probate Beneficiaries*

Unless the estate is supervised, distributions to beneficiaries of the probate estate may be made without a court order.

The Personal Representative *may* deliver a written proposal for distribution to all persons who have a right to object. Any distributee who does not object within 28 days gives up the right to do so.

The Personal Representative may also defer some or all distributions until the estate is to be closed and submit a **Schedule of Distributions and Payment of Claims**, PC 596, to the court for approval.

Provide Annual Accounts

File Notices of Continued Administration

The Personal Representative must provide accounts to beneficiaries which show all receipts and disbursements and which identify property belonging to the estate.

The Personal Representative must file annual notices with the Probate Court if the estate remains open after one year from the date the Personal Representative was appointed.

Make Distributions to Beneficiaries

The Personal Representative must distribute the probate estate to those entitled to receive it, as expeditiously as is consistent with the best interests of the estate.

Close the Probate Estate

The probate estate may be closed by any of the following four methods which apply:

Summary Administration

Sworn Statement

Petition for Settlement Order

Petition for Complete Estate Settlement

⑦ *Close the Probate Estate: Four Methods*

Method #1: Summary Administration

If the value of the entire probate estate, less liens and encumbrances, does not exceed the homestead allowance, family allowance, exempt property, administration costs and expenses, funeral expenses, and expenses of the decedent's last illness, the Personal Representative, without giving notice to creditors, may immediately distribute the estate and file a **Sworn Closing Statement, Summary Proceeding, Small Estates**, PC 590.

If no objection to the closing statement is filed within 28 days, the Personal Representative is entitled to receive a **Certificate of Completion**, PC 592, from the court.

Method #2: Sworn Statement

Unless the estate is supervised, the probate estate can be closed by filing a **Sworn Statement to Close Unsupervised Administration**, PC 591. Copies must be sent to all probate estate distributees. A full account in writing must also be furnished to the distributees, including all amounts paid in fiduciary fees, attorney fees, and other professional fees.

If no objection to the closing statement is filed within 28 days, the Personal Representative is entitled to receive a **Certificate of Completion,** PC 592, from the court.

Absent fraud, misrepresentation, or inadequate disclosure, and unless previously barred by adjudication, an action against the Personal Representative for breach of fiduciary duty must be commenced within six months after the filing of the Sworn Statement.

Method #3: Petition for Settlement Order

Where the Will was admitted *under informal proceedings* and an adjudication of the decedent's testacy status is *not desired*, a **Petition for a Settlement Order** may be filed. The Petition may request the court to consider the final account, to compel or approve an accounting and distribution, to construe the Will, or to adjudicate the estate's final settlement and distribution.

This procedure *only* settles matters between the Personal Representative and the devisees, i.e., the people who were left bequests under the Will. The court may approve settlement, direct or approve estate distributions, and discharge the Personal Representative from further claim or demand of a devisee and those the devisee represents. *There are no forms for this procedure.*

Method #4: Petition for Complete Estate Settlement

The method which offers the greatest protection is to file a **Petition for Order of Complete Estate Settlement**. This method *must* be used if the estate is supervised. Depending on whether testacy has previously been adjudicated, either the **Petition for Complete Estate Settlement, Testacy Previously Adjudicated**, PC 593, or the **Petition for Adjudication of Testacy and Complete Estate Settlement**, PC 594, is filed.

The Petition may request the court to determine testacy, to consider the final account, to compel or approve an accounting and distribution, to construe a Will or determine heirs, and to adjudicate the estate's final settlement and distribution.

The following additional forms must also be filed:

❑   **Waiver/Consent,** PC 561, from each interested person, or **Notice of Hearing**, PC 562

❑   **Schedule of Distributions and Payment of Claims**, PC 596 (if needed)

A filing fee (currently $15) must be paid.

The court may approve settlement, direct or approve estate distribution, and discharge the Personal Representative from further claim or demand of an interested person. On Waivers and Consents or after hearing, the court will issue an **Order for Complete Estate Settlement**, PC 595.

NOTES

"It's not that I'm so smart,
it's just that I stay with problems longer."
–Albert Einstein

SELECTED PROBATE FORMS

Michigan Probate Court forms
mentioned in the text, in numerical order

Probate Court Form 556 (front side)
Petition and Order for Assignment
Reproduced in reduced size for information only
A full size form is required for filing with the Probate Court

Approved, SCAO

OSM CODE: PER, OAA

STATE OF MICHIGAN PROBATE COURT COUNTY OF	PETITION AND ORDER FOR ASSIGNMENT	FILE NO.

Estate of _____ , decedent _____
Social security no.

PETITION

I, _____ , represent that:
Name and relationship

1. Decedent died on _____ .
Date

2. ☐ Decedent was a resident of _____ in this county.
City/Township

   ☐ Decedent lived out of Michigan and left an estate within this county to be administered.

3. Funeral and burial expenses of $ _____
   ☐ have not been paid.
   ☐ have been paid by _____ . (receipt attached)
   Name

   The total value of the decedent's property remaining after payment of funeral and burial expenses does not exceed $15,000 as adjusted for cost of living.

4. The decedent's property and its gross value is as follows:

DESCRIPTION OF PROPERTY	VALUE
Total	0.00

PLEASE SEE OTHER SIDE

Do not write below this line - For court use only

PC 556 (3/00) **PETITION AND ORDER FOR ASSIGNMENT**

MCL 700.1210; MSA 27.11210, 700.1302; MSA 27.11302,
MCL 700.3982; MSA 27.13982

Probate Court Form 556 (reverse side)
Petition and Order for Assignment
Reproduced in reduced size for information only
A full size form is required for filing with the Probate Court

5. The name, age, relationship, and address of each heir is as follows:

NAME	AGE	RELATIONSHIP	ADDRESS

6. **I REQUEST** that the property listed above be assigned as follows:

☐ $ _____ to _____ for funeral and burial expenses.
                 Name(s)

☐ to the surviving spouse, _____ .

☐ to the following heirs: _____

_____

I declare under the penalties of perjury that this petition has been examined by me and that its contents are true to the best of my information, knowledge, and belief.

_____   _____
Attorney signature   Date

_____   _____
Name (type or print)   Bar no.   Petitioner signature

_____   _____
Address   Address

_____   _____
City, state, zip   Telephone no.   City, state, zip   Telephone no.

ORDER ASSIGNING ASSETS

7. **IT IS ORDERED** that the property described above is assigned as follows:

☐ a. $ _____ to _____ for funeral and burial expenses.
               Name(s)

☐ b. to the surviving spouse, _____ .

☐ c. to the following heirs in the stated proportions: _____

_____

_____

_____

_____

For 63 days from the date of this order, the share of each heir other than a surviving spouse or minor child shall be subject to any unsatisfied debt of the decedent up to the value of property received through this order.

_____   _____
Date   Judge   Bar no.

Probate Court Form 558 (front side)
Application for Informal Probate and/or
Appointment of Personal Representative (Testate/Intestate)
Reproduced in reduced size for information only
A full size form is required for filing with the Probate Court

Approved, SCAO		OSM CODE: IPA
STATE OF MICHIGAN **PROBATE COURT** **COUNTY OF**	**APPLICATION FOR INFORMAL PROBATE AND/OR APPOINTMENT OF PERSONAL REPRESENTATIVE (TESTATE/INTESTATE)**	**FILE NO.**

Estate of _____

1. I, _____ , am interested in the estate and make this application as
      Name of applicant

_____ .
Relationship to decedent, i.e., heir, devisee, child, spouse, creditor, beneficiary, etc.

2. Decedent information: _____ _____ m. _____ _____
                  Date of death   Time (if known)   Age   Social Security Number

   Domicile (at date of death): _____ _____ _____
                      City/Township/Village   County   State

   Estimated value of estate assets: Real estate: $_____   Personal estate: $_____

3. So far as I know or could ascertain with reasonable diligence, the names and addresses of the heirs and/or devisees of the decedent, the relationship to the decedent, and the ages of any who are minors are as follows:

NAME	ADDRESS	RELATIONSHIP	AGE (if minor)

Of the above interested persons, the following are under legal disability or otherwise represented and presently have or will require representation:

NAME	LEGAL DISABILITY	REPRESENTED BY Name, address, and capacity

4. ☐ a. Venue is proper in this county because the decedent was domiciled in this county on the date of death.
    ☐ b. The decedent was not domiciled in Michigan, but venue is proper in this county because property of the decedent was located in this county at the date of death.

PLEASE SEE OTHER SIDE

Do not write below this line - For court use only

PC 558 (3/00) **APPLICATION FOR INFORMAL PROBATE AND/OR APPOINTMENT OF PERSONAL REPRESENTATIVE**
       (TESTATE/INTESTATE)   MCL 700.3301; MSA 27.13301, MCL 700.3614; MSA 27.13604, MCR 5.302, MCR 5.309

Probate Court Form 558 (reverse side)
Application for Informal Probate and/or
Appointment of Personal Representative (Testate/Intestate)
Reproduced in reduced size for information only
A full size form is required for filing with the Probate Court

5. ☐ a. The decedent died intestate and after exercising reasonable diligence, I am unaware of any unrevoked testamentary instrument relating to property located in this state as defined under MCL 700.1301.

    ☐ b. I am aware of an unrevoked testamentary instrument relating to property located in this state as defined under MCL 700.1301, but the instrument is not being probated because:

    _____

    The instrument   ☐ is attached to this application.   ☐ is already in the court's possession.

    ☐ c. The decedent's will, dated _____ , with codicil(s) dated _____ , is offered for probate and   ☐ is attached to this application.   ☐ is already in the court's possession.

    ☐ d. An authenticated copy of the will and codicil(s), if any, probated in _____ County, _____ is offered for probate, and documents establishing its probate are attached to this application.
    State

6. To the best of my knowledge, I believe that the instrument(s) subject to this application, if any, was validly executed and is the decedent's last will. After exercising reasonable diligence, I am unaware of an instrument revoking the will or codicil(s).

7. ☐ A personal representative has been previously appointed in _____ County, _____ and the appointment has not been terminated. The personal representative's name and address are: State

Name _____   Address _____

City, state, zip _____

8. ☐ I nominate _____ , as personal representative, who is qualified and has priority
    Name

as: _____ . His/her address is: _____
                                      Address

City, state, zip _____

Other persons having prior or equal right to appointment as personal representative are:

Name _____   Name _____

Name _____   Name _____

9. ☐ The will expressly requests the personal representative serve with bond.

10. ☐ A special personal representative is necessary because _____ .

REQUEST:

11. ☐ Informal probate of the will.

12. ☐ Informal appointment of the nominated personal representative   ☐ with   ☐ without   bond.

13. ☐ The appointment of a special personal representative pending the appointment of the nominated personal representative.

I declare under the penalties of perjury that this application has been examined by me and that its contents are true to the best of my information, knowledge, and belief.

_____
Date

_____   _____
Attorney signature   Applicant signature

_____ _____   _____
Attorney name (type or print)   Bar no.   Applicant name (type or print)

_____   _____
Address   Address

_____ _____   _____
City, state, zip   Telephone no.   City, state, zip   Telephone no.

Probate Court Form 559 (front side)
Petition for Probate and/or Appointment of
Personal Representative (Testate/Intestate)
Reproduced in reduced size for information only
A full size form is required for filing with the Probate Court

---

Approved, SCAO
OSM CODE: PFA

STATE OF MICHIGAN PROBATE COURT COUNTY OF	PETITION FOR PROBATE AND/OR APPOINTMENT OF PERSONAL REPRESENTATIVE (TESTATE/INTESTATE)	FILE NO.

Estate of _____

1. I, _____ , am interested in the estate and make this petition as
   Name of petitioner

   _____ as defined by MCL 700.1105(c).
   Relationship to decedent, i.e., heir, devisee, child, spouse, creditor, beneficiary, etc.

2. Decedent information: _____ _____ m. _____ _____
   Date of death   Time (if known) Age   Social Security Number

   Domicile (at date of death): _____ _____ _____
   City/Township/Village   County   State

   Estimated value of estate assets: Real estate: $_____ Personal estate: $_____

3. So far as I know or could ascertain with reasonable diligence, the names and addresses of the heirs and/or devisees of the decedent, the relationship to the decedent, and the ages of any who are minors are as follows:

NAME	ADDRESS	RELATIONSHIP	AGE (if minor)

Of the above interested persons, the following are under legal disability or otherwise represented and presently have or will require representation:

NAME	LEGAL DISABILITY	REPRESENTED BY Name, address, and capacity

4. ☐ a. Venue is proper in this county because the decedent was domiciled in this county on the date of death.
   ☐ b. The decedent was not domiciled in Michigan, but venue is proper in this county because property of the decedent was located in this county at the date of death.

5. ☐ An application was previously filed and a personal representative was appointed informally.

PLEASE SEE OTHER SIDE

Do not write below this line - For court use only

PC 559 (3/00) **PETITION FOR PROBATE AND/OR APPOINTMENT OF PERSONAL REPRESENTATIVE (TESTATE/INTESTATE)** MCL 700.3402; MSA 27.13402, MCL 700.3502; MSA 27.13502, MCR 5.302(A), MCR 5.308, MCR 5.310(B)

Probate Court Form 559 (reverse side)
Petition for Probate and/or Appointment of
Personal Representative (Testate/Intestate)
Reproduced in reduced size for information only
A full size form is required for filing with the Probate Court

6. ☐ A personal representative has been previously appointed in _____ County, _____
and the appointment has not been terminated. The personal representative's name and address are: _{State}

Name _____ Address _____

City, state, zip

7. ☐ The decedent's will, dated _____ , with codicil(s) dated _____
is offered for probate and is ☐ attached to this petition. ☐ already in the court's possession.
☐ An authenticated copy of the will and codicil(s), if any, probated in_____County, _____
is offered for probate, and documents establishing its probate accompany this petition. State
☐ Neither the original will nor an authenticated copy of a will probated in another jurisdiction accompanies the petition. The
will is lost, destroyed, or otherwise unavailable, but its contents are: (attach additional sheets as necessary)

_____

8. ☐ The decedent's will was ☐ formally ☐ informally probated on_____ in _____ County.
9. To the best of my knowledge, I believe that the instrument(s) subject to this petition, if any, was validly executed and is the
decedent's last will. After exercising reasonable diligence, I am unaware of an instrument revoking the will or codicil(s).
10. ☐ After exercising reasonable diligence, I am unaware of any unrevoked testamentary instrument relating to property located
in this state as defined under MCL 700.1301.

11. ☐ I nominate _____ , as personal representative, who is qualified and has priority
Name

as: _____ . His/her address is: _____
Address

City, state, zip

Other persons having prior or equal right to appointment are:

Name _____ Name _____

Name _____ Name _____

12. ☐ The will expressly requests the personal representative serve with bond.
13. ☐ a. The decedent left a will that directs supervised administration.
☐ b. The decedent left a will that directs unsupervised administration, but supervised administration is necessary for the
protection of persons interested in the estate because: (complete on line below)
☐ c. The decedent died intestate or left a will that does not direct supervised administration, but supervised administration is
necessary because: (complete on line below)

_____

14. ☐ A special personal representative is necessary because _____ .

I REQUEST:
15. ☐ An order determining heirs and that the decedent died ☐ testate. ☐ intestate.
16. ☐ Formal appointment of the nominated personal representative ☐ with ☐ without bond.
17. ☐ Supervised administration.
18. ☐ Appointment of a special personal representative pending the appointment of the nominated personal representative.

I declare under the penalties of perjury that this petition has been examined by me and that its contents are true to the best of my
information, knowledge, and belief.

_____
Date

_____ | _____
Attorney signature | Petitioner signature

_____ | _____
Attorney name (type or print)   Bar no. | Petitioner name (type or print)

_____ | _____
Address | Address

_____ | _____
City, state, zip   Telephone no. | City, state, zip   Telephone no.

Probate Court Form 561
Waiver/Consent
Reproduced in reduced size for information only
A full size form is required for filing with the Probate Court

Approved, SCAO

OSM CODE: WAC

STATE OF MICHIGAN PROBATE COURT COUNTY CIRCUIT COURT - FAMILY DIVISION	WAIVER/CONSENT	FILE NO.

In the matter of _____

1. I am interested in the matter as _____ .

☐ 2. I waive notice of the hearing and consent to the application/petition for _____
Nature of application/petition and name of applicant/petitioner

_____

_____

_____

_____

_____ , and I declare that I have received a copy of this application/petition.

☐ 3. I waive notice of hearing on _____ .
Nature of hearing

Date _____

Signature _____

Attorney name (type or print)	Bar no.	Name (type or print)
Address		Address
City, state, zip	Telephone no.	City, state, zip	Telephone no.

NOTE: Do not use for waivers under MCL 700.3310.

Do not write below this line - For court use only

PC 561 (3/00) **WAIVER/CONSENT**

MCL 700.1402; MSA 27.11402, MGR 5.104(B)

Probate Court Form 562
Notice of Hearing
Reproduced in reduced size for information only
A full size form is required for filing with the Probate Court

---

Approved, SCAO

OSM CODE: NOH

STATE OF MICHIGAN PROBATE COURT _____ COUNTY CIRCUIT COURT - FAMILY DIVISION	NOTICE OF HEARING	FILE NO.

In the matter of _____

TAKE NOTICE: A hearing will be held on _____ at _____ m.,
Date   Time

at _____ before Judge _____
Location   Bar no.

for the following purpose(s): state the nature of the hearing

Aids and services are available, upon reasonable request, to individuals with disabilities - please contact the court prior to the hearing if you would like these accommodations.

_____
Date

Attorney name	Bar no.	Petitioner name	
Address		Address	
City, state, zip	Telephone no.	City, state, zip	Telephone no.

The law provides that you should be notified of this hearing. Unless the check box below is marked, you are not required to attend the hearing, but it is your privilege to do so.

☐ You are required to attend this hearing.

Do not write below this line - For court use only

PC 562 (3/00) **NOTICE OF HEARING**

MCL 700.1401; MSA 27.11401, MCR 5.102

Probate Court Form 565 (front side)
Testimony, Interested Persons
Reproduced in reduced size for information only
A full size form is required for filing with the Probate Court

Approved, SCAO

OSM CODE: TES

STATE OF MICHIGAN PROBATE COURT COUNTY OF	TESTIMONY INTERESTED PERSONS	FILE NO.

Estate of _____

1. My name is:_____ My address is: _____

2. I am related to the decedent (or know his/her family) as follows:_____

3. The date and time of death of the decedent is _____ _____ and at that time, his/her
   Date   Time

   domicile (residence) was: _____
                              Address

NOTE: FOR THE FOLLOWING QUESTIONS TREAT ALL PERSONS WHO DIED WITHIN 120 HOURS AFTER THE DECEDENT AS IF THEY DID NOT SURVIVE THE DECEDENT. List persons who died within 120 hours after the Decedent in item 14 below.

4. The decedent ☐ did ☐ did not leave a surviving spouse named:_____

5. ☐ a. The decedent had the following children, both natural (born in or out of wedlock) and adopted:

   _____

   ☐ b. Of the children listed in 5.a, the following have been adopted by others:_____

   _____

   ☐ c. Of the children listed in 5.a, the following were not children of the surviving spouse: _____

Answer question 6 only if question 5.a. was checked.

6. ☐ a. The following children listed in 5.a. died before the decedent: _____

   ☐ b. Children listed in 6.a. left descendants (either natural or adopted) who survived the decedent. Their name(s) and the name(s) of their deceased parent and the relationship of their parent to the decedent is as follows:

   _____

   _____

   ☐ c. Of the children listed in 6.b, the following were adopted by others: _____

PLEASE SEE OTHER SIDE

Do not write below this line - For court use only

PC 565 (3/00) **TESTIMONY, INTERESTED PERSONS**   MCR 5.104(C), MCR 5.302(B), MCR 5.308(B)(2)(a)

Probate Court Form 565 (reverse side)
Testimony, Interested Persons
Reproduced in reduced size for information only
A full size form is required for filing with the Probate Court

If decedent left no surviving issue, complete 7.

7. The decedent ☐ did ☐ did not   leave a father and/or mother surviving named: _____

If decedent is not survived by spouse, descendants or parents, complete 8. and 9.

8. The decedent ☐ had ☐ did not have   the following brothers or sisters, either natural or adopted, whole blood or half blood, who were not adopted by others and who survived the decedent:

☐ 9. One or more of the brothers and sisters of the decedent died before him/her leaving descendants, either natural or adopted, who were not adopted by others and who survived the decedent. The names of these descendants, and the name(s) of their deceased ancestor are:

If decedent was not survived by spouse, descendants, parent, brother, or sister or children of deceased brother or sister, complete 10. and 11.

10. The decedent ☐ did ☐ did not   leave grandparents (both maternal and paternal) who survived the decedent named:

☐ 11. Both maternal grandparents and/or both paternal grandparents died before decedent. Their surviving descendants and their relationship to the grandparents are:
Maternal grandparents: _____

Paternal grandparents: _____

☐ 12. The following heirs listed above are under legal disability. Their name(s), legal disability, and name of their representative are: _____

☐ 13. The following deceased heirs survived the decedent by more than 120 hours. Their name(s) and the name(s) of those who represent his or her interests are: _____

☐ 14. The following heirs did not survive the decedent by 120 hours. Their name(s), relationship to decedent, and date and time of death are as follows:

NAME	RELATION	DATE OF DEATH	TIME OF DEATH

☐ The decedent left a will and some of the devisees named in the will and codicils are not heirs of the testator. A supplemental testimony form is completed and attached.

Witness signature

Subscribed and sworn to before me on _____ , _____ County, Michigan.
Date

My commission expires: _____ Signature: _____
Date   Judge/Deputy register/Notary public   Bar no.

Attorney signature   Address

Name (type of print)   Bar no.   City, state, zip   Telephone no.

Probate Court Form 566 (front side)
Supplemental Testimony, Interested Persons - Testate Estate
Reproduced in reduced size for information only
A full size form is required for filing with the Probate Court

---

Approved, SCAO

OSM CODE: TSS

STATE OF MICHIGAN PROBATE COURT COUNTY OF	SUPPLEMENTAL TESTIMONY INTERESTED PERSONS Testate Estate	FILE NO.

Estate of _____

USE THIS FORM ONLY IF A DEVISEE NAMED IN THE WILL OR CODICIL IS NOT AN HEIR OF THE TESTATOR

NOTE: TREAT ALL PERSONS WHO DIED WITHIN 120 HOURS AFTER THE DECEDENT AS IF THEY DID NOT SURVIVE THE DECEDENT. List persons who died within 120 hours after Decedent in item 17 below.

15. The names of all devisees named in the will and codicils who are not heirs of the decedent (include testamentary trustees and beneficiaries of testamentary trusts) are: _____

_____

_____

☐ 16. Of the devisees listed in 15, the following died before the decedent. Their name(s) and relationship(s) to the decedent are:

_____

_____

☐ 17. The following devisees died within 120 hours after the decedent. Their name(s), relationships to the decedent, and date and time of death are:

NAME	RELATION	DATE OF DEATH	TIME OF DEATH

☐ 18. The following are descendants of the above predeceased devisees, who survived the decedent:_____

_____

_____

☐ 19. Class gifts in the will or codicils where the members are not specifically identified by name are as follows:

_____

_____

_____

PLEASE SEE OTHER SIDE

Do not write below this line - For court use only

MCL 700.2702; MSA 27.12702, MCL 700.2707-700.2710; MSA 27.12707-27.12710

PC 566 (3/00) **SUPPLEMENTAL TESTIMONY, INTERESTED PERSONS, Testate Estate**

Probate Court Form 566 (reverse side)
Supplemental Testimony, Interested Persons - Testate Estate
Reproduced in reduced size for information only
A full size form is required for filing with the Probate Court

☐ 20. The following devisees listed above are under legal disability. Their name(s), legal disability, and name of their representative are:

_____

_____

☐ 21. The following deceased devisees survived the decedent by more than 120 hours. Their name(s) and the name(s) of those who represent his or her interests are:

_____

_____

☐ 22. The guardian ad litem for each devisee under the will and codicils who is unborn, unknown, or unascertainable is:

_____

_____
Witness signature

Subscribed and sworn to before me on _____ , _____ County, Michigan.
                                  Date

My commission expires: _____ Signature: _____
                  Date   Judge/Deputy register/Notary public

_____
Attorney signature

_____
Name (type of print)   Bar no.

_____
Address

_____
City, state, zip   Telephone no.

Probate Court Form 568
Register's Statement
Reproduced in reduced size for information only
A full size form is required for filing with the Probate Court

---

Approved, SCAO

OSM CODE: RIO

STATE OF MICHIGAN PROBATE COURT COUNTY OF	REGISTER'S STATEMENT	FILE NO.

Estate of _____

1. An application has been filed requesting
   ☐ informal probate of the estate of the above named decedent.
   ☐ the appointment of a personal representative.
   ☐ the estate be reopened.
☐ 2. There is good cause to reopen the estate and reappoint the former personal representative. The estate was not closed under supervised administration.
3. Upon consideration of the application, I determine that all of the following are true:
   a. Venue is proper.
   b. The application is complete and made in accordance with MCL 700.3301.
   c. The applicant appears to be an interested person.
   ☐ d. An original, properly executed, and apparently unrevoked will dated _____ with codicil(s) dated _____ is in my possession.
      ☐ An authenticated copy of the will and codicil(s) probated in _____ County _____ is offered for informal proceedings and documents establishing probate in another state are in my possession.
   e. The application is not within MCL 700.3304.
   ☐ f. A will to which the requested appointment relates has been formally or informally probated.
   ☐ g. The person whose appointment is sought has priority to the appointment.
      ☐ The applicant gave notice of his/her intention to seek an informal appointment to each person having a prior or equal right to an appointment not waived in writing and filed with the court.

☐ 4. The will dated _____ with codicils dated _____ is admitted to informal probate.

☐ 5. _____ is appointed ☐ personal representative ☐ special personal representative of the decedent's estate and upon filing a statement of acceptance, letters shall issue to that personal representative
   ☐ without bond.
   ☐ upon filing a bond in the amount of $ _____ .

☐ 6. The application is denied because:
   ☐ a personal representative has been appointed in this or another county of this state and continues to serve.
   ☐ this or another will of the decedent has been the subject of a previous probate order.
   ☐ the probate relates to one or more of a known series of testamentary instruments, the latest of which does not expressly revoke the earlier.
   ☐ other:

☐ 7. The estate is reopened for _____ days.

Date	Register

Attorney name (type or print)	Bar no.

Address	City, state, zip	Telephone no.

Do not write below this line - For court use only

MCL 700.3302; MSA 27.13302, MCL 700.3303; MSA 27.13303, MCL 700.3304; MSA 27.13304, MCL 700.3305; MSA 27.13305, MCL 700.3308; MSA 27.13308, MCL 700.3601; MSA 27.13601, MCR 5.309

PC 568 (3/00) REGISTER'S STATEMENT

Probate Court Form 569
Order of Formal Proceedings
Reproduced in reduced size for information only
A full size form is required for filing with the Probate Court

Approved, SCAO

OSM CODE: OPF

STATE OF MICHIGAN PROBATE COURT COUNTY OF	ORDER OF FORMAL PROCEEDINGS	FILE NO.

Estate of _____

1. Date of hearing: _____ Judge: _____

Bar no.

THE COURT FINDS:

2. Notice of hearing was given to or waived by all interested persons.

3. Decedent died_____
                    Date

   ☐ a resident of the above named county.
   ☐ a nonresident of Michigan, but left an estate in the above named county.

4. Venue is proper.

☐ 5. Decedent's heirs are determined: _____

6. Decedent died
   ☐ intestate.
   ☐ with a valid, unrevoked will dated _____ with codicil(s) dated _____ .

☐ 7. _____ is entitled to appointment as personal representative.
      Name

8. ☐ The decedent's will directs supervised administration. Since the execution of the will, the circumstances bearing on the need
   for supervised administration ☐ have ☐ have not changed.
   ☐ The decedent's will directs unsupervised administration.
   ☐ Supervised administration ☐ is ☐ is not necessary for the protection of persons interested in the estate.

IT IS ORDERED:

☐ 9. The decedent died intestate.

☐ 10. The will and codicil(s) are valid and admitted to probate.

☐ 11. Estate administration shall be supervised.

☐ 12. _____ is appointed ☐ personal representative ☐ special personal representative
   of the decedent's estate and upon filing a statement of acceptance, letters shall issue to that personal representative
   ☐ without bond
   ☐ upon filing a bond in the amount of $ _____ .

☐ 13. The petition for supervised administration is denied.

☐ 14. Decedent's heirs are: (specify names and relationships)

15. Other:

_____
Date

Judge
_____

_____
Attorney name   Bar no.

_____
Address

City, state, zip   Telephone no.

Do not write below this line - For court use only

MCL 700.3409; MSA 27.13409, MCL 700.3410; MSA 27.13410,
MCL 700.3414; MSA 27.13414, MCL 700.3502; MSA 27.13502, MCL 700.3601; MSA 27.13601

PC 569 (3/00) **ORDER OF FORMAL PROCEEDINGS**

Probate Court Form 571
Acceptance of Appointment
Reproduced in reduced size for information only
A full size form is required for filing with the Probate Court

Approved, SCAO

OSM CODE: AOT

STATE OF MICHIGAN PROBATE COURT COUNTY CIRCUIT COURT - FAMILY DIVISION	ACCEPTANCE OF APPOINTMENT	FILE NO.

In the matter of _____

1. I have been appointed _____ of the person/estate.
   Type of fiduciary

2. I accept the appointment, submit to personal jurisdiction of the court, and agree to file reports and to perform all required duties.

☐ 3. For a period of _____ days from the date of my appointment I exclude from the scope of my responsibility the
   not to exceed 91 days

following real estate or ownership interest in a business entity: _____
   Describe real property or business interest

_____

_____

_____

_____

because I reasonably believe the real estate or other property owned by the business entity is or may be contaminated by a

hazardous substance, or is or has been used in an activity directly or indirectly involving a hazardous substance, that could

result in liability to the estate or otherwise impair the value of property held by the estate.

Date _____

Signature _____

Attorney name (type or print)	Bar no.	Name (type or print)

Attorney address		Address

City, state, zip	Telephone no.	City, state, zip	Telephone no.

Social security no. _____

Driver license no. or other identification _____

_____
Do not write below this line - For court use only

MCL 700.3601; MSA 27.13601, MCL 700.3602; MSA 27.13602,
MCL 700.5214; MSA 27.15214, MCL 700.5301; MSA 27.15301,
MCL 700.5307; MSA 27.15307, MCL 700.5412; MSA 27.15412,
MCL 700.7103; MSA 27.17103, MCR 5.501

PC 571 (3/00) ACCEPTANCE OF APPOINTMENT

Probate Court Form 572
Letters of Authority for Personal Representative
Reproduced in reduced size for information only
A full size form is required for filing with the Probate Court

Approved, SCAO		OSM CODE: LET
STATE OF MICHIGAN PROBATE COURT COUNTY OF	**LETTERS OF AUTHORITY FOR PERSONAL REPRESENTATIVE**	**FILE NO.**

Estate of _____

TO: Name, address, and telephone no.

You have been appointed and qualified as personal representative of the estate on _____ . You are authorized
to do and perform all acts authorized by law except as to the following: Date
☐ Real estate or ownership interests in a business entity excluded from your responsibilities in your acceptance of appointment
☐ Restrictions:

☐ These letters expire: _____ .
               Date

_____
Date

SEE OTHER SIDE FOR NOTICE OF DUTIES.

_____   Judge (formal proceedings)/Register (informal proceedings)   Bar no.

_____
Attorney name (type or print)   Bar no.

_____
Address

_____
City, state, zip   Telephone no.

I certify that I have compared this copy with the original on file and that it is a correct copy of the original and that these letters are
in full force and effect as of the date on the letters.

_____
Date

_____
Deputy register

Do not write below this line - For court use only

MCL 700.3103; MSA 27.13103, MCL 700.3307; MSA 27.13307,
MCL 700.3414; MSA 27.13414, MCL 700.3504; MSA 27.13504,
MCL 700.3601; MSA 27.13601, MCR 5.202(A)

PC 572 (3/00) **LETTERS OF AUTHORITY FOR PERSONAL REPRESENTATIVE**

Probate Court Form 573
Notice of Appointment and Duties of Personal Representative
Reproduced in reduced size for information only
A full size form is required for filing with the Probate Court

---

Approved, SCAO

OSM CODE: NOD

STATE OF MICHIGAN PROBATE COURT COUNTY OF	NOTICE OF APPOINTMENT AND DUTIES OF PERSONAL REPRESENTATIVE	FILE NO.

Estate of _____

TO ALL INTERESTED PERSONS:

1. On _____ I was appointed personal representative as requested in the application or petition for probate of
   Date

   this estate (copy attached unless previously sent). I am serving ☐ without bond. ☐ with bond in the amount of $ _____ .

   The papers related to the estate are on file with the _____ County Probate Court located at

   _____ . This ☐ is ☐ is not a supervised administration.
   Address

☐ 2. Attached is a copy of the will of the decedent which ☐ was ☐ was not admitted to probate and under
   which I will administer, manage, and distribute the estate.

3. The court does not supervise the personal representative in the administration of an estate except in limited circumstances.
4. You or another interested person may petition the court objecting to my appointment and/or demanding that I post a bond or an additional bond. The petition must be filed with the probate court along with the applicable fee. Unless the court grants the petition, I will continue to serve as appointed.
5. You or another interested person may petition for a hearing by the court on any matter at any time during the administration of the estate, including for distribution of assets and allowance of expenses of administration. The petition must be filed with the probate court along with the applicable fee.
6. If you continue to be an interested person (such as an heir of an intestate estate or devisee or beneficiary under the will of the decedent), I will provide you with: 1) a copy of the inventory within 91 days of my appointment; 2) unless waived by you, a copy of an account including fiduciary fees and attorney fees charged to the estate, within 1 year of my appointment; and 3) a copy of the closing statement or settlement petition when the estate is ready for closing.
7. To avoid penalties, I must have paid any federal estate and Michigan estate taxes within 9 months after the date of the decedent's death or another time period specified by law.
8. The estate may not be closed earlier than 5 months after the date of my appointment except in limited circumstances. If the estate is not settled within 1 year after my appointment, within 28 days after the anniversary of the appointment, I must file with the court and send to each interested person a notice that the estate remains under administration and the reason for the continuation of the estate. If you do not receive such a notice, you may petition the court for a hearing on the necessity for continued administration or for closure of the estate.

Date of notice
_____

Attorney name   Name
_____   _____

Address   Address
_____   _____

City, state, zip   Telephone no.   City, state, zip   Telephone no.

ATTENTION: **The above duties are not the only duties required of the personal representative**. This notice of appointment must be served on all interested persons within 14 days after the appointment of the personal representative.

Do not write below this line - For court use only

MCL 700.3705; MSA 27.13705, MCR 5.304

PC 573 (3/00) **NOTICE OF APPOINTMENT AND DUTIES OF PERSONAL REPRESENTATIVE**

Probate Court Form 574
Notice to Creditors - Decedent's Estate
Reproduced in reduced size for information only
A full size form is required for filing with the Probate Court

---

Approved, SCAO

OSM CODE: NCT

STATE OF MICHIGAN PROBATE COURT COUNTY OF	NOTICE TO CREDITORS Decedent's Estate	FILE NO.

Estate of _____ Date of birth: _____

TO ALL CREDITORS: *

NOTICE TO CREDITORS: The decedent, _____ , who lived at

Street address _____ City _____ , Michigan

died _____ .
　　　Date

Creditors of the decedent are notified that all claims against the estate will be forever barred unless presented to

_____ , named personal representative or proposed personal

representative, or to both the probate court at _____
　　　　　　　　　　　　　　　　　　　　　Address　　　　　　　　　　　　　　　　　City

and the named/proposed personal representative within 4 months after the date of publication of this notice.

Date _____

Attorney name (type or print)	Bar no.	Personal representative name (type or print)
Address		Address
City, state, zip	Telephone no.	City, state, zip	Telephone no.

PUBLISH ABOVE INFORMATION ONLY

Publish _____ time(s) in _____ in _____ County
　　　　　　　　　　　　　　Name of publication

Furnish _____ copies to _____

Furnish affidavit of publication to the probate court with copy to _____

Forward statement for publication charges to _____

*NOTE TO PREPARER: If there is a known creditor whose address is unknown and cannot be ascertained after diligent inquiry, insert "including [name of creditor] whose address and whereabouts are unknown:"

Do not write below this line - For court use only

PC 574 (3/00) **NOTICE TO CREDITORS, DECEDENT'S ESTATE** 　　MCL 700.3801; MSA 27.13801, MCR 5.106(A), MCR 5.306(A)(4)

Probate Court Form 576
Notice Regarding Attorney Fees
Reproduced in reduced size for information only
A full size form is required for filing with the Probate Court

Approved, SCAO

OSM CODE: NFA

STATE OF MICHIGAN PROBATE COURT COUNTY OF	NOTICE REGARDING ATTORNEY FEES	FILE NO.

Court address

Court telephone no.

This notice must be completed and mailed by the attorney to all interested persons whose interests will be affected by the payment of attorney fees within 14 days after the appointment of a personal representative or within 14 days after the retention of an attorney by a personal representative, whichever is later.

Estate of _____

TO ALL AFFECTED INTERESTED PERSONS:

1. The attorney named below has been retained to provide services on behalf of the personal representative of this estate. A copy of the agreement for payment of attorney fees is attached for your information.

2. The attorney will send a statement for services to the personal representative before payment is made. The statement shall include time records consisting of the identity of the person performing the services, the date the services were performed, the amount of time spent performing the services, and a brief description of the services. You have the right to copies of all statements and can request them from either the attorney or the personal representative.

3. The attorney fees will be paid ☐ monthly. ☐ quarterly. ☐ other _____.

4. You have the right to object to the fees within one of the time frames stated below depending on the type of estate administration.

   • If this is a supervised administration, you may object to the attorney fees at any time before the probate court allows the fees.

   • If this is an unsupervised administration, you may object to the attorney fees at any time before the allowance of the fees by the court or within 28 days after the personal representative files the sworn closing statement with the court.

5. If you want to make an objection it must be made in writing or at a hearing. See below for directions on written objections.

   • If this is a supervised administration, a written objection must be filed with the probate court along with a $15.00 filing fee. You may file your objection by mail or in person at the above court address. A copy of the written objection must also be sent to either the personal representative or attorney named below. If you want a hearing on your objection, you must file a motion with the court requesting a time and date for the hearing. You must notify all interested persons of the hearing time and date.

   • If this is an unsupervised administration, a written objection must be filed with the probate court along with a $15.00 filing fee. You may file your objection by mail or in person at the above court address. A copy of the written objection must also be sent to either the personal representative or attorney named below. The court will not hold a hearing on your objection unless you or another person request one. To request a hearing you must file a petition for a formal proceeding with the probate court along with a $15.00 filing fee. A copy of the petition must also be sent to either the personal representative or the attorney named below.

Date

Attorney signature

Fiduciary name (type or print)

Attorney name (type or print)   Bar no.

Title

Address

Address

City, state, zip   Telephone no.

City, state, zip   Telephone no.

PC 576 (3/00) **NOTICE REGARDING ATTORNEY FEES**

MCL 700.3415; MSA 27.13415, MCL 700.3502; MSA 27.13502, MCL 700.3721; MSA 27.13721, MCR 8.303(D)

Probate Court Form 577 (front side)
Inventory
Reproduced in reduced size for information only
A full size form is required for filing with the Probate Court

---

Approved, SCAO

OSM CODE: INV

STATE OF MICHIGAN **PROBATE COURT** **COUNTY** CIRCUIT COURT - FAMILY DIVISION	**INVENTORY**	**FILE NO.**

In the matter of _____

I, _____ , _____ submit the following
  Name (type or print)   Title

as a complete and accurate inventory of all the assets of the estate and the fair market valuations as of the:

☐ date of death (decedent's estate only).
☐ date of qualification as fiduciary (all other estates).

PERSONAL PROPERTY AND REAL ESTATE (If property is encumbered, show nature and amount of lien)	ESTATE'S INTEREST
TOTAL ASSETS	0.00

PLEASE SEE OTHER SIDE

Do not write below this line - For court use only

PC 577 (3/00) **INVENTORY**

MCL 700.3706; MSA 27.13706, MCL 700.3707; MSA 27.13707, MCL 700.5417; MSA 27.15417,
MCR 5.307, MCR 5.310

Probate Court Form 577 (reverse side)
Inventory
Reproduced in reduced size for information only
A full size form is required for filing with the Probate Court

The following property has been appraised:

_____
Description of property

_____
Name of appraiser

_____
Address of appraiser

_____
City, state, zip

_____
Description of property

_____
Name of appraiser

_____
Address of appraiser

_____
City, state, zip

_____
Description of property

_____
Name of appraiser

_____
Address of appraiser

_____
City, state, zip

_____
Description of property

_____
Name of appraiser

_____
Address of appraiser

_____
City, state, zip

I declare under the penalties of perjury that this inventory has been examined by me and that its contents are true to the best of my information, knowledge, and belief.

_____
Date

_____   _____
Attorney signature   Signature

_____   _____
Attorney name (type or print) Bar no. Name (type or print)

_____   _____
Address   Address

_____   _____
City, state, zip   Telephone no.   City, state, zip   Telephone no.

Probate Court Form 578
Notice to Known Creditors
Reproduced in reduced size for information only
A full size form is required for filing with the Probate Court

Approved, SCAO

OSM CODE: NKC

STATE OF MICHIGAN PROBATE COURT COUNTY OF	NOTICE TO KNOWN CREDITORS	FILE NO.

Estate of _____

TO: _____
Name

_____
Address

_____
City, state, zip

The fiduciary believes you may be a creditor of the estate. The attached notice to creditors was published _____ .
Date

You have 4 months from the above date of publication or 1 month from the date this notice is sent to you, whichever is later, to present your written claim or it will be forever barred. You may use the Statement and Proof of Claim (Form PC 579) to submit your claim. The written claim must be timely delivered or mailed to the fiduciary listed below. You may also send it to the probate court for filing along with a filing fee of $15.00. You may also commence a suit against the estate in a court.

Date _____

Name of fiduciary to whom claim should be presented _____

Attorney name (type or print) _____ Bar no. _____

Title _____

Address _____

Address _____

City, state, zip _____ Telephone no. _____

City, state, zip _____

PROOF OF SERVICE

I certify that on _____ I served a copy of this notice on the creditor by
Date

☐ delivering personally to the creditor.
☐ mailing, with postage prepaid, to the address indicated in this notice.

I declare that this proof of service has been examined by me and that its contents are true to the best of my information, knowledge, and belief.

Date _____

Signature _____

Do not write below this line - For court use only

PC 578 (3/00) **NOTICE TO KNOWN CREDITORS**

MCL 700.3801; MSA 27.13801, MCL 700.3803, MSA 27.13803, MCL 700.3804; MSA 27.13804, MCR 5.306(B)

Probate Court Form 581
Notice to Spouse of Rights of Election and
Allowances, Proof of Service, and Election
Reproduced in reduced size for information only
A full size form is required for filing with the Probate Court

OSM CODE: NSE

Approved, SCAO

STATE OF MICHIGAN PROBATE COURT COUNTY OF	NOTICE TO SPOUSE OF RIGHTS OF ELECTION AND ALLOWANCES, PROOF OF SERVICE, AND ELECTION	FILE NO.

Estate of _____

NOTICE

TO: _____

As surviving spouse you have the right to elect between certain property interests in this estate.

☐ 1. Your spouse died leaving a will. You may elect one of the following:
   a. To abide by the terms of the will.
   b. To take half of the share that would have passed to you had your spouse died without a will, reduced by half of the value of all property derived from your spouse by any other means other than testate or intestate succession upon his/her death.
   c. If you are a widow, to take your dower right as provided by law.
☐ 2. Your husband died leaving no will. You may elect one of the following:
   a. To take your intestate share.
   b. To take your dower right as provided by law.
3. This election shall be made within 63 days after the date for presentment of claims, or within 63 days after service of inventory upon you, whichever is later. Send a copy of this election to the personal representative. You may also file a copy with the court.
4. You may also have the right of priority to homestead, certain property, and a family allowance.

Attorney name (type or print) _____   Signature of personal representative _____

Address _____   Address _____

City, state, zip _____   Telephone no. _____   City, state, zip _____

PROOF OF SERVICE OF NOTICE

☐ by mail
I served ☐ personally the above notice on the spouse on _____ .
                                                    Date
I declare under the penalties of perjury that this proof of service has been examined by me and that its contents are true to the best of my information, knowledge, and belief.

Date _____   Signature _____

Choose only one box.   **SPOUSE'S ELECTION**
☐ 1. I will abide by the terms of the will.
☐ 2. I will take half of the share that would have passed to me had the testator died intestate, reduced by half of the value of all property derived from the decedent by any means other than testate or intestate succession upon the decedent's death.
☐ 3. I, as widow, take my dower right as provided by law.
☐ 4. I, as widow, take my intestate share (no will) as prescribed by law.

Date _____   Signature _____

PROOF OF SERVICE OF ELECTION

☐ by mail
I served ☐ personally the above spouse's election on the personal representative on _____ .
                                                                          Date
I declare under the penalties of perjury that this proof of service has been examined by me and that its contents are true to the best of my information, knowledge, and belief.

Date _____   Signature _____

Do not write below this line - For court use only

MCL 558.1-558.29; MSA 26.221-26.245, MCL 700.2202; MSA 27.12202, MCL 700.3705; MSA 27.13705, MCR 5.305

PC 581 (3/00) **NOTICE TO SPOUSE OF RIGHTS OF ELECTION AND ALLOWANCES, PROOF OF SERVICE, AND ELECTION**

Probate Court Form 582 (front side)
Selection of Homestead Allowance and Exempt Property, and Petition and Order for Family Allowance
Reproduced in reduced size for information only
A full size form is required for filing with the Probate Court

Approved, SCAO

OSM CODE: FAM/FAG

STATE OF MICHIGAN PROBATE COURT COUNTY OF	SELECTION OF HOMESTEAD ALLOWANCE AND EXEMPT PROPERTY, AND PETITION AND ORDER FOR FAMILY ALLOWANCE	FILE NO.

Estate of _____

SELECTION AND PETITION

1. I, _____ , am interested in this estate as _____
Petitioner name (type or print)   Relation

_____ of the decedent.

☐ 2. I select the following property as my homestead allowance:_____

_____

_____

_____

_____

_____

_____

☐ 3. I select the following exempt property under MCL 700.2404:

PERSONAL PROPERTY ITEM	VALUE

☐ 4. The following persons are the surviving spouse, minor children, and other persons whom the decendent was obligated to support and, was in fact, supporting at the time of death:

NAME	BIRTH DATE	RELATIONSHIP	NAME	BIRTH DATE	RELATIONSHIP

(PLEASE SEE OTHER SIDE)

Do not write below this line - For court use only

PC 582 (3/00) **SELECTION OF HOMESTEAD ALLOWANCE AND EXEMPT PROPERTY, AND PETITION AND ORDER FOR FAMILY ALLOWANCE**
MCL 700.2401-700.2405; MSA 27.12401-27.12405

Probate Court Form 582 (reverse side)
Selection of Homestead Allowance and Exempt Property,
and Petition and Order for Family Allowance
Reproduced in reduced size for information only
A full size form is required for filing with the Probate Court

5. The reasons for the need of a family allowance of $ _____ per _____ are: _____
                                                                week or month

_____

_____

_____

_____

6. The interested persons, addresses, and their representatives are identical to those appearing on the initial application/petition, except as follows:

7. ☐ a. **I request** that the selected homestead and exempt property be assigned.

   ☐ b. **I request** that $ _____ per _____ be allowed as family allowance.
                                            week or month

I declare under the penalties of perjury that this document has been examined by me and that its contents are true to the best of my information, knowledge, and belief.

_____ Attorney signature	_____ Date
_____ Attorney name (type or print)　　　　Bar no.	_____ Petitioner signature
_____ Address	_____ Address
_____ City, state, zip　　　　Telephone no.	_____ City, state, zip　　　　Telephone no.

WAIVER AND CONSENT

8. As personal representative, I waive notice of the hearing and consent to allowing the petition.

_____
Date

_____
Signature

ORDER

IT IS ORDERED:

☐ 9. _____ is allowed homestead and
        Name (type or print)

   exempt property of the decedent as selected. The selection is assigned as requested.

☐ 10. A family allowance of $ _____ per _____ is granted from the estate of the decedent
                                                        week or month

   for the support and maintenance of those persons identified in the petition during the settlement of the estate or other period as limited by statute*, but in no event more than one year after decedent's date of death if the estate is inadequate to discharge allowed claims.

_____
Date

_____
Judge　　　　Bar no.

*NOTE: Death, settlement of the estate, etc., may terminate this allowance (see MCL 700.2403; MSA 27.12403 for limitations).

Probate Court Form 583 (front side)
Account of Fiduciary
Reproduced in reduced size for information only
A full size form is required for filing with the Probate Court

Approved, SCAO

OSM CODE: ACC

STATE OF MICHIGAN PROBATE COURT COUNTY CIRCUIT COURT - FAMILY DIVISION	ACCOUNT OF FIDUCIARY	FILE NO.

☐ _____ Number Annual ☐ Final ☐ Interim

Estate of _____

1. I, _____ Name , am the _____ Title

of the estate and submit the following as my account, which covers the period from_____ Month, day, year

to _____ Month, day, year (may not exceed 12 months).

COLUMN 1. INCOME AND OTHER RECEIPTS		COLUMN 2. EXPENSES AND OTHER DISBURSEMENTS	
	$		$
Total Column 1	0	Total Column 2	0

PLEASE SEE OTHER SIDE

Do not write below this line - For court use only

PC 583 (3/00) **ACCOUNT OF FIDUCIARY**

MCL 330.1631; MSA 14.800(631), MCL 700.3703(4); MSA 27.13703(4), MCL 700.5418; MSA 27.15418, MCR 5.308, MCR 5.310(C), MCR 5.769, MCR 8.303

Probate Court Form 583 (reverse side)
Account of Fiduciary
Reproduced in reduced size for information only
A full size form is required for filing with the Probate Court

2. Balance on hand from last account (or value of inventory, if first account) .... $ _____

   Add Total Column 1 (Income and Other Receipts) from the other side of this form .... $ 0 _____

   Subtotal of Balance on hand and Total Column 1 .... $ 0 _____

   Subtract Total Column 2 (Expenses and Other Disbursements) from the other side of this form .... $ 0 _____

   Balance of assets on hand (itemize below) This line must equal the last line in item 3. .... $ 0 _____

3. The balance of assets on hand are:

ITEMIZED ASSETS REMAINING AT END OF ACCOUNTING PERIOD	
	$
Total balance on hand. This line must equal the last line in item 2.	$ 0

4. The interested persons, addresses, and their representatives are identical to those appearing on the initial application/petition, except as follows:

5. This account lists all income and other receipts and expenses and other disbursements which have come to my knowledge.
6. ☐ a. No Michigan estate tax or inheritance tax is due.
   ☐ b. Michigan estate tax or inheritance tax ☐ is due. ☐ has been paid in full (evidence of full payment from Michigan Department of Treasury is attached).
7. ☐ This account is not being filed with the court.
8. ☐ My fiduciary fees for this accounting period are $_____. Attached is a written description of the services performed.
9. ☐ Attorney fees for this accounting period are $_____. Attached is a written description of the services performed.

I declare under the penalties of perjury that this account has been examined by me and that its contents are true to the best of my information, knowledge, and belief.

_____
Date

_____
Attorney signature

_____
Fiduciary signature

Attorney name (type or print) _____ Bar no.

Fiduciary name (type or print)

Address

Address

City, state, zip _____ Telephone no.

City, state, zip _____ Telephone no.

For accounts that must be filed with the court. | **NOTICE TO INTERESTED PERSONS** |

1. You must bring to the court's attention any objection you have to this account. The court will not review the account otherwise.
2. You have the right to review proofs of income and disbursements at a time reasonably convenient to the fiduciary and yourself.
3. You may object to all or part of an accounting by filing a written objection with the court before the court allows the account. You must pay a $15.00 filing fee to the court when you file the objection.
4. If an objection is filed and is not otherwise resolved, the court will conduct a hearing on the objection.

Probate Court Form 584 (front side)
Account of Fiduciary
Reproduced in reduced size for information only
A full size form is required for filing with the Probate Court

Approved, SCAO

OSM CODE: ACC

STATE OF MICHIGAN PROBATE COURT _____ COUNTY CIRCUIT COURT - FAMILY DIVISION	ACCOUNT OF FIDUCIARY ☐ _____ Annual ☐Final ☐Interim Number	FILE NO.

Estate of _____

1. I, _____ , am the _____
    Name   Title

of the estate and submit the following as my account, which covers the period from _____
                                                                                                                        Date

to _____ . This account contains a correct statement of all income and disbursements which
    Date

have come to my knowledge.

2. **SUMMARY**

Balance on hand from last account (or value of inventory if first account) .... $ _____

Add income in this accounting period (total from Schedule A) .... $ 0.00 _____

Total assets accounted for .... $ 0.00 _____

Subtract disbursements in this accounting period (total from Schedule B) .... $ 0.00 _____

Total balance of assets remaining (itemize and describe in Schedule D) .... $ 0.00 _____

If additional sheets are required for Schedules A or B, place all itemization on those sheets and include only category totals on these schedules.

SCHEDULE A: Income in this accounting period		SCHEDULE B: Expenses and other disbursements, including distributions to devisees and beneficiaries	
Net gain, if any, from Schedule C	GAIN	Net loss, if any, from Schedule C	
Total Income	0.00	**Total Expenses and Disbursements**	0.00

PLEASE SEE OTHER SIDE

Do not write below this line - For court use only

PC 584 (3/00) **ACCOUNT OF FIDUCIARY**

MCL 330.1631; MSA 14.800(631), MCL 700.3703(4); MSA 27.13703(4),
MCL 700.5418; MSA 27.15418, MCR 5.308(A), MCR 5.310(C), MCR 5.769, MCR 8.303

Probate Court Form 584 (reverse side)
Account of Fiduciary
Reproduced in reduced size for information only
A full size form is required for filing with the Probate Court

SCHEDULE C: Gains and losses on disposition of assets (use only if needed)

DESCRIPTION	DATE ACQUIRED	DATE SOLD	VALUE AT TIME ACQUIRED BY FIDUCIARY	NET SALES PRICE	GAIN (LOSS)
					0.00
					0.00
					0.00
					0.00
TOTAL GAIN (LOSS)			0.00	0.00	0.00

If gain, transfer to Schedule A; if loss, transfer to Schedule B.

SCHEDULE D: Itemized assets remaining at end of accounting period
If additional sheets are required, indicate on Schedule "See attached sheets".

BALANCE OF ASSETS REMAINING (show this amount on summary) ....

3. The interested persons, addresses, and their representatives are identical to those appearing on the initial application/petition, except as follows:

4. This account lists all income and other receipts and expenses and other disbursements which have come to my knowledge.
5. ☐ a. No Michigan estate tax or inheritance tax is due.
   ☐ b. Michigan estate tax or inheritance tax ☐ is due. ☐ has been paid in full. (evidence of full payment from Michigan Department of Treasury is attached)
6. ☐ This account is not being filed with the court.
7. ☐ My fiduciary fees for this accounting period are $_____ . Attached is a written description of the services performed.
8. ☐ Attorney fees for this accounting period are $_____ . Attached is a written description of the services performed.

I declare under the penalties of perjury that this account has been examined by me and that its contents are true to the best of my information, knowledge, and belief.

Date _____

_____
Attorney signature

_____
Fiduciary signature

_____ Bar no. _____
Attorney name (type or print)

_____
Fiduciary name (type or print)

_____
Address

_____
Address

_____ Telephone no. _____
City, state, zip

_____ Telephone no. _____
City, state, zip

For accounts that must be filed with the court. | **NOTICE TO INTERESTED PERSONS** |

1. You must bring to the court's attention any objection you have to this account. The court will not review the account otherwise.
2. You have the right to review proofs of income and disbursements at a time reasonably convenient to the fiduciary and yourself.
3. You may object to all or part of an accounting by filing a written objection with the court before the court allows the account. You must pay a $15.00 filing fee to the court when you file the objection.
4. If an objection is filed and is not otherwise resolved, the court will conduct a hearing on the objection.

Probate Court Form 587
Notice of Continued Administration
Reproduced in reduced size for information only
A full size form is required for filing with the Probate Court

---

Approved, SCAO

OSM CODE: RIP

STATE OF MICHIGAN PROBATE COURT COUNTY OF	NOTICE OF CONTINUED ADMINISTRATION	FILE NO.

Estate of _____

1. The original appointment of the personal representative occurred on _____ .

Date

   ☐ The administration has been continued annually since the date of the original appointment.

2. The estate remains under administration. The continued administration is necessary because:

3. The interested persons, addresses, and their representatives are identical to those appearing on the initial application/petition except as follows:

Date _____

Attorney signature _____

Personal representative signature _____

Attorney name (type or print) _____ Bar no. _____

Name (type or print) _____

Address _____

Address _____

City, state, zip _____ Telephone no. _____

City, state, zip _____ Telephone no. _____

CERTIFICATE OF MAILING

I certify that a copy of this notice was served on the interested persons of record or their attorneys by ordinary mail at their last known address(es).

Date _____

Signature _____

Do not write below this line - For court use only

PC 587 (3/00) **NOTICE OF CONTINUED ADMINISTRATION**   MCL 700.3951; MSA 27.13951, MCR 5.307(B), (D), MCR 5.310(C)(6)

Probate Court Form 590
Sworn Closing Statement, Summary Proceeding - Small Estates
Reproduced in reduced size for information only
A full size form is required for filing with the Probate Court

Approved, SCAO		OSM CODE: CIS
STATE OF MICHIGAN PROBATE COURT COUNTY OF	SWORN CLOSING STATEMENT, SUMMARY PROCEEDING Small Estates	FILE NO.

Estate of _____

1. I am the personal representative and upon filing this sworn closing statement with the court, this estate will be closed without a hearing.

2. The interested persons, addresses, and their representatives are identical to those appearing on the initial application/petition except as follows:

3. The estate is not under supervised administration and I have not been prohibited by court order from filing this statement.

4. To the best of my knowledge the value of the entire estate less liens and encumbrances did not exceed homestead allowances, family allowances, exempt property, costs and expenses of administration, reasonable funeral expenses, and reasonable, necessary medical and hospital expenses of the last illness of the decedent. The value of the estate is shown on the inventory that I sent to all of the interested persons.

5. I fully administered the estate by disbursing and distributing it to the persons entitled to it.

6. I delivered a copy of this sworn closing statement to the distributees of the estate and to all claimants and demandants, of whom I am aware, whose claims are not barred and have not been paid. I furnished a written full account of the administration to the distributees whose interests are affected.

_____
Personal representative signature

Sworn to before me on _____ , _____ County, Michigan.
                  Date

My commission expires: _____ Signature: _____
                       Date

NOTICE TO INTERESTED PERSON(S): You may object to this sworn closing statement by filing written objections with the above mentioned probate court along with a $15.00 filing fee. If an objection is not filed within 28 days after this sworn closing statement is filed with the court, the probate register will issue a certificate stating that it appears I have fully administered this estate. The certificate does not preclude any action against me or the surety on a bond I may have obtained. If an action or proceeding involving me is not pending in this court one year after this sworn closing statement is filed, my appointment ends.

_____
Attorney signature

Attorney name (type or print)	Bar no.	Personal representative name (type or print)
Address		Address
City, state, zip	Telephone no.	City, state, zip Telephone no.

Do not write below this line - For court use only

PC 590 (3/00) **SWORN CLOSING STATEMENT, SUMMARY PROCEEDING, Small Estates**

MCL 700.3988; MSA 27.13988, MCR 5.311(A)

Probate Court Form 591
Sworn Statement to Close Unsupervised Administration
Reproduced in reduced size for information only
A full size form is required for filing with the Probate Court

Approved, SCAO

OSM CODE: SST

STATE OF MICHIGAN PROBATE COURT COUNTY OF	SWORN STATEMENT TO CLOSE UNSUPERVISED ADMINISTRATION ☐ SUPPLEMENTAL	FILE NO.

Estate of _____

Social security no.

1. I am the personal representative of this estate and upon filing of this sworn statement with the court, this estate will be closed without a hearing. More than five months have passed since the date of my original appointment as personal representative.

2. I have published notice to creditors as required by law and the time for presentment of claims has expired.

3. I have fully administered this estate by paying, settling, or disposing of claims which were presented, expenses of administration and all other taxes. I have distributed the assets of the estate to the persons entitled to assets.*

4. The interested persons, addresses, and their representatives are identical to those appearing on the initial application/petition, except as follows:

5. ☐ a. No Michigan estate or inheritance tax is due.
   ☐ b. Michigan estate tax or inheritance tax has been paid in full (evidence of full payment from Michigan Department of Treasury is attached).

6. I sent a copy of this sworn statement to all distributees and to all claimants whose claims are neither paid nor barred and to all demandants. I furnished a full account in writing to the distributees whose interests are affected by the administration.

☐ 7. I reopened the estate and have completed the administration.

_____
Signature of personal representative

Sworn to before me on_____ , _____ County, Michigan.
Date

My commission expires:_____ Signature: _____
Date

_____
Attorney signature

Attorney name (type or print)	Bar no.	Name of personal representative (type or print)

Address		Address

City, state, zip	Telephone no.	City, state, zip	Telephone no.

NOTICE: NOTICE TO INTERESTED PERSON(S): You may object to this sworn statement by filing written objections with the above mentioned probate court along with a $15.00 filing fee. If an objection is not filed within 28 days after this sworn statement is filed with the court, the probate register may issue a certificate stating that it appears that I have fully administered this estate. The certificate does not preclude any action against me or the surety on a bond I may have obtained. If an action or proceeding involving me is not pending in this court one year after this sworn statement is filed, my appointment ends.

*Note: Specify any exceptions. If any claims remain undischarged, state whether the estate was distributed subject to possible liability with the agreement of the distributees, or state in detail other arrangements which were made to accommodate outstanding liabilities.

Do not write below this line - For court use only

MCL 700.3954; MSA 27.13954, MCL 700.3958; MSA 27.13958,
MCR 5.311(A), (C)

PC 591 (3/00) **SWORN STATEMENT TO CLOSE UNSUPERVISED ADMINISTRATION**

Probate Court Form 592
Certificate of Completion
Reproduced in reduced size for information only
A full size form is required for filing with the Probate Court

Approved, SCAO

OSM CODE: CIC

STATE OF MICHIGAN PROBATE COURT COUNTY OF	CERTIFICATE OF COMPLETION ☐ SUPPLEMENTAL	FILE NO.

Estate of _____

I certify that:

1. The ☐ sworn closing statement, summary proceeding, small estates
   ☐ sworn statement to close unsupervised administration

   of _____ , the personal representative(s) of the estate, was
   _____Name_____

   filed on _____ , more than 28 days ago.
   _____Date_____

2. No objection has been filed.

3. The personal representative(s) appear(s) to have fully administered the estate.

_____   _____
Date   Register

_____
Do not write below this line - For court use only

MCL 700.3954; MSA 27.13954, MCL 700.3958; MSA 27.13958,
MCL 700.3988; MSA 27.13988; MCR 5.311(C)

PC 592 (3/00) **CERTIFICATE OF COMPLETION**

Probate Court Form 593
Petition for Complete Estate Settlement,
Testacy Previously Adjudicated
Reproduced in reduced size for information only
A full size form is required for filing with the Probate Court

Approved, SCAO

OSM CODE: PCS

STATE OF MICHIGAN **PROBATE COURT** **COUNTY OF**	**PETITION FOR** **COMPLETE ESTATE SETTLEMENT,** **TESTACY PREVIOUSLY ADJUDICATED**	**FILE NO.**

Estate of _____

1. I am the personal representative appointed on _____ by ☐ the court. ☐ the register.
   Date

2. Testacy has previously been formally adjudicated.

3. The interested persons, addresses, and their representatives are identical to those appearing on the initial application/petition except as follows:

4. The time for presenting claims that arose prior to the decedent's death has expired.

5. ☐ All claims properly presented have been paid, settled, or disposed of.
   ☐ A schedule for payment of properly presented claims is filed and served with this petition.

6. A final account
   ☐ has been served on all interested persons.
   ☐ is filed and served with this petition.

7. ☐ All estate assets have been distributed as set forth in the final account.
   ☐ A schedule for the distribution of all remaining assets of the estate is filed and served with this petition.

8. ☐ No Michigan estate or inheritance tax is due.
   ☐ Any Michigan estate tax or inheritance tax has been paid in full (evidence of full payment from Michigan Department of Treasury is attached).

I REQUEST:

9. ☐ The final account be approved and that any fiduciary fees and/or attorneys fees set forth in the final account be approved.

   ☐ The distributions previously made and/or all distributions as set forth in the schedule of distributions and payment of claims be approved.

   ☐ The personal representative be discharged.

I declare under the penalties of perjury that this petition has been examined by me and that its contents are true to the best of my information, knowledge, and belief.

_____
Date

_____ Attorney signature	_____ Petitioner signature
_____ Attorney name (type or print) Bar no.	_____ Petitioner name (type or print)
_____ Address	_____ Address
_____ City, state, zip Telephone no.	_____ City, state, zip Telephone no.

Do not write below this line - For court use only

MCL 700.3952; MSA 27.13952, MCR 5.311(B)

PC 593 (3/00) **PETITION FOR COMPLETE ESTATE SETTLEMENT, TESTACY PREVIOUSLY ADJUDICATED**

Probate Court Form 594 (front side)
Petition for Adjudication of Testacy and Complete Estate Settlement
Reproduced in reduced size for information only
A full size form is required for filing with the Probate Court

---

Approved, SCAO

OSM CODE: PAC

STATE OF MICHIGAN PROBATE COURT COUNTY OF	PETITION FOR ADJUDICATION OF TESTACY AND COMPLETE ESTATE SETTLEMENT	FILE NO.

Estate of _____

1. I am the personal representative appointed on _____ by ☐ the court. ☐ the register.
    Date

2. Testacy has not been formally adjudicated.

3. The interested persons, addresses, and their representatives are identical to those appearing on the initial application/petition except as follows:

4. The time for presenting claims which arose prior to the decedent's death has expired.

5. ☐ All claims properly presented have been paid, settled, or disposed of.
    ☐ A schedule for payment of properly presented claims is filed and served with this petition.

6. ☐ The decedent did not leave a will.

7. ☐ The decedent's will, dated _____ , with codicil(s) dated _____
    is offered for probate and is ☐ attached to this petition. ☐ already in the court's possession.

    ☐ Neither the original will nor an authenticated copy of a will probated in another jurisdiction accompanies the petition. The will is lost, destroyed, or otherwise unavailable, but its contents are: (attach additional sheets as necessary)

    _____

8. ☐ The decedent's will was informally probated on _____ in _____ County.

9. To the best of my knowledge, I believe that the instrument(s) subject to this petition, if any, was validly executed and is the decedent's last will. After exercising reasonable diligence, I am unaware of an instrument revoking the will or codicil(s).

10. ☐ After exercising reasonable diligence, I am unaware of any unrevoked testamentary instrument relating to property located in this state as defined under MCL 700.1301.

11. ☐ A final account
    ☐ has been served on all interested persons.
    ☐ is filed and served with this petition.

12. ☐ All estate assets have been distributed as set forth in the final account.
    ☐ A schedule for the distribution of all remaining assets of the estate is filed and served with this petition.

13. ☐ No Michigan estate or inheritance tax is due.
    ☐ Any Michigan estate tax or inheritance tax has been paid in full (evidence of full payment from Michigan Department of Treasury is attached).

PLEASE SEE OTHER SIDE

Do not write below this line - For court use only

MCL 700.3402; MSA 27.13402, 700.3952; MSA 27.13952, MCR 5.311(B)

PC 594 (3/00) **PETITION FOR ADJUDICATION OF TESTACY AND COMPLETE ESTATE SETTLEMENT**

Probate Court Form 594 (reverse side)
Petition for Adjudication of Testacy and Complete Estate Settlement
Reproduced in reduced size for information only
A full size form is required for filing with the Probate Court

I REQUEST:

14. ☐ An order determining heirs and that the decedent died ☐ testate. ☐ intestate.

15. ☐ The final account be approved and that any fiduciary fees and/or attorneys fees set forth in the final account be approved.

☐ The distributions previously made and/or all distributions as set forth in the schedule of distributions and payment of claims be approved.

☐ The personal representative be discharged.

I declare under the penalties of perjury that this petition has been examined by me and that its contents are true to the best of my information, knowledge, and belief.

_____
Date

_____   _____
Attorney signature   Petitioner signature

_____   _____
Attorney name (type or print)   Bar no.   Petitioner name (type or print)

_____   _____
Address   Address

_____   _____
City, state, zip   Telephone no.   City, state, zip   Telephone no.

Probate Court Form 595
Order for Complete Estate Settlement
Reproduced in reduced size for information only
A full size form is required for filing with the Probate Court

Approved, SCAO		OSM CODE: OES
STATE OF MICHIGAN PROBATE COURT COUNTY OF	ORDER FOR COMPLETE ESTATE SETTLEMENT	FILE NO.

Estate of _____

1. Date of hearing: _____ Judge:_____
   Bar no.

THE COURT FINDS:
2. Notice of hearing was given to or waived by all interested persons.
3. The time for presenting claims has expired.
4. ☐ The final account is correct and ought to be allowed.
5. ☐ The assets of the estate have been distributed, and all claims properly presented have been paid, settled, or disposed of.
   ☐ The schedule for distribution and payment of claims correctly identifies the manner in which assets remaining in the estate shall be paid and/or distributed.
6. ☐ a. No Michigan estate or inheritance tax is due.
   ☐ b. Michigan estate tax or inheritance tax has been paid in full (evidence of full payment from Michigan Department of Treasury is attached).
☐ 7. Decedent's heirs are determined: _____

_____

_____

8. Decedent died
   ☐ intestate.
   ☐ with a valid, unrevoked will dated _____ with codicil(s) dated _____.

IT IS ORDERED:
9. ☐ The decedent died intestate.
10. ☐ The will and codicil(s) are valid and admitted to probate.
11. ☐ The final account is approved.
12. ☐ Fiduciary fees and/or attorney fees are approved except: _____

13. ☐ Distributions already made or as set forth in the schedule for distribution and payment of claims are approved.
14. ☐ The appointment of the personal representative is terminated, the personal representative is discharged, and the bond, if any, is cancelled. Estate administration is closed.
15. ☐ Upon filing evidence of payment of the claims and distributions as set forth above (if any) the appointment of the personal representative may be terminated and an order of discharge entered.
16. ☐ Decedent's heirs are: (specify names and relationships)

_____   _____
Date   Judge   Bar no.

_____   Bar no.
Attorney name (type or print)

_____
Address

_____   Telephone no.
City, state, zip

Do not write below this line - For court use only

PC 595 (3/00) **ORDER FOR COMPLETE ESTATE SETTLEMENT**   MCL 700.3952; MSA 27.13952, MCR 5.311(B)

Probate Court Form 596
Schedule of Distributions and Payment of Claims
Reproduced in reduced size for information only
A full size form is required for filing with the Probate Court

Approved, SCAO

OSM CODE: SDP

STATE OF MICHIGAN PROBATE COURT COUNTY OF	SCHEDULE OF DISTRIBUTIONS AND PAYMENT OF CLAIMS	FILE NO.

Estate of _____

1. I, _____ , am the personal representative.
   <small>Name</small>

☐ 2. The following properly presented claims have not been paid, settled, or disposed of. If approved by the court, these claims will be paid.

CREDITOR (Name and Address)	AMOUNT OF DEBT	AMOUNT TO BE PAID
	$	$
	$	$
	$	$
	$	$

☐ 3. Distributions to the following devisees/heirs have been made:

ASSET	DOLLAR AMOUNT OR VALUE	DATE OF DISTRIBUTION	NAME OF RECIPIENT
	$		
	$		
	$		
	$		

☐ 4. The following fees and costs will be paid before final distribution:

Attorney $ _____   Personal Representative $ _____

☐ 5. If approved by the court, the remaining estate will be distributed to the following devisees/heirs in the following amounts:

ASSET	DOLLAR AMOUNT OR VALUE	NAME OF RECIPIENT
	$	
	$	
	$	

Date _____

Attorney signature _____

Petitioner signature _____

Attorney name (type or print) _____ Bar no. _____

Petitioner name (type or print) _____

Address _____

Address _____

City, state, zip _____ Telephone no. _____

City, state, zip _____ Telephone no. _____

PC 596 (4/00) **SCHEDULE OF DISTRIBUTIONS AND PAYMENT OF CLAIMS**

MCL 700.3952; MSA 27.13952,
MCL 700.3953; MSA 27.13953

Probate Court Form 598
Affidavit of Decedent's Successor for Delivery
of Certain Assets Owned by Decedent
Reproduced in reduced size for information only
A full size form is required for filing with the Probate Court

---

Approved, SCAO

AFFIDAVIT OF DECEDENT'S SUCCESSOR
FOR DELIVERY OF CERTAIN ASSETS OWNED BY DECEDENT

Estate of _____

1. I am decedent's successor as surviving ☐ spouse ☐ adult child ☐ other heir _____
specify

   ☐ devisee under the will dated _____ .

   ☐ fiduciary or representative of _____ who is an heir or devisee and has a legal incapacity.
   Name

2. Decedent died a resident of _____ on _____ .
   City, township, or village and county and state   Date

   More than 28 days have passed since decedent's death.

3. No real property is included in the estate.

4. Decedent's estate, less liens and encumbrances, does not exceed $15,000 (as adjusted for cost of living as provided in MCL 700.1210).

5. An application/petition for the appointment of a personal representative is not pending or has not been granted in any jurisdiction. A petition for assignment of an estate not exceeding $15,000 (as adjusted for cost of living) has not been filed with a court.

6. I am entitled to payment or delivery of the property described as: _____ .

7. The name and address of each other person entitled to a share of the property and his/her proportion is as follows:

NAME	ADDRESS	RELATIONSHIP	SHARE %

8. A copy of the death certificate is attached.

_____
Signature

_____
Name (type or print)

_____
Address

_____
City, state, zip

Subscribed and sworn to before me on _____ , _____ County, Michigan.
Date

My commission expires: _____ Signature: _____

NOTICE: A false statement on this affidavit may subject the person swearing to the statement to prosecution for perjury.

MCL 700.3983; MSA 27.13983

PC 598 (3/00) **AFFIDAVIT OF DECEDENT'S SUCCESSOR FOR DELIVERY OF CERTAIN ASSETS OWNED BY DECEDENT**

CHAPTER 16

. . . .

PROTECT
AND
PRESERVE
ESTATE
ASSETS

Protect and Preserve Estate Assets

In Your Hands

If you are the Personal Representative, you have a duty to protect and preserve the property in the probate estate. If you are the Trustee, it is incumbent on you to safeguard the assets of the trust. The decedent's property, in other words, is in your hands.

While you must guard against loss, that is not sufficient. You are also expected to make the property productive. It is anticipated that the assets will earn income and appreciate in value while in your custody as a result of wise investments on your part.

This is an awesome responsibility, and one which must not be taken lightly. Should you fail to meet the standards set forth in the Will or trust instrument, or established by state statute or case law, you could be personally liable to the beneficiaries for any damages.

In this chapter, we discuss the concerns that should be addressed in managing the most common types of estate property.

What Are Your Duties?

If you are a fiduciary, a number of duties or standards of behavior are imposed by statute or common law. Some of these are summarized in an earlier chapter. (See Chapter 6, "Who Should Administer the Estate?") Many of these duties or standards relate directly or indirectly to the management of property and you should familiarize yourself with them.

The Will or trust instrument may impose specific duties related to property management. You should read these documents carefully to determine what directions they may contain.

Under Michigan law, except as otherwise provided by the Will, the Personal Representative must take all steps reasonably necessary for the management, protection, and preservation of the estate in the Personal Representative's possession.

Unless otherwise provided by the governing instrument, *all* fiduciaries— Personal Representatives and Trustees— are bound by Michigan's Prudent Investor Rule.

Property which the decedent owned jointly with others with rights of survivorship automatically passes to the survivors by operation of law and neither the Personal Representative nor the Trustee is responsible for it. However, to prevent any misunderstanding, we recommend you notify the survivors that the property is now theirs and that they are responsible for its management.

Before you do so, however, make sure the property was truly joint and that the survivors claim ownership. It may be that an asset was held jointly for convenience only. This is often done with bank accounts. In that case, the asset should be treated as belonging to the decedent and the Personal Representative should manage it as part of the probate estate. (See Chapter 11, "Inventory the Assets.")

The decedent's trust, or possibly his probate estate, may be the beneficiary of pensions, retirement plans, IRAs, and various types of annuities. If you are the fiduciary, you may be responsible for making investment choices for an account. You may also have to select a settlement option, a matter which we take up in a later chapter. (See Chapter 21, "Transfer Remaining Assets to Beneficiaries.")

If other beneficiaries are named, then the Personal Representative or Trustee has no responsibility. Nevertheless, it would be a good idea for you to notify the beneficiaries, provide them with relevant information, and give them at least a general warning about the advisability of seeking professional advice before making any elections.

Setting Priorities

The first step is to determine priorities and make note of any items which may be time sensitive. The following are some examples:

❑ If the decedent owned perishable items, these should be attended to before they become worthless.

❑ If property or casualty insurance is expiring, it must be renewed without delay.

❑ If investments such as certificates of deposit are maturing, they may be automatically renewed unless action is taken.

❑ Stock options may have to be exercised by a given date.

❑ Contractual obligations may have to be fulfilled on a specified date or dates.

❑ Leases may have to be renewed, or lease options exercised.

❑ There may be a right to sell stock or other business or investment interests under a Buy-Sell Agreement, or a partnership or other agreement, which must be exercised by a certain date.

Establishing Authority

The decedent's assets may be in various entities with different types of ownership. Before you can act with respect to any asset, you must establish your authority to do so.

Assets in Decedent's Name

For assets owned in the decedent's sole name, you may have to present evidence of your appointment as Personal Representative. (See Chapter 15, "To Probate or Not to Probate.") You may also have to retitle sole-name assets into your name as Personal Representative.

For sole-name assets which pass under the Will to a beneficiary or which "pour over" to a trust, it may be possible to leave the assets titled in the name of the decedent until the time comes to transfer them to the beneficiary or the trust. This will avoid the need to retitle the asset twice.

Assets in Trust Name

For assets in the name of a trust, you will have to prove that you are the Successor Trustee.

Joint Assets

For assets owned jointly by the decedent with others with rights of survivorship, all the survivors normally need to do is provide proof of the decedent's death and identify themselves as the survivor.

Retirement Accounts

For assets held in an IRA, pension, or profit sharing plan, or other retirement account, if there is a named beneficiary that person is the only one with authority over that account.

Even though the Personal Representative or Trustee will generally have authority over all assets of the estate, you will not have any authority over these accounts, as Personal Representative or Trustee, unless the estate or trust is the beneficiary.

Bank Accounts
Opening New Accounts

In order to accomplish receipts, disbursements, and other cash management functions over the course of the administration, it will be necessary to open one or more new bank accounts.

If there is a probate estate, accounts should be opened in the name of the Personal Representative. (For example: "Mary A. Jones, Personal Representative/Estate of John R. Jones, Deceased.")

A Taxpayer Identification Number (TIN), also called an Employer Identification Number (EIN), will have to be obtained for the estate from the Internal Revenue Service. This is accomplished by filing IRS Form SS-4 with the IRS office in the district where the estate is being administered.

Your attorney or accountant will generally prepare Form SS-4 for you. It should be filed with the IRS as soon as possible so that the number can be obtained and the new accounts opened. Banks will sometimes open an account indicating "applied for" where the Taxpayer Identification Number is to be inserted, but often they will insist on having the number at the time the account is opened.

If the decedent had a revocable living trust, it became irrevocable— and became a separate entity for legal and tax purposes— at the decedent's death. Accounts should be opened in the name of the Trustee. (For example: "Mary A. Jones, Trustee/ John R. Jones Irrevocable Trust.")

A Taxpayer Identification Number will have to be obtained for the irrevocable trust. (There are different ways of titling such a trust after the decedent's death, with some attorneys preferring to add the date of the original trust or the date of death, when it became irrevocable, after the trust name. Follow your attorney's advice on this point.)

As a minimum, there should be a checking account. If there is both a probate estate and a trust, there should be a checking account for each. All cash and checks that are received should be promptly deposited to the checking account for the probate estate or the trust, as appropriate, and all disbursements for that entity should be made from this account.

Because most financial transactions flow through the checking account, keeping separate checking accounts for the probate estate and the trust will facilitate the record keeping which is required of you as Personal Representative of the estate and/ or Trustee of the trust:

You must provide accounts, at least annually, to beneficiaries. (See Chapter 14, "Keep the Beneficiaries Informed.")

You must also provide information required for the preparation of the various tax returns. (See Chapter 19, "The Tax Man Cometh.") Your records must be sufficient for both of these purposes.

If significant funds accumulate in the checking account, consideration should be given to putting some of the excess into a money market account, certificates of deposit, or other fairly liquid, secure investments. If the amounts are very large, you should consider whether multiple accounts should be opened with different institutions to benefit from Federal insurance of the accounts.

Why Separate Accounts?

If you are not detail oriented by nature, you may question the need for separate accounts and meticulous records. You may think it would be simpler to just run everything through your own personal accounts and keep any relevant information "in your head."

As a fiduciary, you are simply not allowed to commingle or mix funds of the estate or trust with your own funds.

Also, a probate estate and a trust are separate entities for legal and tax purposes. It would be quite time consuming and expensive for an attorney or accountant to comb through your personal records to ferret out the transactions that apply to the probate estate or the trust.

Furthermore, without separate records, it would be more difficult for you to defend yourself against a charge of financial malfeasance or to prove figures on a tax return to an auditor.

If you are not of a temperament to observe formalities, recognize distinctions between entities, and keep complete records, you should enlist a family member or an outside professional to handle the details of the administration for you. As an alternative, you may wish to add a bank or trust company as co-fiduciary, agent, or custodian. Finally, you may want to step aside in favor of someone who is more suited to this type of work.

Existing Accounts

Accounts in Decedent's Name

Accounts in the decedent's sole name should be retitled in the name of the probate estate or, if appropriate, in the name of the trust. You may instead close the account and transfer the funds to one or more other accounts already standing in the name of the probate estate or the trust. Accounts should not remain in the decedent's name and you should not write checks or withdraw funds under a power of attorney since your authority to act under the power expired at the decedent's death.

Accounts in Trust Name

Accounts in the name of a trust that was revocable by the decedent should be retitled. The pre-death trust was not a separate tax entity. All transactions of the trust were attributed to the decedent. The trust may even have had the decedent's Social Security Number as its Taxpayer Identification Number (TIN). By contrast, the post-death trust is a separate taxable entity. Its name should include the word "irrevocable" and it must have its own TIN.

Joint Accounts

Accounts that were joint with rights of survivorship should be retitled in the name(s) of the surviving joint tenant(s). If the account was joint for convenience only and the surviving tenant does not claim ownership, the account should be treated as being in the decedent's sole name. (See Chapter 11, "Inventory the Assets.")

Certificates of Deposit

If there are certificates of deposit, the Personal Representative, Trustee, or surviving joint owner should be aware of the terms and the maturity dates. There is no need to prematurely cash in a certificate of deposit which is paying an attractive rate of interest.

However, if it is desired to withdraw the funds, banking regulations generally allow this to be done in advance of the maturity date without the usual penalty.

Other Financial Assets

Other financial assets typically include stocks, bonds, and mutual funds. They may be held individually (in certificate form) or in one or more brokerage accounts.

Securities in Brokerage Accounts

Securities in a brokerage account in the decedent's sole name should generally be transferred to a new brokerage account in the name of the Personal Representative of the estate. Securities in a brokerage account in the name of the decedent's revocable trust, which became irrevocable upon his death, should generally be transferred to a new brokerage account in the name of the Trustee of the irrevocable trust. The procedure in both cases is the same as for bank accounts, discussed above.

Securities in Certificate Form

Securities owned by the decedent or his trust in certificate form (not held in a brokerage account) may remain in that form until a decision is made as to who should receive that security or if it is to be sold. There is generally no need to retitle those securities prior to distribution.

Jointly Owned Securities

Securities owned jointly by the decedent and others may generally be transferred to the surviving joint owners, in the same manner as a joint bank account, as discussed above. If the securities are in a brokerage account, a new account may be opened by the surviving joint owners and the securities transferred to it. If the securities are in certificate form, contact the issuing company, agency, or a stock brokerage for guidance in how to retitle the security.

Mutual Funds

Mutual fund shares are held in accounts, either directly with the issuing mutual fund, or by a stock brokerage firm in an account which may hold several mutual funds and other securities.

In either case, mutual funds in the decedent's sole name should generally be transferred to a new brokerage account in the name of the Personal Representative of the estate.

Mutual funds in the name of the decedent's revocable trust, which became irrevocable upon his death, should generally be transferred to the name of the Trustee of the irrevocable trust.

Contact the brokerage firm, if the mutual fund is held in a brokerage account, or the mutual fund directly, if the mutual fund is held directly at the issuing mutual fund company. You will need to establish your authority in either event, and provide a new Taxpayer Identification Number for the estate or irrevocable trust. Titling of the account will be the same as the bank accounts, discussed above.

IRAs and Other Retirement Accounts

Many types of securities, including stocks, bonds, and mutual funds, may be held in IRA or other kinds of retirement accounts.

However, even though you may see the decedent's name in the title of the IRA or other retirement account, you should *not* retitle those accounts in the name of the Personal Representative. Unless the estate is the beneficiary of the account, those accounts do not belong to the estate and should remain titled as they are, until action is taken by the beneficiary.

Management of Financial Assets

If you are the Personal Representative or the Trustee, you must see that the financial assets of the probate estate or trust are properly managed. If the probate estate or trust is the beneficiary of a retirement plan, IRA, or annuity, and you as fiduciary are empowered to choose investments for the account, you must see that this is done wisely.

If you are the surviving joint owner of an investment portfolio, you owe it to yourself to look after these assets for which you are now responsible.

If you are the beneficiary of a retirement plan, IRA, or annuity, and you have authority to select investments, it is in your interest to do so in a manner which best suits your needs.

If you are not experienced in investment management, you should seek a competent advisor. (See Chapter 10, "Where to Turn for Help.")

Whether you work with an advisor or on your own, there are certain things to be kept in mind as you decide what to do with the investments.

How Much Cash is to Be Raised?

Cash will be needed to pay debts of the decedent, claims against the estate, expenses of administration, and possibly estate taxes. If you are unable to develop an estimate of these amounts on your own, you should work with your attorney to come up with an estimate of the amount that will be required to discharge these obligations.

If the Will or trust instrument provide for cash bequests, funds will be needed to pay them.

Beyond these needs for cash, you may wish to liquidate all or a portion of the securities. You may be concerned about potential fiduciary liability in the event of a market downturn. You may be the sole beneficiary or the surviving joint tenant and you may not wish to hold the securities going forward.

In any event, before you sell, make sure you have the requisite authority. Normally this is not a problem. Many Wills and trust instruments give the fiduciary broad authority to sell assets and to make distributions to beneficiaries in cash or in kind, or partly in each.

Nevertheless, Michigan law requires that, unless the Will indicates a contrary intention, a decedent's probate estate should be distributed *in kind* to the extent possible. That means the securities themselves would be distributed to the beneficiaries, and not the cash resulting from the liquidation of the securities. Also, beneficiaries may have strong feelings on the matter and

---

Estimating Cash Needs

To prepare an estimate of the cash that will be required, begin with an estimate of the gross estate for Federal Estate Tax purposes.

Subtract estimated fees and and other administration expenses, and any known debts of the estate. (If no estimate of fees and expenses is available, use 3% of the gross estate.)

The result will be the estimated taxable estate.

Calculate the Federal Estate Tax and the state death taxes.

To the amount of the combined taxes, add the estimated fees, administration expenses, debts, and claims.

Finally, add any cash bequests that must be paid under the Will or trust instrument.

should be consulted or at least advised before you embark on a liquidation program.

When it is determined how much cash is to be raised, plans must be made to do so. It must be decided what securities will be sold and when this will be accomplished. Your investment advisor can help you with this.

When selecting securities to be sold, look first to those which have a full step-up in basis in order to minimize gain for income tax purposes. (See Chapter 11, "Inventory the Assets.") If all or a large portion of the portfolio is to be disposed of, it should be done over a period of time, sometimes several months, a practice known as *dollar cost averaging*. In theory, and sometimes in practice, this helps assure that you are not selling at the bottom of the market.

The proceeds of securities sales should be placed in a money market account so that a market rate of interest can be earned with minimal exposure to loss of principal.

What is the Extent of Your Investment Authority?

Many Wills and most trust instruments give the Personal Representative or Trustee authority to invest in such assets as they deem advisable. This seemingly broad authority may be limited, however, by the requirement that the fiduciary invest and manage assets as a prudent investor would.

In Michigan, this requirement has been codified as the Prudent Investor Rule. The statute sets forth duties with respect to portfolio strategy, risk and return objectives, diversification, loyalty, impartiality, investment costs, and delegation of investment and management functions.

The Prudent Investor Rule may be expanded, restricted, eliminated, or otherwise altered by the Will or trust instrument.

We recommend you seek the advice of your attorney concerning the extent of your investment authority in light of the language in the Will or trust instrument and the requirements of the Prudent Investor Rule.

Even if you believe you have full authority, you should consider getting approval of major investments, or of the overall investment plan, from the beneficiaries. By getting the beneficiaries to sign off, you will be better able to defend yourself from "Monday morning quarterbacks" who might criticize your actions if the investments go awry.

If investments have passed to you as the sole surviving joint tenant, you have complete authority with respect to those assets.

What Types of Investments Make Sense?

For investments in the probate estate or the trust, which are held in a fiduciary capacity, safety is paramount. Speculative or very risky investments should be avoided.

If you are the Personal Representative or Trustee, you must decide how much safety is required. Must everything be reduced to cash and held in Federally insured bank accounts? Must the money be spread among different financial institutions so that the amount on deposit in any one institution is within the Federal deposit insurance limit?

Are U.S. Government securities acceptable? High-grade corporate bonds? "Blue chip" stocks?

Your decision should take into account the expectations of the beneficiaries as well as your own risk tolerance.

Tax-exempt investments may or may not be desirable for the probate estate or for the trust, depending on the tax situations of the estate or trust and the beneficiaries. This should be discussed with your accountant.

The needs and investment objectives of the beneficiaries should also be considered in deciding what investments make sense. How long do you anticipate being involved as fiduciary? Is there a need to generate income for the beneficiaries during this period?

Are there or will there be continuing trusts which will go on for years after administration of the estate, and should investments be made with a view to satisfying the objectives of those trusts and their beneficiaries?

Your attorney and investment advisor should be able to assist you in this regard.

What is the Overall Plan?

Keep in mind that investments may be found in the probate estate, in one or more trusts, and in retirement plans, IRAs, or annuities. These various "pots" of investments should not be dealt with in isolation. All of them should be taken into account in designing a comprehensive financial plan.

Where possible, assets within a single entity (e.g., the probate estate or the trust) should be consolidated for convenience. Assets held individually or in multiple small brokerage accounts may be consolidated into a single brokerage account.

How Will Assets Be Managed Going Forward?

When the administration of the estate is concluded, there will likely be some investments for which you are responsible. There may be investments in your own name (or in the name of your own revocable living trust) which you received from the decedent's probate estate or trust, or which became yours as the surviving joint tenant. There may be investments in a continuing trust of which you are Trustee.

These assets will have to be managed going forward. You will have to decide how much responsibility you want to take on yourself, and how much you are willing to delegate to a professional money manager.

You can hold assets individually, in certificate form, but most people find this cumbersome. A popular alternative is to hold the assets in a brokerage account. Various types of brokerage accounts are possible. You can manage the account yourself or you can allow the broker or other money manager to do so. You can, if you wish, require that you approve transactions before they are made.

Another alternative is a trust, agency, or custodial account at a bank or trust company. It is a popular myth in some circles that "stodgy bankers" are overly conservative and produce only mediocre investment returns. You may be surprised by the investment track records that some banks and trust companies have compiled.

We recommend you talk to two or three brokerage companies and a like number of banks or trust companies. Your attorney can refer you to several of each.

Personal Property

If there is a surviving spouse, personal property will typically pass to the spouse, either because the spouse is considered to have owned it jointly with the decedent with rights of survivorship or because the Will or trust instrument leaves it to the spouse. If this is the case, the spouse will normally assume responsibility for the property and there is no need for the Personal Representative or Trustee to be concerned about it.

If there is no surviving spouse, or if the spouse does not receive all of the personal property, as in a second marriage, the situation is different. Any property which is determined to be joint with rights of survivorship is the responsibility of the surviving joint owner or owners. (An automobile, for example, may be registered jointly. Also, it is possible that the decedent executed an assignment making his children, or others, joint owners of all or part of his personal property.)

However, the Personal Representative or Trustee must take charge of any remaining property.

If there is both a Personal Representative and a Trustee, it must be decided who is responsible for the personal property. This depends on several factors and should be discussed with your attorney.

If you are responsible for the decedent's personal property, you must see that it is safeguarded. Consider immediately taking the following steps to safeguard the property:

❑   If the property is in a home or apartment, make sure the premises are secure. If there is any question about the number or identity of people who have keys, consider changing the locks.

❑ Arrange for a prompt inventory of all items. (See Chapter 11, "Inventory the Assets.") A written inventory, in addition to its other uses, is an important control which will enable you to keep track of all of the items and make a claim against the insurance if something is stolen or lost in a fire. Also consider making a videotape of the personal property, and possibly even have that done by a professional to provide added authority.

❑ Be sure all family members and friends who have access to the premises understand who is entitled to the property and when and how it is to be distributed. (See Chapter 21, "Transfer Remaining Assets to Beneficiaries.") Otherwise, they may mistakenly believe they are free to take whatever they wish.

❑ Valuable items, such as fine jewelry, artwork, or collectibles, should be placed in safe storage. You should also check to make sure these items are insured.

❑ Potentially dangerous items such as guns or drugs may require special handling.

❑ If any personal property is to be sold, beneficiaries should be notified in advance, preferably by certified mail, return receipt requested.

Financial Records

Consider removing the decedent's financial records from the premises if you are the fiduciary and you will not be living there. This should certainly be done if the premises will be vacant.

In any event it will be easier for you to work with those records if they are at your home or office, or the office of your attorney or accountant.

If the residence is going to be sold, you certainly don't want people passing through to be able to see these records when they open drawers.

Real Estate

Who is responsible for real estate will depend on how it was titled.

Real estate that was owned by a husband and wife as tenants by the entireties passes to the surviving spouse and is the responsibility of the spouse. Property that is joint with rights of survivorship is the responsibility of the surviving joint tenant(s). Real property that is in the probate estate or the trust is the responsibility of the Personal Representative or the Trustee.

You should verify how the property is actually titled since it may be different than you or other family members may have thought. (See Chapter 11, "Inventory the Assets.")

In the case of a partial or fractional interest in real estate, or a home held in a personal residence trust, you should consult with your attorney to determine the responsibilities for the property following the death of the decedent.

Safeguarding Real Estate

If you are responsible for a residence or other real property, whether in Michigan or in another state, you must see that it is safeguarded and maintained until it is either sold or deeded to a beneficiary. If there is an apartment, it will need to be safeguarded until vacated. Review the lease to determine the decedent's obligations and make necessary arrangements with the apartment management.

Be sure there is adequate homeowner's or renter's insurance in force. The existing policy may have lapsed with the decedent's death. You should check with the agent to determine what coverage there is and how long it will continue.

If a residence or apartment is vacant, consider living in the home temporarily to "house sit" or having another family member or other person do so. If this cannot be arranged, you or another family member should look in on the premises regularly.

Consider notifying the police that the house is vacant. Whether or not the house is occupied, you should continue the utilities. Continue or arrange for landscaping and snow removal. Be sure that the bills for these services, as well as those for prop-

erty insurance, property taxes, and any mortgages or home equity loans, are paid promptly.

Sale of Real Estate

If the property is to be sold, you should meet with a real estate broker as soon as possible and take steps to place it on the market.

If the property is in the probate estate, the Personal Representative may have to get permission from the Probate Court to make the sale. You may want to get a court order even if it is not required, and even if there is no probate estate, to protect yourself against charges that the property should not have been sold, or that it was sold at too low a price. As an alternative, you could obtain the written agreement of the beneficiaries to sell at the proposed price. However, a court order will provide greater protection.

Any proposed sale should be reviewed by your attorney before you sign any documents. This is especially true if the sale is to be made to a family member or other "insider" at a below-market price. Such a sale involves a host of property rights issues and potential Gift Tax questions which must be sorted out before a deal is finalized.

Potentially Contaminated Property

If any real property is suspected of being contaminated by environmentally hazardous substances, and if you are the Personal Representative or Trustee, you should consult with your attorney before taking any action with respect to the property. Ideally, this should be done even before you agree to serve as a fiduciary.

Once you become an "owner" of the contaminated land, you may be financially liable for its cleanup. The cost of remediating the site to the satisfaction of state and Federal authorities could exceed the value of the land itself. Your attorney will advise you how best to handle the matter.

Rental Property

If the probate estate or the trust contains rental property, the Personal Representative or Trustee must see to the collection of rents, the maintenance of the property, and compliance with all the landlord's obligations.

Business Interests

If the decedent had a business interest in his sole name or in his trust, the Personal Representative or Trustee is responsible for preserving this interest.

If the decedent was in business with others, the surviving owners may decide to terminate the enterprise or to continue it. Either way, there could be a Buy-Sell Agreement or other document which spells out how this is to be done and sets forth the rights of the decedent.

You should obtain copies of any such documents and have them reviewed by your attorney. You should then monitor the actions of the surviving owners to ensure that they comply with the terms of the agreement and that the decedent's probate estate or trust gets the settlement to which it is entitled.

If the decedent or his trust was the sole owner of a business, the Personal Representative or Trustee will have to see to the continuation of the concern until arrangements can be made to sell it or transfer ownership to beneficiaries.

A fiduciary does not automatically have authority to continue a business. Authority is often granted in the Will or trust instrument. If it is not, you must look to state law.

In Michigan, a Personal Representative may continue a sole proprietorship or partnership for four months, but must then either reorganize the sole proprietorship or partnership as a corporation or other limited liability entity or obtain Probate Court approval to continue in business beyond the four-month limit. A Trustee, on the other hand, is permitted to continue a business in any form and for any length of time.

If you are the fiduciary, unless you feel that you are capable of running the business yourself, you must make sure that there are people in place to handle day-to-day operations. If there is no one inside the business who can be relied upon to do so, you should consider bringing in someone from the outside to provide the needed management.

CHAPTER 17

. . . .

DEALING WITH CREDITORS

Dealing with Creditors

Should you be under the impression that estate administration is only about gathering assets and distributing them to beneficiaries, we must remind you of another major aspect of handling an estate: The second admonition in the standard definition of estate administration is to "pay debts, expenses, and taxes." Almost every estate will have some creditors and most will have expenses of administration and funeral expenses.

The debts of the decedent must be settled; they are not automatically extinguished on death. Creditors must be reckoned with and you and family members need assurances that all liabilities of the decedent have been put to rest and are behind you. You do not want to receive unpaid bills long after the estate has been distributed.

The legal, moral, and ethical thing to do, if there are enough funds in the estate, is to pay all creditors in full. If you know with certainty who all the creditors are and have estate funds to pay them, that's fine. However, you may not be able to pay them all, and you may not be 100% certain that a claim won't be filed which would come as a complete surprise to you.

In this chapter you will learn:

❑   Why you should not rush to pay liabilities of the estate from personal funds.

❑   The various types of creditors' claims and how they differ.

❑   What your legal obligations are to notify creditors of the decedent.

❑   When creditors must present claims and what happens if they are late.

❑   Which types of claims are entitled to priority, if estate assets aren't sufficient to pay everyone.

❑   How you may be personally liable if you don't handle claims properly.

❑   How you can avoid personal liability for claims.

❑   When revocable trust assets may be subject to claims.

❑   What types of assets are generally not subject to claims.

While you may think that spicy topics such as Will contests would fill the court dockets, claims against estates are a more frequent source of Probate Court litigation. As you will see, this is an area in which the support and guidance of an attorney is usually required.

Are There Other Sources of Payment?

Before your start to tally estate assets and potential claims, consider whether other sources of payment of some items exist. In some cases certain of the decedent's debts may be covered, at least in part, by other sources, so that you need not pay them in full from the estate.

Consider the following possible sources of payment of the decedent's debts and obligations:

❑   The decedent may have prepaid funeral expenses in what is known as *pre-need* planning.

❑   The decedent may have left life insurance for the specific purpose of paying funeral and burial expenses. This may provide a source of cash, but if payable to the estate will become an estate asset and subject to the claims rules discussed in this chapter.

❑   Burial assistance may be available from the Veteran's Administration. (See Chapter 8, "Veteran's Benefits.")

Which "Estate" is Subject to Claims of Creditors?

As you know from other chapters, the term "estate" has different meanings, depending on the context.

In the context of our discussion of claims, we are generally referring to the decedent's probate estate.

It is the probate estate that is generally subject to claims. It is the Personal Representative who generally has the responsibility of dealing with creditors.

In Michigan, however, a decedent's revocable trust may also be available to pay claims and, if there is no probate estate, the Trustee is responsible for the notification of creditors and payment of claims.

Why is the Claims Process So Important?

The claims process can protect the interests of the family, creditors with priority, and other creditors as well. Aside from validating the Will, and determining who are the beneficiaries of the estate, determining what claims should be paid prior to distribution to beneficiaries ranks high on the list of reasons why the probate process exists.

Consider the following case in which proper use of the claims process was essential to the well-being of the decedent's family:

Thelma's husband, Edgar, died suddenly. This was a second marriage and the couple kept their financial affairs separate and filed separate tax returns. Thelma had no knowledge of Edgar's finances and stepped up to the plate to handle his estate.

Edgar didn't leave a Will, and Thelma had herself appointed Personal Representative. She spent a considerable amount of time diligently searching his records for assets and liabilities. To her surprise and great chagrin, she found that Edgar owed back taxes to the IRS and the state taxing authorities, going back many years, including interest and penalties. She also determined that Edgar left very few assets.

Edgar's employer did provide $100,000 of group term life insurance on his life, which Edgar had always assured Thelma would pass to her. However, the employer couldn't find any beneficiary designation, and so it paid the $100,000 to the estate rather than to Thelma.

Thelma was prepared to pay the funeral expenses out of her own funds, and use the insurance money to pay the taxes, and intended to distribute the small balance to herself and Edgar's adult child.

However, after consulting an attorney Thelma learned that certain claims had priority. She paid the funeral expenses from the estate's funds. She exercised her rights as surviving spouse and took her lawful homestead, family allowance, and exempt property. She paid herself a reasonable Personal Representative fee, and paid a reasonable fee to the attorney and accountant. She then paid the small balance to the taxing authorities.

Without knowledge of the claims process, Thelma would have used the insurance money to pay the back taxes, paid the funeral and other expenses from her own pocket, and had very little left for herself or Edgar's son. What Thelma did was just what the law allowed her to do, and was approved by the Probate Court every step of the way.

❑ The decedent may have had credit life insurance, which would pay the balance on the home mortgage, the balance on a car or boat loan, credit card balances, or the balance on an automobile lease.

❑ Medical bills may be covered by health insurance, Medicare, or in some cases by automobile or homeowners insurance.

❑ Estate taxes may be reimbursable from trusts which are included in the decedent's gross estate and the assets of which give rise to those taxes.

Pay Estate Liabilities From Estate Funds

A Personal Representative is generally not personally liable for the decedent's obligations, or for obligations incurred by the Personal Representative during administration of the estate. Before you rush to pay any of these from your own funds, consider why you want to do that.

If there is a timing issue, you may ask the creditor to wait until you can liquidate estate assets. If the decedent's debts are large, you may have to sell assets to raise the cash to pay them. However, those types of decisions should be made as part of an overall plan, with an understanding of what is needed and when. (See Chapter 16, "Protect and Preserve Estate Assets.")

You may even have to take loans against assets to pay obligations, including taxes. (See Chapter 19, "The Tax Man Cometh.")

If you are concerned that estate assets may be insufficient to pay the claim, then you certainly should know this:

As a general rule, neither the fiduciary nor survivors have any obligation to pay claims against the estate out of their personal funds.

As Personal Representative, you could be personally liable under a contract you enter into with regard to estate matters if you don't indicate that you are dealing on behalf of the estate. You could also be personally liable to creditors if you don't follow the priority rules for paying creditors, discussed below, or

Reimbursement of Estate Taxes

When Helen's husband, Bruce, died, his Personal Representative made an election on Bruce's Federal Estate Tax return to treat the marital trust (which Bruce had provided for Helen) as QTIP property. It therefore qualified for the marital deduction, with the result that no Federal Estate Tax was due at Bruce's death.

When Helen died, Bruce's marital trust was includible in Helen's gross estate. Federal Estate Tax of $450,000 was payable in Helen's estate. Of that amount, $275,000 was attributable to Bruce's marital trust.

Under provisions in Bruce's trust instrument and the Internal Revenue Code, Bruce's marital trust reimbursed Helen's estate for the $275,000.

if you otherwise violate your fiduciary duties. Survivors may also be liable if they were also parties to a contract with the decedent, if joint obligations were involved, or they take joint property which is subject to a mortgage.

However, the general rule is that you are not personally liable for the obligations of the estate.

You May Be Able to Deal With Friendly Creditors

There are probably a number of the decedent's creditors who will be happy to work out some kind of arrangement. Before we embark on the formal claims process, we should survey those possibilities:

❑ Credit card companies will be happy to hear from you with a request for the final account balance and instructions to close the account. Carefully review the last bill and recent bills, especially those covering any period of incapacity, and the post-death period as well. Try to identify any charges that may have been made without the decedent's authorization.

❑ Subscriptions to magazines can sometimes be canceled and a refund given for the balance of the subscription term.

❑ Cable television, Internet service, cable modem, telephone, and cellular telephone service contracts should be reviewed to determine whether and how they can be terminated. Often a telephone call to the company will result in immediate termination without penalty. If an amount has been prepaid, ask for a prorated refund due to death. You may get it.

❑ Apartment rental contracts may be somewhat more difficult to terminate. Review the contract and discuss the matter with the landlord.

Dealing with the Landlord

Even if the estate is technically liable under the lease, the landlord has an obligation to try to rent the property and cannot merely sit back and collect rents from the estate. If you are having problems with the landlord's position, see your attorney.

However, sometimes there is such demand for the unit that you will have to negotiate for time to move the furniture and personal belongings to another location.

❑ Consider refinancing mortgages or other obligations, or paying them off, perhaps with insurance proceeds.

Joint Debts; Obligations That Go With the Property

There may be some types of debts for which the decedent and someone else were jointly liable. A loan taken out by both the decedent and spouse would be a prime example. Although the estate remains liable for the debt, the joint debtor is also liable and, if it is not paid, the creditor can proceed against both the estate and the joint debtor.

There may also be debts which are secured by property, and the property is to be distributed to a beneficiary. A mortgage on real estate would be an example. If the estate does not pay the mortgage debt, the real estate remains subject to the debt when the property is distributed to the beneficiary.

Overview of the Claims Process

The claims process may be broken down into seven steps. (As indicated below, the same process may be applicable, with modifications, to the Trustee of the decedent's revocable trust.)

① The Personal Representative determines who are creditors of the estate. (See Chapter 12, "Are There Liabilities?")

② The Personal Representative *publishes* a notice to creditors that the decedent has died and the creditors must present their claims by a certain date or they will be barred.

③ The Personal Representative provides *actual notice* to known creditors. (The notice process is discussed in detail below and is summarized in Chapter 15, "To Probate or Not to Probate.")

Taking Over the Home ...with the Loan

George and Elise owned their residence as tenants by the entireties (joint tenancy between husband and wife).

There was a mortgage on the home in their joint names.

When Elise died, George became the sole owner of the property. George also remained liable on the mortgage debt.

④   The claimant either files a claim as directed in the notice, or begins a lawsuit to collect the claim within the time limit for presenting claims.

⑤   The Personal Representative *allows* the claim (i.e., agrees with the claimant that the claim is owed), settles the claim for a lesser amount, or *disallows* the claim (i.e., rejects the claim as not owed).

⑥   If the Personal Representative has disallowed a claim and the claimant wants to pursue the claim, the claimant must file a lawsuit to do so.

⑦   If a claimant has submitted a claim late, the claim will generally be barred. We discuss below the relevant time periods and possible ways a claimant may get around the time limitation.

If a claim is valid, and if estate property has been distributed to beneficiaries prior to satisfying the estate's debts, those who received the property may have to give it back to the estate to satisfy the claim. It is also possible that the Personal Representative will be *personally liable* for the amount of the claim.

Various Types of Claims, With Different Implications

The definition of a *claim* under Michigan law is very broad. Claims include liabilities of the estate that arose before, at, or after the death of the decedent. Claims can be based on contracts (agreements that the decedent made or that the estate makes) or on a tort (something that the decedent did to someone in violation of a duty, such as injuring someone in an accident). For further examples of the types of liabilities which may give rise to claims, see Chapter 12, "Are There Liabilities?"

Claims also include funeral and burial expenses and expenses of administration. They do not include estate taxes, which are subject to other procedures.

Complicating things further, different types of claims are subject to different claims procedures. It's also important to know what kind of claim it is because the statute provides an order of priority for payment based on the category of claim.

Different Types of Claims Have Different Priorities

As a general rule, Michigan statute provides the following order of priority in which claims against the estate of a decedent must be paid if estate property is insufficient to pay all claims in full:

①   Administrative expenses, funeral, and burial expenses.

②   Certain statutory allowances for the family. (See discussion of these family allowances below and also in Chapter 18, "Putting the Horror Stories in Perspective.")

③   Debts and taxes with priority under Federal law.

④   Medical and hospital expenses incurred in connection with the decedent's last illness, including compensation of people who attended to the decedent.

⑤   Debts and taxes with priority under Michigan law.

⑥   Other claims.

The priority of administrative expenses, funeral and burial expenses, and family allowances is very important to the family. It means that even if there are not enough assets in the estate to satisfy all claims, the decedent can be buried, the people administering the estate can be paid, and the family can get certain amounts (defined by statute) before anything at all is paid to creditors.

No preference can be given in payment of a claim over another claim of the same class, and a claim due and payable is not entitled to preference over a claim which is not yet due.

In certain circumstances, nonprobate property may be liable for claims. Nonprobate property might include revocable trust assets and joint property, in some cases. In those cases the Personal Representative may have an obligation to pursue collection of the equitable share of the claims from the nonprobate property.

We will now review the various types of potential claims and some of the characteristics of each.

Administrative Expenses

Administrative expenses are those which are necessary to administer the estate. They include reasonable attorney and accountant fees, court fees, costs of publication, costs for multiple copies of the death certificate, and reasonable fiduciary fees. Many other types of expenses may also fall within this category. If you need to incur an expense to administer the estate, it's probably an administrative expense, and you should ask your attorney if in doubt.

It is generally not necessary to file a claim against the estate for administrative expenses. This is because payment of the various types of administrative expenses is specifically authorized by law and Court Rules.

That does not mean, however, that all administrative expenses will necessarily be allowed. There is always a means for someone to complain to the Probate Court about excessive or unnecessary administrative expenses.

For example, if the estate is in a supervised probate proceeding, the expenses will be included in an account, and will be subject to review by the Probate Court as part of that account. If, on the other hand, the estate is being administered in a nonsupervised probate, an account will have to be provided to interested persons, any of whom can ask the Probate Court to review the expenses and disallow them.

Fiduciary Fees

A Probate Judge once said that some Personal Representatives consider their letters of authority a license to steal by taking unreasonably high fiduciary fees.

Judges are aware of the tendency of some people to put their hands into the estate's "cookie jar." These people sometime rationalize excessive payments to themselves based on a close relationship with the decedent, years of service prior to the decedent's death without charging, or a desire to adjust their share of the estate because of a belief that the other beneficiaries are not worthy of their shares.

None of this has any place in determining reasonable fiduciary fees. (See discussion regarding fiduciary fees in Chapter 20, "Should You Take Fiduciary Fees?") The courts view fiduciary fees in the context of what would be reasonable if another fiduciary were handling the matter, generally without regard to all of the emotional or personal baggage a particular individual may bring to a situation.

You should therefore be aware that someone could be looking over your shoulder, and that you are always subject to "a higher authority"—the Probate Court.

Attorney Fees

A Personal Representative may employ an attorney to perform necessary legal services or to assist the Personal Representative in the performance of the Personal Representative's administrative duties. The same rule applies to a Trustee. The attorney is entitled to reasonable compensation for that employment, which would include reimbursement of necessary costs.

Michigan Court Rules require attorneys to have written fee agreements with a Personal Representative of a probate estate. If a probate estate is involved, the attorney must serve all interested persons with a copy of the fee agreement, and a notice regarding attorney fees. (A copy of the Probate Court form, **Notice Regarding Attorney Fees**, PC 576, is included at the end of Chapter 15, "To Probate or Not to Probate.")

Strictly speaking, the Successor Trustee of a revocable trust which became irrevocable on the decedent's death is not required to provide a copy of the fee agreement to the beneficiaries. However, if you are the Successor Trustee you should discuss with your attorney the advisability of providing the fee agreement in any event.

It may be better to let the beneficiaries know up front what kinds of fees will be incurred, rather than deal with objections after the fact from beneficiaries who are surprised by legal services required and the basis upon which the Successor Trustee contracted for them.

Attorney fees are always subject to Probate Court review and must be reasonable. In appropriate circumstances, they may be adjusted by the court. There are various factors to be taken into account in determining the reasonableness of attorney fees; the number of hours of service is not the sole criterion. However, regardless of the fee agreement, Michigan Court Rules require that every attorney who represents a Personal Representative must maintain time records reflecting what was done, by whom, when, and how much time it took to perform the services.

Funeral and Burial Expenses
Normal Estate Administration

There will generally be no issue in determining what constitutes reasonable funeral and burial expenses. If the estate is insolvent, however, some courts outside Michigan have held that the rights of the estate's creditors should be taken into account in determining if the funeral and burial expenses are reasonable and therefore entitled to priority, and a Michigan court might do so as well.

This is an area in which common sense will take you far. If there's going to be an issue concerning ability to pay all the creditors, don't incur extravagant funeral or burial expenses. If the estate is going to be a taxable estate, don't assume that all the funeral-related expenses will be deductible on the estate tax return.

Even in large estates, where payment of creditors is not an issue, expenses for lavish funeral luncheons are a prime target for disallowance on IRS audits of estate tax returns.

Special Rules for Small Estates

If the value of the estate is $15,000 or less *after payment of funeral and burial expenses*, it can be handled under an expedited small estate proceeding. (See the discussion of small estates in Chapter 15, "To Probate or Not to Probate.")

Another procedure, Summary Administration, can apply even if the value of the estate is over $15,000. This procedure allows distribution of the estate without giving notice to creditors, if it appears from the inventory and appraisal that the value of the entire estate, less liens and encumbrances, does not exceed certain expenses and statutory allowances.

If that is the case, then the Personal Representative may, without giving notice to creditors, immediately distribute the assets to those persons entitled to them and file a closing statement. Under this procedure, except for creditors holding mortgages, liens, and encumbrances the assets are not subject to creditors' claims. (For further discussion of Summary Administration see Chapter 15, "To Probate or Not to Probate.")

Statutory Spousal and Family Allowances

Michigan statute provides for certain allowances to assure that the surviving spouse and children are not left totally without means. These statutory allowances, which are granted very high priority, are the following:

① The homestead allowance.

② The family allowance.

③ The exempt property allowance.

Administration costs and expenses, and reasonable funeral and burial expenses have priority over these statutory allowances. The homestead allowance has priority over all other claims.

The family allowance has priority over all claims against the estate except the homestead allowance, and administration costs and expenses, and reasonable funeral and burial expenses.

Rights to exempt property (or other assets needed to make up any deficiency in exempt property) have priority against all claims against the estate, again with the exception of administration costs and expenses, and reasonable funeral and burial expenses. However, the right to assets to make up a deficiency in exempt property is reduced as necessary to permit payment of the homestead allowance and family allowance.

The amounts of these allowances and who may be entitled to them are discussed in detail in Chapter 18, "Putting the Horror Stories in Perspective."

Other Types of Claims
Claims for Taxes

Federal, state, and local governments do not have to file claims against the estate in order to pursue their claims for the decedent's tax obligations which accrued during his lifetime, nor to perfect their claims for income taxes for which the estate may be liable, nor for estate taxes.

The decedent's tax liabilities are certainly not wiped out as a result of death. On the contrary, if there are any deficiencies which arose during the decedent's lifetime, the taxing authorities can proceed against the Personal Representative of the estate.

Moreover, if the decedent made a taxable gift during his lifetime, or if there is estate tax due on the decedent's estate, a lien for those taxes automatically arises at time of the gift (for gift taxes), and at the date of death (for estate taxes).

The assets may be released from the lien if the assets are used to pay certain charges against the estate and reasonable administration fees, and in certain other circumstances. However, if the Personal Representative distributes estate assets without having first paid the tax, or without getting the property released from the tax lien, the Personal Representative may be held *personally* liable for the unpaid tax, interest, and penalties.

Secured Debts

The decedent may have given security for a debt. For example, a mortgage is security for a mortgage loan. A creditor whose debt is secured by mortgage, pledge, or other lien does not have to file a claim within the statutory claims period.

Unsecured Debts

Unsecured debts will include most of the debts of the decedent, as described in Chapter 12, "Are There Liabilities?" If a debt does not fall into any of the preceding categories, it is probably an unsecured debt without priority.

Those types of debts must be the subject of a claim filed within the statutory claims period. However, if the Personal Representative knows or should know of the creditor, then actual notice of the claims period must be given to the creditor; published notice will not suffice. See the discussion below regarding notice to creditors.

Claims Not Due and Contingent or Unliquidated Claims

Some claims are not due until a future date, or may become due only if certain things happen or do not happen. For example, an obligation under a promissory note due in five years is not presently due. Likewise, if the decedent signed a guaranty of a bank loan of a third party, the estate is not presently liable under the guaranty if payments under the loan are being made by the person primarily responsible for it.

Nonetheless, persons with claims that are not presently due, or are contingent, or unliquidated (not presently representing a fixed amount) still must present their claims within the statutory claims period.

Notice to Creditors

No Notice Required in Small Estates

Estates which qualify for the small estate procedure (value of the estate under $15,000 after payment of funeral and burial expenses), as well as those which qualify for Summary Administration, don't have to publish a claims notice nor give actual notice to known creditors. All other probate estates must publish a claims notice.

This notice advises creditors that all claims against the decedent's estate must be presented within four months of the date of publication or they will be barred. With the exception of these small estates, publication of notice is required for every probate estate.

Publication of Notice to Creditors

The Personal Representative must publish a notice which informs creditors that they have four months from the date of publication to present their claims or the claims will be barred. The notice must appear only one time, in a newspaper defined by Court Rules. Probate Court form, **Notice to Creditors, Decedent's Estate,** PC 574 (reproduced at the end of Chapter 15, "To Probate or Not to Probate"), contains the required information.

The Personal Representative does not have to publish notice if the estate has no assets, the decedent has been dead for more than three years, or notice was previously published in the Michigan county where the decedent was domiciled.

Actual Notice to Known Creditors and Trustee

The Personal Representative must also give actual notice to each known creditor. Notice must either be served personally or by mail.

A creditor is considered to be *known* to the Personal Representative if the Personal Representative has actual notice of the creditor or if the creditor's existence is reasonably ascertainable by the Personal Representative based on an investigation of the decedent's available records for the two years immediately preceding death and the decedent's mail following death.

Actual notice should also be given to the Trustee of a revocable trust of the decedent. Technically the statute defines the type of trust as one which the decedent reserved the right to revoke at his or her death, and revocable trusts usually provide the right to revoke the trust at any time *during life* but not *at death.*

We nonetheless recommend considering the usual revocable trust as one whose Trustee should be given actual notice.

Actual notice must be given within the four-month period following publication of the notice to creditors. However, if the Personal Representative first knows of an estate creditor less than 28 days prior to the expiration of this time period, actual notice may be given within 28 days after the Personal Representative first knows of the creditor.

Actual notice to known creditors and to the Trustee can be given by sending a copy of Probate Court form, **Notice to Creditors, Decedent's Estate,** PC 574, a copy of which is reproduced at the end of Chapter 15, "To Probate or Not to Probate."

Generally there is no personal liability on the Personal Representative or the estate's attorney for failure to give the required notice, if they believe, in good faith, that notice to that person is not required. However, the estate may be liable for failure to give the notice.

Don't Forget the Hospital

When giving notices to known creditors, consider giving notice to all hospitals and physicians who attended the decedent during his or her last illness and the two years prior to death.

This notice will give them an opportunity to submit their bills within the claims period or be barred.

Otherwise, because of the long delays sometimes incurred in the medical billing and insurance reimbursement process, you could receive bills many months or even years after the decedent's death.

Presentment of Claims

If a claim is presented to the estate the Personal Representative should determine whether the claim has been presented in a timely manner, properly stated, properly served, and represents a bona fide claim.

As this is a practical guide and not a legal treatise, we will not address those details here. The claim should be promptly forwarded to your attorney for a determination as to whether it should be allowed or disallowed (and possibly litigated), or an attempt made to settle the claim.

Timing is critical. If the Personal Representative fails to notify the claimant of any disallowance within 63 days after the expiration of the time for original presentation of the claim, or 63 days after appointment of the Personal Representative, whichever is later, the claim will be considered to have been allowed. Under the statute, the Personal Representative can later change the allowance to a disallowance, but we recommend taking the appropriate action within the initial time limits if possible.

Certain Types of Claims Do Not Have to be Presented

Claims need not be presented in several circumstances:

①　If a claim is being made in a proceeding against the decedent that is pending at the time of death, the claimant need not present the claim to the Personal Representative.

②　A creditor who has a mortgage, pledge, or other lien on estate property can pursue the collateral without filing a claim.

③　A creditor who wants to establish the liability of the decedent or the Personal Representative, where the liability is covered by insurance, can pursue the liability without presenting a claim, but only to the extent of the insurance protection limits.

④　Post-death claims for compensation for services rendered and reimbursement of expenses advanced by the Personal Representative or by an attorney, and certain others providing services to the Personal Representative, need not be presented at all. The statute specifically provides that this type of claim is not affected by the notice to creditors.

When Are Claims Barred?

Pre-Death Claims

Claims may be barred at different times, depending on when the claim arose, and whether the required notices to creditors were given. Here are typical scenarios dealing with claims that arose *before* the death of the decedent:

① If the applicable statute of limitations had already run at the time of the decedent's death, the claim is barred.

It is therefore important that any claims be referred to your attorney to determine if the statute of limitations had already expired when the decedent died. If the statute of limitations had not run as of the time of the decedent's death, it is suspended for four months after the decedent's death, after which time it starts to run again.

② If proper notice to creditors was given and the claim is not properly presented, in a timely manner, then the claim will be barred.

③ If the requirements of the notice to creditors are not met, the claim will be barred three years after the decedent's death.

This means that if proper notice is not given, claims may be presented for up to *three years*. Therefore, publishing notice to creditors and giving actual notice to known creditors will considerably shorten the period during which a creditor may make a claim. Once a claim is barred, the liability may not be asserted against the Personal Representative, the persons receiving the estate, or the persons who receive nonprobate assets.

Post-Death Claims

Claims arising *after* the decedent's death will be barred unless presented within certain time limits as well:

① Claims based on a contract with the Personal Representative must be presented within four months after performance by the Personal Representative is due.

② For almost all other claims, the claim must be presented within four months after the claim arises or four months after the date of publication of the notice to creditors, whichever is later.

③ There is no time limit for presentation of claims for compensation for services rendered and reimbursement of expenses advanced by the Personal Representative or by an attorney, and certain others providing services to the Personal Representative.

The Personal Representative May Be Personally Liable

The law requires the Personal Representative to pay claims in the order of priority provided by law. This is to be done after the expiration of four months after the publication date of the notice to creditors, and after providing for the statutory allowances (homestead and family allowance and exempt property), for claims already presented that have not yet been allowed or whose allowance has been appealed, and for unbarred claims that may yet be presented. The Personal Representative is also to provide for costs and expenses of administration.

At the same time, however, the Personal Representative is permitted to pay a claim that is not barred at any time, whether or not the claim is formally presented. However, if the Personal Representative pays a claim in any of the following circumstances, he or she may be personally liable to another claimant whose claim is allowed and who is injured by the payment:

①   If payment of a claim is made before the expiration of the above time limit and the Personal Representative does not require the claimant who is paid to give adequate security for the refund of any portion of the payment necessary to pay another claimant; or

②   If payment of a claim is made, due to the negligence or willful fault of the Personal Representative, in a manner than deprives the injured claimant of priority.

Further, a Personal Representative who does not comply with all of the statutory requirements with regard to allowances and priority of payment of claims, and distributes estate property in a manner which causes damages to anyone who would have been entitled to those allowances or payment of claims, could be held personally liable for breach of fiduciary duty.

Claims Against the Decedent's Revocable Trust

If no Personal Representative of the decedent's probate estate has been appointed, and if the decedent created a revocable trust, then the Trustee of that trust must publish the same notice to creditors, and give actual notice to known creditors, in the same manner as discussed above.

If the property in the probate estate is insufficient to pay the following expenses, claims, and allowances, the property in the decedent's revocable trust (which became irrevocable on the decedent's death) may be subject to:

①   The administration expenses of the decedent's estate, including funeral and burial expenses.

②   Enforceable and timely presented claims of creditors of the settlor (the decedent).

③   Homestead, family, and exempt property allowances.

Trust Assets Can Be Liable for Claims

It is very common, as a result of careful estate planning, for all of a decedent's assets to be in his or her revocable trust.

In this case there is no probate estate.

However, the Successor Trustee of the decedent's trust is then responsible for providing notice to creditors, and the trust is liable for their claims.

Certain Property May Be Exempt From Claims

There are two general types of property which may be exempt from claims of creditors:

Property Passing Under Beneficiary Designation

Certain assets pass on the decedent's death under a beneficiary designation, by operation of law. Those would include life insurance, IRAs, pension and profit sharing plan benefits, annuities, deferred compensation plans, and U.S. Savings Bonds with a Payable on Death designation. Unless the decedent's estate is the named beneficiary, those assets would typically not become part of the probate estate, and thus would not be subject to claims of creditors.

The Personal Representative would generally not have any authority over the proceeds of those types of assets. In limited circumstances, however, the statute does allow a creditor to reach life insurance premiums paid if the creditor can show that the premium dollars were transferred fraudulently to an insurance or annuity policy.

Joint Property

Absent a fraudulent conveyance, property owned jointly with rights of survivorship will automatically pass to the surviving joint owner or owners upon the decedent's death. That type of property also passes by operation of law, outside the probate estate, and will not generally be subject to claims. The surviving joint owner would generally become the owner of the property free from the claims of the creditors of the deceased joint owner unless, for example, the property is subject to a mortgage, pledge, or other lien.

A transfer may be held to be a fraudulent conveyance if it is done with the intent to defraud creditors. This might be found to be the case, for example, where property is transferred to joint tenancy at a time when the owner of the property is insolvent.

CHAPTER 18

. . . .

PUTTING THE HORROR STORIES IN PERSPECTIVE

Putting the Horror Stories in Perspective

We have all heard stories about how someone died and the family couldn't touch the assets, that everything was "tied up" in Probate Court for years, and the family was in a desperate situation, even though the estate was ample. In another allegedly true story, some property had to be sold and, as the story goes, that also dragged on for months or years. In another story, everything had to be sold to pay estate taxes. In yet another the creditors or the tax authorities got the entire estate and the family got nothing.

And how often do we hear of the second wife who was cut out by the husband's Will and his children by a prior marriage took the entire estate?

In every story there is probably a grain of truth, but the facts become distorted as the story is told and retold. Anyhow, it doesn't really matter what someone says happened in a case they heard about. What matters is that if you find yourself in a similar situation, here and now, you need to know what really can happen. It may not always be rosy, but often it's not exactly as the folks will tell you.

Providing for the Family's Cash Needs

The first myth is that after someone dies everything is frozen, tied up in probate or with the IRS, and nothing can be touched, not a penny spent, until the process is completed years down the road.

The reality is that in most situations, even if there is a probate estate the family's cash needs can be met from several sources, if not immediately then with only minor delays. Consider the following examples:

Joint Accounts

Joint accounts owned by the decedent and the surviving spouse automatically become the property of the surviving spouse and can continue to be accessed just as prior to the death.

Credit Cards

Credit cards owned by the surviving spouse can continue to be used to charge expenses. The decedent may have expired but if the card hasn't the survivor can generally continue to use either joint credit cards or credit cards in the surviving spouse's name alone.

Life Insurance

Often there will be life insurance payable directly to the surviving spouse. That has nothing to do with probate and the cash received by the surviving spouse can generally be spent. Insurance proceeds can usually be obtained within a couple of weeks after application is made. (See Chapter 9, "Life Insurance.")

Revocable Trust Assets

If the decedent had a revocable trust, the Successor Trustee can access the assets of that trust, including the trust's bank accounts, without any involvement with the Probate Court at all.

Obtain Probate Authority

Finally, even if everything is in the decedent's sole name—there are no joint accounts, no credit cards, no life insurance, and no revocable trust assets—obtaining authority from the Probate Court will still not involve the draconian process so often described.

Please take a moment to peruse the small estate procedures outlined in Chapter 15, "To Probate or Not to Probate." These are truly expedited procedures. However, even if the estate does not qualify for any of these procedures, within a couple of days the necessary probate pleadings can be prepared, an estate opened, and Letters of Authority issued to the Personal Representative, who will then have very broad authority to use estate assets. Generally no court hearing is necessary and it's merely a matter of getting the documents together and the facts straight, and starting the process.

Yes, it is true that in a taxable estate liquidity—cash— will have to be raised to pay estate taxes, due nine months after the date of death. However, estate taxes will only be due if the estate is relatively large. (See Chapter 19, "The Tax Man Cometh.") The stories we have all heard paint a picture of a modest estate where, due to probate or the IRS, the poor widow is left without cash to buy a meal.

The bottom line is that today, in Michigan at least, these horror stories just do not represent reality.

Estate Property Can Be Sold

A related story is that certain estate property has to be sold, and there is a buyer but the sale will fall through because of the delay in "going through probate."

Again, today this type of situation should generally not happen. The Personal Representative has the authority, under the law, to sell estate property, including both personal property and real estate, without permission or other action of the court in all types of probate administration, including supervised administration.

There could be an exceptional case where the Probate Court has restricted the ability of the Personal Representative to sell real estate or personal property. That type of restriction would appear clearly upon the Letters of Authority and would be the exception, not the rule.

Even if there is such a restriction, or if some interested person is objecting to the proposed sale, the Personal Representative may ask the court to confirm a sale of personal property or real estate in a formal proceeding. Interested persons would have to be given notice of the hearing, and the matter would be resolved. It could take a few weeks to schedule a hearing. In most cases an interested buyer will understand this modest delay.

The Need to File An Estate Tax Return Doesn't Freeze the Estate

Even in cases where the estate is large enough to require filing of a Federal Estate Tax return, this still doesn't freeze the estate.

The Federal Estate Tax return is generally not filed until the due date, which is nine months after the date of death. That return is sometimes filed on extension up to six months later than that, or a total of 15 months after the date of death. It is true that a prudent Personal Representative should not distribute the entire estate until an IRS closing letter is received, which could take six months after the estate tax return is filed. This means that the Personal Representative will not be in a position to make final distribution until at least 15 months to two years after the date of death, maybe longer if there is a protracted audit.

However, this does not mean the estate is frozen during the period of administration. Partial distributions of estate assets can generally be made, and in most cases would be made if there is a surviving spouse. Even in other cases, once the estate assets are known and liabilities, including tax liabilities, are determined, the Personal Representative will have a sense of what can safely be distributed on an interim basis.

Expediting Partial Distributions

If partial distributions are contemplated, it is important to assemble the information needed to prepare the Federal Estate Tax return as early as possible.

This is so the amount of tax can be estimated and it can be decided how much of the estate may be safely distributed.

The Surviving Spouse and Children Generally Won't Be Left Penniless

It is possible that the decedent may have left nothing at all. In that case, of course, there will be nothing for the surviving spouse and children. But in almost all other cases the surviving spouse and children have certain rights which rank so high on the list of priorities that, whether there is a Will or no Will at all, they will get something.

What the statute allows for the surviving spouse and children may not seem like a lot, but everything is relative. If the concern is that creditors will take the estate and the surviving spouse and children will literally be thrown out into the cold, this is not quite so. Even if the decedent left the estate to others, the family still has certain rights.

The amounts mentioned in this chapter are effective for estates of individuals who died after March 31, 2000, which is the effective date of Michigan's Estates and Protected Individuals Code. If a person died before that date, you'll need to refer to smaller amounts as provided under the Revised Probate Code which was in effect prior to that date.

Also, the allowances and exempt property we describe are available for a decedent who dies while domiciled in Michigan. If the decedent died domiciled outside of Michigan, rights to homestead allowance, family allowance, and exempt property, if any, will be governed by the law of the decedent's domicile at the time of death.

Homestead Allowance

The surviving spouse is entitled to receive a homestead allowance of $15,000. This amount will be adjusted annually for inflation.

If there is no surviving spouse, each minor child and each dependent child of the decedent is entitled to a homestead allowance equal to $15,000, as adjusted annually for inflation, divided by the number of the decedent's minor and dependent children. A dependent child means an adult child who was dependent upon the decedent.

The homestead allowance has priority over all claims against the estate, including other allowances and other claims, with the sole exception of administrative costs and expenses, and funeral and burial expenses. Therefore, it is virtually the top priority for disbursement from an estate.

Also, the homestead allowance is in addition to any share passing to the surviving spouse or minor or dependent child under the decedent's Will, unless otherwise provided, by intestate succession, or by elective share. We will discuss below what assets can be used to satisfy the homestead allowance.

Family Allowance

A reasonable family allowance is payable to the decedent's surviving spouse and minor children whom the decedent was obligated to support, and children of the decedent or another who were in fact being supported by the decedent. The family allowance is intended to provide support and maintenance for these people during the period of estate administration.

If the estate is inadequate to discharge allowed claims, the family allowance is not to continue for a period of more than one year. It is payable to the surviving spouse, if living, for the use of the surviving spouse and minor and dependent children. Otherwise, it is payable to the children or persons having their care and custody.

The statute does not set an amount for the family allowance. It simply says that a "reasonable" family allowance is payable, either in a lump sum or in installments. The Personal Representative may determine the family allowance in a lump sum not exceeding $18,000 or periodic installments not exceeding 1/12 of that amount per month for one year. This amount will be adjusted annually for inflation.

The Personal Representative may disburse the funds of the estate to pay the family allowance in that amount or a lesser amount without court order. It is possible that a greater amount of family allowance may be payable, but only if approved by the Probate Court. If someone who is entitled to family allowance dies, that person's rights to any allowance which has not yet been paid terminate. However, remarriage does not cut off rights to unpaid family allowance.

The family allowance has priority over all claims against the estate, except administrative costs and expenses, funeral and burial expenses, and the homestead allowance. It is not chargeable against a benefit or share passing to the surviving spouse or children by the Will of the decedent, unless otherwise provided, by intestate succession, or by way of elective share.

Exempt Property

The decedent's surviving spouse is also entitled to household furniture, automobiles, furnishings, appliances, and personal effects from the estate up to a value not to exceed $10,000 more than the amount of any security interests to which the property is subject. The $10,000 amount will be adjusted annually for inflation. If there is no surviving spouse, the decedent's children are entitled jointly to the same value. All children are allowed to receive this allowance, not just minor or dependent children.

If encumbered assets (assets subject to a security interest) are selected and the value in excess of security interests, plus that of other exempt property, is less than $10,000, or if there is not $10,000 worth of exempt assets in the estate, the spouse or children are entitled to other assets of the estate, if any, necessary to make up the $10,000 value. Rights to exempt property and assets needed to make up a deficiency of exempt property generally have priority over all claims. However, the right to assets to make up a deficiency of exempt property may have to be reduced to permit payment of homestead and family allowances.

The rights to exempt property are in addition to a benefit or share passing to the surviving spouse or children by the decedent's Will, unless otherwise provided, by intestate succession, or by elective share. A specific devise of personal property to the spouse or children without a further indication that it replaces this exemption is not to be interpreted as within the phrase "unless otherwise provided."

What Assets Are Used to Satisfy the Allowances?

If the estate is otherwise sufficient, property specifically devised is not to be used to satisfy rights to homestead allowance or exempt property. Subject to this restriction, the surviving spouse, fiduciaries, or others who have the care and custody of minor children, or children who are adults may select property of the estate as homestead allowance and exempt property.

Selection can be made using a Probate Court form, **Selection of Homestead Allowance and Exempt Property, and Petition and Order for Family Allowance,** PC 582. (A copy of PC 582 is reproduced at the end of Chapter 15, "To Probate or Not to Probate.") The Personal Representative may make those selections if the surviving spouse, the adult children, or those acting for the minor children are unable or fail to do so within a reasonable time. The Personal Representative may execute a deed of distribution or other instrument to establish the ownership of property taken as homestead allowance or exempt property.

If an interested person is not satisfied with the selection, determination, payment, proposed payment, or failure to act with respect to any of these allowances, that person may file a petition in the Probate Court for appropriate relief.

Spousal Election vs. Revocable Trusts

Under current Michigan law, the property subject to the spousal election is only the property subject to the Will, i.e., the probate estate.

Thus, for example, property the decedent may have transferred to his or her revocable trust during lifetime will not be subject to the spousal election.

Spousal Elections

The surviving spouse of a decedent who was domiciled in Michigan and who dies testate (with a Will) may file with the court an election in writing that the spouse elects one of the following:

① That the spouse will abide by the terms of the Will.

② That the spouse will take one-half of the sum or share that would have passed to the spouse had the decedent died intestate (without a Will), reduced by one-half of the value of all property derived from the decedent by any other means other than testate or intestate succession upon decedent's death. The property "derived by the surviving spouse from the decedent" includes the following:

a. A transfer made within two years before the decedent's death to the extent that the transfer is subject to Federal Gift or Estate Tax.

b. A transfer made before the date of death subject to a power retained by the decedent that would make the property, or a portion of the property, subject to Federal Estate Tax.

c. A transfer effectuated by the decedent's death through joint ownership, tenancy by the entireties, insurance beneficiary, or similar means.

③ If a widow, that she will take her dower right as provided by law. The dower election, which is available only to a surviving widow, entitles her to one-third part of all the lands in which her husband was seized of an estate of inheritance at any time during the marriage, which she can use during her lifetime.

Within 28 days after the Personal Representative is appointed, notice must be given to the surviving spouse of the rights of election, allowances, and exempt property.

Remember to Consider Possible Reductions in the Spouse's Elective Share

At the time Sidney died he was in the middle of a divorce with his third wife, Evelyn. However, because the divorce was not finalized they were still legally married and Evelyn had all the rights of a surviving spouse.

A few days before Sidney died he wrote a new Will, in which he left everything to his children by his first marriage.

After Sidney died, Evelyn made an election against the Will, hoping to take her elective share of a relatively large estate. However, Evelyn was the beneficiary under Sidney's Profit Sharing Plan beneficiary designation, which Sidney did not and could not change. Under Federal law such a change required his wife's consent, and in view of the pending divorce Sidney didn't even bother to ask Evelyn to consent.

In computing the amount of Evelyn's elective share, the Profit Sharing account was considered as part of "property derived by the spouse from the decedent by any means other than testate or intestate succession upon the decedent's death."

As a result, Evelyn's elective share was reduced by one-half the Profit Sharing Plan balance she received, substantially reducing the amount of her elective share of estate assets.

The Probate Court form **Notice to Spouse of Rights of Election and Allowances, Proof of Service, and Election,** PC 581, may be used for this purpose. (A copy of PC 581 is reproduced at the end of Chapter 15, "To Probate or Not to Probate.")

The Court Rules provide that proof of service of the notice does not need to be filed with the court, and that no notice need be given in the following situations:

①   The right of election is made before notice is given.

②   The spouse is the Personal Representative or one of the Personal Representatives.

③   There is a waiver of the rights and allowances.

If the spouse exercises the right of election, the spouse must serve a copy of the election on the Personal Representative personally or by mail. The same form used to notify the spouse of his or her spousal rights (PC 581) may be used to make election. The election must be made within 63 days after the date for presentment of claims or within 63 days after the service of the inventory upon the surviving spouse, whichever is later. The election may be filed with the Probate Court, but that is not required unless the estate is in supervised administration.

If the spouse dies before making the election, the election may no longer be exercised. This may seem obvious but would otherwise be an issue where one death followed the other closely in time, and the estate of the second to die wanted to exercise the election in the first estate.

If the surviving spouse fails to make an election within the time specified, it is generally conclusively presumed that the surviving spouse elects to abide by the terms of the Will or to accept his or her intestate share. However, that presumption will not apply in the following cases:

①   Assets are discovered after the estate has been closed.

②   If the spouse petitions during estate administration for allowance of claims against the estate, because of estate litigation, or other good cause.

Rights of a Spouse Who Was Omitted in a Premarital Will

What happens if a person makes a Will and then marries and the spouse is not mentioned in the Will? Under Michigan law, there is some relief for the spouse who was omitted from the premarital Will.

If the spouse of the testator (the person who made the Will) marries the testator after the testator executes his or her Will, the surviving spouse is entitled to receive, as an intestate share, not less than the value of the share of the intestate estate the surviving spouse would have received if the testator had died without a Will (the intestate estate) as to that portion of the testator's estate, if any, which does not fall into either of the following categories:

① Property devised to a child of the testator who was born before the testator married the surviving spouse and who is not the surviving spouse's child.

② Property devised to a descendant of such a child.

However, this rule will not apply in three situations:

a. It appears, either from the Will or other evidence, that the Will was made in contemplation of the testator's marriage to the surviving spouse.

b. The Will expresses the intention that it is to be effective notwithstanding the subsequent marriage.

c. The testator provided for the spouse by transfer outside the Will, and the intent that the transfer be a substitute for leaving something in the Will can be established, either by statement of the testator, or can be reasonably inferred by the amount of the transfer or other evidence.

Remember that even if this election is not worthwhile, either because of the exclusion of amounts left to children and descendants from the estate for these purposes, or because it just doesn't apply in view of the above conditions, the surviving spouse can still elect against the Will and take the elective share.

Rights of Children Omitted in a Parent's Will

As a general rule, a parent has no obligation to leave anything to a child, and a child who receives nothing under the parent's Will has no right to any of the estate. However, there are exceptions where the child is born or adopted after the execution of the Will.

If the testator does not provide in his or her Will for a child who is born or adopted after the execution of the Will, the omitted after-born or after-adopted child will be entitled to a share of the estate unless:

①   It appears from the Will that the omission was intentional. (For example, a person might specifically say that he intends to leave nothing to any after-born or after-adopted children, or that the only children who are to take under the Will are those who are in being at the time of execution of the Will.)

②   The testator provided for the omitted after-born or after-adopted child by transfer outside the Will and the intent that the transfer be a substitute for leaving something in the Will can be established, either by statement of the testator, or can be reasonably inferred by the amount of the transfer or other evidence.

③   The Will left all or substantially all of the estate to the other parent of the omitted child and that other parent survived the testator and is entitled to take under the Will.

If none of the above apply, the omitted child is entitled to a share, generally determined as follows:

a. If the parent had no child living when the Will was executed, the omitted child will receive an intestate share.

b. If the parent had one or more living children at the time the Will was executed, and one or more of them was left something under the Will, the omitted child is entitled to the same share as the child to whom a bequest was made.

In other words, the omitted child is written into the Will, in the same manner as the other children.

CHAPTER 19

. . . .

THE
TAX MAN
COMETH

The Tax Man Cometh

Death and Taxes

It has been said that the only two certainties in life are death and taxes. Nowhere is this more apparent than in the administration of an estate. When an individual dies, there is a plethora of different tax returns that may have to be filed. These include the following:

①   Federal, state, and local individual income tax returns for years prior to death.

②   Federal, state, and local individual income tax returns for the year of death.

③   Federal and state fiduciary income tax returns for the probate estate.

④   Federal and state fiduciary income tax returns for any trusts.

⑤   Federal Gift Tax returns.

⑥   Federal Estate Tax return.

⑦   State estate or inheritance tax returns.

⑧   Generation-Skipping Transfer Tax returns.

⑨   Tax returns for household employees.

⑩   Business tax returns.

Taxes are best taken seriously. The Government has super-preferred creditor status and takes priority over most other claimants. Taxes must be paid or provided for before any distributions are made to beneficiaries. If you are a fiduciary, you may be *personally liable* for unpaid taxes to the extent of any distributions to beneficiaries. If you are a beneficiary, you may be liable for unpaid taxes to the extent of any property you received.

If you are a fiduciary, the filing of timely, correct, and complete returns and the payment of tax when due is one of your most important responsibilities. You need not prepare the returns yourself. However, you should have a general understanding of each return, what it shows, and when it is due. You should also be aware of any elections that have been made and any questions or issues and the positions that have been taken with regard to them.

In this chapter, we explain the basics of each tax and highlight the things you must do or consider to discharge your duties as Personal Representative or Trustee.

For each tax, we identify elections or issues that should be considered. Many of these elections are subject to time limits. If you think any of the elections or issues may apply to the decedent's situation, you should bring this to the attention of your attorney at once. To be safe, you may want to have the attorney review this list and tell you which of the elections or issues may apply to your situation.

Individual Income Tax Returns

Federal, state, and local individual income tax returns must be filed for the year of death and for any prior year for which the decedent had not filed. Returns may have to be filed for more than one state or locality depending on the sources of the decedent's income.

Individuals are normally required to make installment payments of the tax that is expected to be due. However, the IRS has indicated that such payments need not be continued after death, although payments would still be required of a surviving spouse.

The Federal return (Form 1040) is generally due on April 15th of the year following the tax year. The return for Michigan

Iɴᴅɪᴠɪᴅᴜᴀʟ
Iɴᴄᴏᴍᴇ Tᴀx
Rᴇᴛᴜʀɴs

(Form MI-1040) and many other states is also generally due on April 15th. The dates for local returns may vary, but many are due on either April 15th or April 30th.

An automatic two-month extension of the Federal return may be obtained. Additional extensions may be requested, but are at the discretion of the IRS. Extensions may also be requested for the Michigan return and for most other state and local returns. An extension of time to file does not extend the time for paying the tax. An estimate of the tax due should be paid with the extension form to avoid the running of interest.

Returns should be signed by the Personal Representative, if there is one. Otherwise, the Trustee or anyone who is in charge of the decedent's property may sign.

If there is a surviving spouse, he or she may file a joint return with the decedent for the year of death (if the surviving spouse did not remarry in that year) and for any prior year. The surviving spouse signs the return. If there is a Personal Representative, the Personal Representative must also sign. If there is more than one Personal Representative, all should sign.

The decedent's regular tax accountant may be best able to prepare these returns because of his or her familiarity with the decedent's income and deductions.

There are two elections that should be considered:

Medical Expense Deduction

Medical expenses of the decedent paid after death may be deducted on the decedent's final Federal Income Tax return. However, any such expenses deducted for income tax purposes cannot also be deducted on the decedent's Federal Estate Tax return. It must be decided which is more advantageous.

U.S. Savings Bond Interest

Accrued interest on Series E or EE U.S. Savings Bonds owned by the decedent may be reported on the decedent's final Federal Income Tax return. Depending on various factors, this may result in less income tax being paid, and the income tax will be deductible for Federal Estate Tax purposes. For example, if the decedent had excess charitable contributions in the year of death, or carried over from prior years, accelerating the income onto the decedent's final return is a way to get some benefit from those charitable deductions.

It may also result in the income tax being paid by the estate, rather than the beneficiaries who receive the bonds, the implications of which should be considered in each case.

Fiduciary Income Tax Returns

FIDUCIARY
INCOME TAX
RETURNS

If there is a probate estate or a trust, a Federal fiduciary income tax return must generally be filed for the entity for the years it is open. One or more state fiduciary income tax returns must generally be filed as well. A Michigan return must generally be filed for an estate or trust which is considered a Michigan resident, or an estate or trust with income from Michigan sources. Filing requirements for other states may vary.

Like individuals, estates and trusts must make installment payments of the tax that is expected to be due. However, estates are excused from this requirement for tax years ending less than two years after the decedent's death. A trust which was revocable by the decedent and which received the residue of the decedent's probate estate is likewise allowed a two-year reprieve.

The Federal return (Form 1041) is generally due on April 15th of the year following the tax year. The return for Michigan (Form MI-1041) and many other states is also generally due on April 15th. If an estate or trust has adopted or elected a *fiscal year* (discussed below), returns are generally due the 15th day of the fourth month after the close of the tax year.

An extension of time to file the Federal return may be requested. The forms and procedures for estates are different than those for trusts. However, the extension for either an estate or a trust is limited to six months. Extensions may also be requested for the Michigan return and for most other state returns. An extension of time to file does not extend the time for paying the tax. An estimate of the tax due should be paid with the extension form to avoid the running of interest.

**FIDUCIARY
INCOME TAX
RETURNS**

Returns for the estate must be signed by the Personal Representative. Returns for the trust must be signed by the Trustee. If there is more than one Personal Representative or Trustee, all should sign.

While the decedent's regular tax accountant may be best able to prepare the individual returns, the fiduciary returns are another matter. Fiduciary income tax is a specialized area and most tax practitioners have had only limited exposure to it. Even at the risk of bruised feelings, you should insist that the fiduciary returns be prepared by someone who is experienced in this field.

An estate or a trust is a separate entity for tax purposes and must have its own Taxpayer Identification Number (TIN). Taxpayer Identification Numbers are usually obtained for the probate estate and/or the trust early in the administration in order to open bank, brokerage, and other accounts in the name of the probate estate or trust. However, if a TIN has not already been obtained, a number will have to be secured before a fiduciary return may be filed.

A fiduciary income tax return is a hybrid type of return that attributes taxable income either to the estate or trust or to the beneficiaries. Income and capital gains, in other words, can either be taxed to the estate or trust or "carried out" to the beneficiaries.

A special form, known as a K-1, is prepared for each beneficiary as part of the 1041. The K-1 notifies the beneficiary of the amount of income and capital gains that the beneficiary must include in his or her Federal taxable income for the year. A similar form is used with the MI-1041 to notify beneficiaries of items that must be included on their Michigan returns.

You or your attorney should advise the beneficiaries that their tax situation will be slightly different because of the estate or trust, and particularly:

① A portion of the income and capital gains of the estate or trust may be taxed to them.

② They will be receiving a K-1 after the end of the estate or trust's taxable year, which they must give to their tax preparer when received. If the estate or trust will be on a fiscal year—rather than a calendar year—let them know what fiscal year has been elected and approximately when they can expect to receive their K-1s.

③ They cannot finalize their own taxes until the K-1 is received.

④ They cannot determine the amount to include in income by simply adding up the distributions they received for the year. This will not, except by coincidence, equal the figure on the K-1.

Make sure to tell them that none of this is your fault, or the fault of your attorney or accountant. It's simply the system which the Congress has put into place and the IRS administers.

Issues that should be considered in connection with the fiduciary income tax returns include the following:

Adoption of Fiscal Year for Estate

An estate may adopt a *fiscal year* and this may present opportunities for tax planning. It may be possible to defer the liability of the beneficiaries for taxes on the estate's income which is allocated to them. It may also be possible to reduce taxes by spreading income over two fiscal years.

Election to Treat Trust as Part of Estate

An election may be made to treat the trust as part of the estate for income tax purposes for two years after the decedent's death. (If there is no probate estate, the election may still be made.) This effectively allows a trust's income to be reported on a fiscal year basis, but only for two years.

FIDUCIARY INCOME TAX RETURNS

What's on a K-1?

The most common items of income shown on a K-1 are interest and dividends, which the beneficiary is instructed to report on Schedule B on his or her Federal Income Tax return.

Short-term or long-term capital gain may also appear.

The K-1 for the final year of the estate or trust may indicate deductions or loss carryovers which may be used by the beneficiary.

Where to Deduct Administration Expenses

Most of these expenses may be taken on the fiduciary income tax return in the year paid. However, any such expenses deducted for income tax purposes cannot be deducted on the decedent's Federal Estate Tax return. It must be decided which is more advantageous.

Avoiding Taxation at Estate or Trust Level

The fiduciary tax brackets are severely compressed and most of the income of an estate or trust is taxed at the highest rate. For example, for the 2000 tax year a married couple filing jointly would have to have $288,350 of taxable income to reach the 39.6% marginal Federal Income Tax bracket, while a trust would reach that bracket with only $8,650 of taxable income. Therefore, plans should be made to distribute enough to the beneficiaries to ensure that all the income of the estate or trust is "carried out" to the beneficiaries (see discussion above) so that it will be taxed to them instead of the estate or trust. This assumes that the marginal tax rates of the beneficiaries are lower than that of the estate or trust, which is often the case.

Plan for the Final Year

You should ask for bills for anticipated legal and accounting work that will be done after the final year of the estate or trust, e.g., preparation of fiduciary income tax returns for the year. These bills should be paid before the end of the year so they can be deducted on the final return.

Federal Gift Tax Returns

If the decedent made any gifts during his or her life, Federal Gift Tax returns may have to be filed. Generally no returns are required for gifts to qualified charities, outright gifts to a U.S. citizen spouse, or gifts that are within the annual gift tax exclusion amount, currently $10,000 per donee per year. If the decedent was married at the time of the gift the exemption may be doubled to $20,000 per donee per year.

However, the definition of a gift in the Internal Revenue Code and Treasury Regulations is very broad and there are some transfers which you might not think are gifts which are considered gifts for gift tax purposes. Also, there are exceptions to the general rules pertaining to charitable and marital deductions and the allowance of the annual exclusion.

There may also be a question as to whether gifts made at the end of the decedent's life were complete as of his or her demise. Consequently, any transfers made by the decedent should be reviewed by your attorney.

Only a handful of states have a *state* gift tax, and Michigan is not among them.

Any gift tax liability must be paid not later than the due date of the return.

The Federal Gift Tax return is officially known as a United States Gift (and Generation-Skipping Transfer) Tax Return, Form 709. The form is also used to compute Generation-Skipping Transfer Tax (GST Tax) on those gifts which are also generation-skipping transfers and to allocate GST exemption. The decedent's final gift tax return is due by April 15th of the year following the year of death or, if a Federal Estate Tax return must be filed, the due date (with extensions) of the Federal Estate Tax return, *whichever is earlier*. If the decedent made any gifts in years prior to his or her death which were not reported on a gift tax return, the necessary returns must be filed as soon as possible.

An extension of time of up to six months may be requested to file the gift tax return, either by letter or by requesting an extension of the final *Federal Income Tax* return. However, the due date of the gift tax return may not be extended beyond the

The Gifts That Weren't

At his attorney's urging, Sam made a large number of $10,000 gifts to all of his children, their spouses, and their children, just a few days before he passed away.

These gifts were each intended to qualify for the $10,000 annual Gift Tax exclusion. By removing this money from Sam's gross estate for Federal Estate Tax purposes, his family would have saved a huge amount of taxes.

Unfortunately, many of the family members felt it was inappropriate to cash the checks while Sam was so ill. So they held onto the checks and cashed them after he passed away.

The IRS took the position that the gifts were not completed gifts, because Sam could have stopped payment on the checks.

The money represented by the checks uncashed at the date of death was included in Sam's gross estate, and Federal Estate Tax had to be paid on those amounts.

FEDERAL
GIFT TAX
RETURNS

due date (with extensions) of the Federal Estate Tax return, if a Federal Estate Tax return has to be filed. An extension of time to file does not extend the time for paying the tax. Therefore, an estimate of the tax due should be paid with the extension request to avoid the running of interest.

Gift tax returns should be signed by the Personal Representative, if there is one. If not, the Trustee or anyone who is in charge of the decedent's property should sign.

If the decedent's regular tax accountant has prepared gift tax returns in the past and is comfortable doing so, you may wish to have this individual prepare the final gift tax return and any gift tax returns that may be required for prior years. If the accountant is not accustomed to gift tax returns, we recommend you ask the attorney to either prepare the gift tax returns, especially if the attorney will be preparing the estate tax return or, at a minimum, to review the drafts prepared by the accountant prior to filing.

Three major issues that should be considered in connection with the gift tax return are as follows:

What Should Be Reflected on the Gift Tax Return?

Although what is a taxable gift may appear to be a very basic question, sometimes the answer is not so simple, and even counter-intuitive.

Lending money to a family member and then discharging or forgiving the loan is a taxable gift. Giving money to a family member which the family member then uses to pay medical expenses is a taxable gift, though paying the medical expenses directly to the medical service provider qualifies for an unlimited gift tax exemption. Giving a child money to pay a grandchild's college or private elementary or secondary school tuition is a taxable gift, though paying that tuition directly to the school may qualify for an unlimited gift tax exemption. Giving someone expensive jewelry is a taxable gift. Buying someone a car is a taxable gift.

Taxable Gift But No Gift Tax To Be Paid?

A person may make a taxable gift and still owe no gift tax.

This is because each person has a lifetime estate and gift tax exemption, which covers a certain amount of lifetime gifts or, if not used during lifetime, covers gross estate on death.

That exemption covers $675,000 in 2000, and is scheduled to increase in stages to $1 million by 2006.

In many cases these gifts will be valued under the $10,000 annual gift tax exclusion amount, and so no gift tax return would be required if there were no other gifts to the person in the same year which brought total gifts over $10,000. Also, if the decedent was married at the time of the gift, the spouse's annual $10,000 gift tax exclusion may also be available.

The best approach is to discuss with your attorney all significant transactions made by the decedent and let the attorney advise you as to which would have required a gift tax return.

FEDERAL
GIFT TAX
RETURNS

Should Gift Splitting Be Elected?

Should gifts made by the decedent be *split* with the decedent's spouse? Splitting gifts with the spouse has the effect of doubling the amount of the annual exclusion that is available. The spouse must consent to this treatment by signing— in a specified place— the decedent's return. The spouse may also have to file a gift tax return.

Should GST Exemption Be Allocated?

Here we tread on really esoteric ground, but extremely relevant to some estates:

Should a portion of the decedent's Generation-Skipping Transfer Tax exemption be allocated on the return? This will affect larger estates only and deals with transfers which currently or in the future may benefit persons more than one generation lower than the decedent, e.g., grandchildren.

Federal Estate Tax Return
Significance of the
Federal Estate Tax Return

FEDERAL
ESTATE TAX
RETURN

If a Federal Estate Tax return is to be filed, you will find that it "drives" the administration of the estate. Required information must be gathered. Assets must be valued. Issues and questions involving the interpretation of Federal and state law must be addressed. Available elections must be considered. Cash must be raised to pay the tax. All of this must be completed in time to meet the filing deadline.

**FEDERAL
ESTATE TAX
RETURN**

After filing, the administration of the estate is effectively on hold until the Internal Revenue Service reviews the return, which normally does not occur for approximately six months. At that time, the IRS may either issue a closing letter indicating the return has been accepted as filed or send correspondence advising that the return has been selected for audit.

In general, if the estate was large enough to require a Federal Estate Tax return, your chances for an audit are very good.

The audit could take anywhere from a week to several months, or even longer. The audit could result in changes to asset values, inclusion of additional assets, or disallowance or changes in the amount of deductions.

If the estate's representatives disagree with the audit changes, they may appeal to the IRS Appeals Office. If this does not resolve the matter, the estate's representatives may take the case to a Federal Court. Consequently, it could be years before a final determination of Federal Estate Tax liability is obtained.

We hasten to reassure you, however, that this is a worst case scenario. Many returns are accepted as filed. Where there is an audit, it sometimes amounts only to a request for additional information, and once that information is provided then the return is accepted. In other cases, where issues are raised by the auditor, a satisfactory settlement can usually be negotiated.

The receipt of a closing letter from the IRS means that the asset values reported on the return, or as adjusted on audit, are the values "as finally determined for Federal Estate Tax purposes." The Will or trust instrument may direct that bequests or *spinoff* trusts be funded using these values. Also, these values are presumed to be the new income tax basis for the assets included in the gross estate.

Is a Return Required to Be Filed?

A Federal Estate Tax return must be filed if the decedent's *gross estate* plus *adjusted taxable gifts* equals or exceeds the *applicable exclusion amount*.

The *gross estate* is a defined term in the Internal Revenue Code and should not be confused with the *probate estate*. The gross estate is very broad and may include the decedent's residence, joint property, life insurance, annuities, IRAs, and retirement plans, in addition to cash and investments. It may even include property the decedent no longer owned at death, such as certain types of transfers made during life, including transfers to the decedent's trust.

Adjusted taxable gifts refers to gifts the decedent made during life for which a gift tax return was required to be filed.

The *applicable exclusion amount* is the sum which may pass free of estate tax. The exclusion is $675,000 for deaths in 2000. Under current law, it is to gradually increase, reaching $1,000,000 in 2006.

A return *may* be filed even if the estate is under the threshold. This should be considered for the following reasons. First, filing a return starts the statute of limitations running. Second, it avoids a failure to file penalty if assets or taxable gifts are subsequently discovered which put the estate over the filing amount. Third, by filing a return, the estate's representatives will receive a closing letter from the IRS. Finally, filing a return will establish a presumed basis for the assets reported.

When Must the Tax Be Paid?

Any Federal Estate Tax that is due must be paid not later than the due date of the return.

When Does the Return Have to Be Filed?

The Federal Estate Tax return is officially called a United States Estate (and Generation-Skipping Transfer) Tax Return, Form 706. The form is also used to compute Generation-Skipping Transfer Tax (GST Tax) on those transfers which are also generation-skipping transfers and to allocate GST exemption. The return must be filed nine months after the death of the decedent.

FEDERAL ESTATE TAX RETURN

Can an Extension of Time Be Obtained?

One or more extensions of time to file may be requested. The total of these extensions cannot exceed six months. An extension of time to pay the tax may also be requested. However, interest will accrue on any amount not paid on the nine-month date. An estimate of the tax due should be paid with the extension form to avoid the running of interest.

Who is Responsible for the Return?

The *executor* is responsible for the return and signs the return for the estate. The executor is also responsible for paying the tax. The executor is a defined term in the Internal Revenue Code. If there is a Personal Representative *who has been appointed and is acting*, then the Personal Representative is the executor. If there is no Personal Representative, then any person in actual or constructive receipt of property of the decedent, including but not limited to the Trustee of the decedent's trust, is an executor.

Who Should Prepare the Return?

The Federal Estate Tax return can be very complex. Moreover, it is outside the scope of experience of most tax practitioners. It is the province of estate planning attorneys and bank or trust company tax departments who deal on a daily basis with the preparation of these returns and the issues that relate to them, as well as arguing these issues with the IRS in audits.

It would be a serious mistake to allow an inexperienced practitioner to prepare this return and an even more serious mistake to try to do it yourself. Missing a single election could cost the estate thousands of dollars in taxes.

What Issues Should Be Considered?

There are a variety of issues that should be considered in connection with the Federal Estate Tax return. Entire books have been written on this topic. It is not our intention to make you an expert on any of these issues, many of which are quite technical and involved, and you should keep in mind the old adage that a little knowledge is a dangerous thing.

We wish only to sensitize you to these matters so you will be better able to assist and communicate with the preparer of the return. To reiterate our warning at the beginning of this chapter, many elections are subject to time limits. If you think an issue may apply, you should notify your attorney promptly.

Listed below, in alphabetical order, are the more common issues you are likely to encounter:

Administration Expenses

These expenses include executor's commissions, attorney and accountant fees, appraiser fees, court costs, and other such expenditures. They may be taken as deductions on the Federal Estate Tax return or the fiduciary income tax return in the year paid, or they may be split between the two.

Alternate Valuation

Assets are normally shown at their date-of-death values. An election may be made to instead use the values six months after death, or on the date sold, exchanged, distributed, or otherwise disposed of, if such occurred during the six-month period.

The election may only be made if the result of the election is to decrease both the gross estate and the estate tax payable. For example, if there is no estate tax due because everything passes to the surviving spouse, and values have increased significantly during the six-month period, you cannot elect alternate valuation to obtain a higher income tax basis for the property.

Apportionment

Although the Federal Estate Tax is paid by the executor, it must be determined who actually bears the burden of the tax. If the tax is apportioned, then all beneficiaries are charged their share. If the tax is *not* apportioned, then the entire burden falls on the residuary beneficiaries. Whether or not there is apportionment depends on provisions in the governing instrument, state law, and the Internal Revenue Code.

Who bears the burden of the estate tax can also affect the tax itself. For example, if the surviving spouse or charities are charged with tax, that will decrease the amount of the marital or charitable estate tax deduction, which will in turn increase the estate tax. That will increase the amount of tax borne by the spouse or charity, again affecting computation of the tax, and on and on. It is a circular or *interrelated* computation that must be solved algebraically, or by repeated trial and error, or by using specialized computer software.

Disclaimers

The intended recipient of property may *renounce* or *disclaim* it. (See Chapter 13, "Who Shares in the Estate?") If there is to be a *qualified disclaimer*, the rules of Section 2518 of the Internal Revenue Code must be complied with. This is important. If a disclaimer fails to meet these criteria, it is deemed to be a gift from the person disclaiming (the *disclaimant)* for gift tax purposes.

As a general rule a disclaimer must be made within nine months of the death, although there are other rules and a number of specific requirements to be satisfied.

The effect of a qualified disclaimer is that the disclaimed property passes without being considered a taxable gift from the person disclaiming. Generally it will pass in the same manner as if the disclaimant predeceased the decedent. In the right circumstances a disclaimer can be an excellent post-mortem planning tool. A series of disclaimers can even be used to pass property down several generations.

Equalization of Estates

Upon the death of a married individual, there may be no Federal Estate Tax payable as the result of a reduce-to-zero marital bequest to the surviving spouse. A strategy for reducing the total amount of tax paid (by the two spouses combined) is to pay *some* tax at the first death. This allows both spouses to take advantage of the lower brackets.

Exclusion of Certain Retirement Plans

Certain retirement plans may be excluded from the gross estate under a transition rule if the decedent began receiving payments prior to 1985.

Generation-Skipping Transfer Tax (GST) Exemption

Allocation of the decedent's GST Exemption may be made on or before the date for filing the Federal Estate Tax return, including extensions. After this date, the automatic allocation rules of Section 2632(c) of the Internal Revenue Code will apply.

Installment Payments of Estate Tax

If the estate consists largely of an interest in a closely held business, an election may be made to defer payment of the Federal Estate Tax for up to five years, then pay the tax in as many as ten annual installments. Interest must be paid, but a portion of the interest is at a preferential rate.

Medical Expenses Paid After Death

These may be deducted either on the Federal Estate Tax return or on the decedent's final Federal Income Tax return, or they may be split between the two.

Postpone Tax on Value of Remainder or Reversionary Interest

If the estate includes a remainder or reversionary interest, an election may be made to postpone payment of the Federal Estate Tax attributable to that interest until six months after the precedent interest in the property terminates.

Qualified Conservation Easement Exclusion

An election may be made to exclude from the gross estate part of the value of land subject to a qualified conservation easement.

FEDERAL ESTATE TAX RETURN

Qualified Domestic Trust

Property passing to a surviving spouse who is not a United States citizen will not qualify for the marital deduction unless the property is in a Qualified Domestic Trust. (Abbreviated QDT or QDOT). Steps can be taken to create such a trust after death, but time limits apply.

Qualified Family-Owned Business Interest

A deduction may be available, subject to limitations, for the adjusted value of a family-owned business interest.

QTIP Election

QTIP is short for Qualified Terminable Interest Property. If certain requirements are met, property which does not otherwise qualify for the marital deduction may be made to qualify by electing to treat it as QTIP property.

Reasonable Cause Extension

The IRS may, for reasonable cause, extend the time for payment of Federal Estate Tax for up to ten years. Interest would accrue on the amount unpaid.

Redemption of Stock

Stock in a closely held corporation may be redeemed to raise cash to pay Federal Estate Tax, state death tax, and funeral and administration expenses. Called a *Section 303 redemption*, it qualifies as a sale and avoids having to treat the sales proceeds as a dividend.

Reformation

The Internal Revenue Service is normally not bound by post-death *reformation*, or court ordered modification, of a decedent's Will or trust instrument.

In certain cases, however, a reformation will be recognized. Examples include dividing a trust for GST purposes and reforming a trust to qualify as a charitable remainder trust.

If the decedent's estate plan doesn't seem to be working, or wasn't done properly, ask your attorney if reforming the Will or trust might provide some benefit.

Selling Expenses

Expenses for selling property of the estate are deductible on the Federal Estate Tax return if the sale is necessary to pay the decedent's debts, administration expenses, or taxes, to preserve the estate, or to effect distribution. If these expenses are not deducted on the Federal Estate Tax return, they may be offset against the proceeds of sale in determining gain or loss. In no case, however, will a double deduction be allowed.

Special Use Valuation

An election may be made to value farm property or real estate used in a closely held business at its value for farm or business use instead of its highest and best use. Specific requirements must be met for the property to qualify for the election.

An Introduction to Form 706

In this section, we introduce you to the United States Estate (and Generation-Skipping Transfer) Tax Return, Form 706, often referred to simply as the 706.

You should be aware of what goes on the form so you will be able to assist the preparer in assembling the necessary information. Also, if you are the executor (discussed above) you will have to sign the return and you should have a general understanding of the form and what is on it. Finally, the 706 is an important document with ongoing significance for income tax and Generation-Skipping Transfer Tax purposes and for trust funding purposes. You should know where to find the information it contains and what it means.

Form 706 consists of three summary pages followed by schedules for each type of asset and deduction. Various supporting documents must be included with the return as attachments.

If you would like to obtain a copy of Form 706 and the instructions, ask your attorney or your accountant, or call the IRS at:
1-800-TAX-FORM
(1-800-829-3676)

You can also download the form and instructions from the IRS Web site:
http://www.irs.gov

Make sure your printer has plenty of paper! The basic Form 706 has 44 pages and the instructions run 26 pages.

Page 1, the face page, shows the actual computation of the tax. It is also the signature page.

Page 2 provides a "check the box" section for certain elections, including the election for alternate valuation. This page shows the marital status and other information about the decedent. It also shows the beneficiaries of the estate and the amount received by each.

Page 3 has a series of questions that must be answered "yes" or "no" and it contains a recapitulation of the various schedules and the amount reported on each.

Schedules A through I are used to report assets which comprise the decedent's gross estate. As explained earlier, the gross estate goes well beyond assets owned in the decedent's name. The schedules and the assets reported on each are listed below.

Schedule A—Real Estate

This schedule includes real estate owned in the decedent's sole name. The full legal description should be shown. Property should be appraised. Some Michigan practitioners use twice the State Equalized Value (SEV) if the result is reasonable and valuation is not likely to be an issue. If property is purchased or sold within a reasonable time before or after death, the purchase price or sales price should be used.

Schedule B—Stocks and Bonds

This schedule includes stocks and bonds owned in the decedent's sole name. Listed securities should be valued at mean market values, adjusted for ex-dividends. Accrued dividends and accrued interest should be listed separately. Mutual funds should be shown at net asset value (NAV), sometimes called the bid price.

Schedule C—Mortgages, Notes, and Cash

This schedule includes mortgages, notes, and cash owned in the decedent's sole name. Accrued interest should be shown separately.

Schedule D—Insurance on the Decedent's Life

This schedule includes policies in which the decedent had any incidents of ownership. Values should be taken from Forms 712 received from the insurance company.

Schedule E—Jointly Owned Property

Part 1 includes property of which the decedent and the decedent's spouse were the only joint tenants. Only one-half of this property is included in the gross estate.

Part 2 includes all other joint property. The amount included in the gross estate is proportionate to the consideration which the decedent contributed to acquire the property.

Schedule F—Other Miscellaneous Property Not Reportable Under Any Other Schedule

This schedule includes items such as:

❏ Household furniture and furnishings, art work, and personal effects. These should be appraised and a waiver of inspection should be requested from the IRS.

❏ Refunds, accounts and loans receivable.

❏ Unincorporated business interests.

❏ Property for which a QTIP election was previously made. (Typically a QTIP marital trust)

Schedule G—Transfers During Decedent's Life

This schedule includes transfers which were revocable by the decedent. Most typical would be the decedent's revocable living trust. Transfers in which the decedent retained an interest would also be listed here.

FEDERAL ESTATE TAX RETURN

Schedule H—Powers of Appointment

This schedule includes property subject to a general power of appointment, typically a power of appointment marital trust.

A general power is one which is exercisable in favor of the decedent, his estate, his creditors, or the creditors of his estate, unless it is limited by an ascertainable standard or it is exercisable only in conjunction with the creator of the power or a person having an interest that is substantially adverse to that of the power holder.

Schedule I—Annuities

This schedule includes pensions and other annuities. Also included are IRAs and retirement plans.

Schedules J through T are used to report deductions. The schedules and the deductions listed on each are described below.

Schedule J—Funeral Expenses and Expenses Incurred in Administering Property Subject to Claims

This schedule includes funeral, burial, and related expenses. Also reported here are administration expenses not deducted on the fiduciary income tax return.

Schedule K—Debts of the Decedent, and Mortgages and Liens

This schedule includes amounts paid or payable for any pre-death goods and services, pre-death legal or trust fees, and various types of taxes. Debts must be enforceable against the estate to be deductible. Mortgages and other loans are also shown on this schedule.

Schedule L—Net Losses During Administration and Expenses Incurred in Administering Property Not Subject to Claims

This schedule is seldom used. Only rarely does an estate suffer a loss of the type that can be deducted. Only a few practitioners bother to separately report those expenses that relate to property not subject to claims. Most practitioners ignore the distinction and include all allowable expenses on Schedule J.

Schedule M—Bequests, etc., to Surviving Spouse

This schedule lists all property qualifying for the marital deduction. The marital deduction is generally available for all property passing to the surviving spouse.

Gifts to the surviving spouse can be outright or in a trust which qualifies for the marital deduction. There are two types of trusts which qualify:

Trusts over which the surviving spouse possesses a general power of appointment.

Trusts for which QTIP treatment is elected.

A bequest to the surviving spouse is often expressed as a formula which is designed to leave the spouse only what is necessary to reduce the Federal Estate Tax to zero.

If the surviving spouse is not a U.S. Citizen, no marital deduction is available unless the property passing to the spouse is in the form of a Qualified Domestic Trust (QDT or QDOT).

Schedule O—Charitable, Public, and Similar Gifts and Bequests

This schedule lists all property qualifying for the charitable deduction. The charitable deduction is generally available for all property passing to a qualified charity under a provision in the Will or trust instrument.

No deduction may be taken on the estate tax return if the executor or family members *voluntarily* donate the decedent's property to charity, although the beneficiary to whom the property has passed may be able to take a charitable deduction on his or her income tax return.

Schedule P—Credit for Foreign Death Taxes

This schedule is used to compute the credit for death taxes paid to a foreign country.

Schedule Q—Credit for Tax on Prior Transfers

This schedule is used to compute the credit for estate tax paid on property bequeathed to the decedent by another person who died not more than ten years before the decedent.

Schedule R—Generation-Skipping Transfer Tax

This schedule is used to calculate Generation-Skipping Transfer Tax (GST Tax) and to allocate the decedent's GST Exemption to transfers made at death.

Schedule T—Qualified Family-Owned Business Interest Deduction

This schedule is used to calculate the net value of *qualified family-owned business interests.*If more than 50% of a person's estate consists of qualified family-owned business interests, the Personal Representative may elect to deduct the value of such interests from the gross estate up to a maximum deduction of $675,000. The eligibility requirements and the net effect of the deduction are complex and should be discussed with your attorney.

Schedule U—Qualified Conservation Easement Exclusion

This schedule is used to calculate the portion of the value of the land subject to the easement which may be excluded. Schedule U is unique. It is not used to report a *deduction*, but an *exclusion*, which reduces the amount of the gross estate.

Required Attachments

Certain documents must be included with the return as attachments. What will be required will depend on the facts of each situation. However, the following are the most common attachments:

> ### File a "Complete" 706
>
> A complete Federal Estate Tax return, which includes all the necessary information and an index to attachments, will be easier for the IRS to review.
>
> It may permit approval of the return as filed without requiring the IRS to ask for any further information.
>
> This will expedite the closing of the estate, and save you professional fees by avoiding further contact with the IRS with regard to the return.

- ❑ Death Certificate.

- ❑ Last Will and Testament.

- ❑ Governing instruments for trusts of which decedent was settlor.

- ❑ Governing instruments for trusts of which the decedent was a trustee, beneficiary, or power holder.

- ❑ Appraisals.

- ❑ Forms 712 for insurance policies.

- ❑ Gift Tax returns.

- ❑ Proof of payment of state death tax.

- ❑ Approved extension request.

Before You Sign

When you sign the 706, you acknowledge the following statement:

Under penalties of perjury, I declare that I have examined this return, including accompanying schedules and statements, and to the best of my knowledge and belief, it is true, correct, and complete.

Before signing, you should review the 706 *in detail* with the preparer. Depending on the complexity of the return, this could take several hours. Make sure all assets of which you are aware are included and that you know how the values were determined. Check the deductions against your records, or at least review them for reasonableness. Ask questions about any elections or other matters you don't understand.

Even though you may not have prepared the return, if you are the Executor or a Co-Executor you are responsible for it. It is a responsibility you should take seriously.

Review the Draft Federal Estate Tax Return

Take the time to review the draft Federal Estate Tax return carefully and reflect on what is included and how it is valued, what is excluded, and what deductions are taken. This return is your representation to the IRS and you are responsible for it.

Some seemingly unimportant events, of which you may be aware but your preparer may not, can have serious consequences.

For example, if any stock splits have taken place after the date of death, make sure that the preparer was made aware of them in evaluating whether to use the alternate valuation date.

Stock values tend to drop radically after a stock split, and it may appear as if the gross estate has decreased in value when, in fact, there are merely more shares with each having a lower value.

State Estate or Inheritance Tax Returns

The majority of the states, including Michigan, have adopted an *estate tax* which "piggybacks" on the *Federal* Estate Tax. The Internal Revenue Code allows a credit against the Federal Estate Tax for death taxes paid to a state. The maximum credit depends on the amount of the Federal gross estate and is determined by reference to a table. The state estate tax is equal to the amount of the maximum Federal credit. If the Federal credit is zero, the state estate tax is also zero.

This type of state death tax is known as a "pickup tax" because the state "picks up" the amount of the Federal credit. It is relatively painless because the state merely takes what would otherwise go to the IRS. It is also simple. The state return that is required to be filed is very brief, generally only one page.

The remaining states impose an *inheritance tax*, which is based on the amount passing to each beneficiary. There are typically lower rates for property going to immediate family members and higher rates for amounts received by more distant relatives or nonrelatives. These states may have an estate tax as well. The usual rule in such cases is that, if the inheritance tax is less than the Federal credit, there is an estate tax equal to the difference between the two. The total state death tax, then, would be equal to the Federal credit.

A Michigan Estate Tax return must be filed if a Federal Estate Tax return is required and the decedent either was a resident of Michigan or owned property having a tax situs in Michigan.

Real property and tangible personal property, such as furniture, furnishings, automobiles, and jewelry, have a tax situs in the state where they are located. Intangible personal property, which consists of financial assets such as securities and bank accounts, has a tax situs in the state where the decedent was domiciled at the time of his death.

If no return is required to be filed, you should submit a Request for Certificate of No Michigan Estate Tax Liability, Form 2356, to the Michigan Department of Treasury. This is especially important if there is a probate estate as the certificate will be needed to close the estate with the Probate Court.

Estate or inheritance tax returns may have to be filed in other states if the decedent was a resident of another state or owned property with a tax situs in one or more other states.

Michigan Estate Tax must be paid not later than the due date of the return. Other states may have different requirements.

The Michigan Estate Tax return must be filed nine months after the death of the decedent. There are two different forms. Form MI-706 is used if the decedent was a Michigan resident and all property was located in Michigan. Form 706A is used if the decedent was a Michigan resident with out-of-state property, or a nonresident with property in Michigan. A copy of the Federal Estate Tax return must be included with the MI-706 or MI-706A. Other states may have different requirements.

A Federal extension of time to file or to pay automatically applies to Michigan as well. Interest will accrue on any amount not paid on the nine-month date. An estimate of the tax due should be paid on a Michigan Estate Tax Estimate Voucher, Form 2527, to avoid the running of interest. Copies of all approved Federal extensions must be attached to the Michigan return when it is filed. Other states may have different requirements.

The Personal Representative is responsible for the Michigan Estate Tax return and signs the return for the estate. If there is no court-appointed Personal Representative, then every person who receives part of the estate is considered a Personal Representative. Other states may have different requirements.

The Michigan Estate Tax return and any other state estate or inheritance tax returns should be prepared by the same person or office that is preparing the Federal Estate Tax return, if a Federal 706 is required. If returns will have to be filed with states other than Michigan, the preparer should get forms and instructions from these states as soon as possible so he or she will know what information will be required, as well as the time requirements for filing and payment.

The only major issue that should be considered in connection with Michigan Estate Tax involves a so-called *reduce-to-zero* marital provision. It must be asked if it was the decedent's

If you would like to obtain copies of forms related to the Michigan Estate tax, ask your attorney or your accountant, or call the Michigan Department of Treasury Forms by Phone Service, at 1-800-FORM-2-ME (1-800-367-6263), or in Lansing 517-373-6598.

Forms may also be obtained by fax by calling Forms by Fax: 517-241-8730.

You can also download the forms from the Michigan Department of Treasury Web site:

http://www.treas.state. mi.us/formspub/ estind.htm

Internet Links To Sources Cited

www.carobtreepress.com

STATE ESTATE OR
INHERITANCE TAX
RETURNS

GENERATION-SKIPPING
TRANSFER TAX
RETURNS

intention to pay no *Federal* Estate Tax, in which case some *Michigan* Estate Tax could still be payable, or to pay no Federal *or* Michigan Estate Tax. This must be determined by reference to the reduce-to-zero language in the decedent's Will or trust instrument. This and other issues may arise in connection with estate or inheritance tax under the laws of other states.

Generation-Skipping Transfer Tax (GST) Returns
What is the GST?

The Federal Generation-Skipping Transfer Tax (GST) is a tax which is imposed on transfers to persons who are more than one generation below the person making the transfer. It is separate from, and in addition to, the other two Federal transfer taxes—the Federal Gift Tax and the Federal Estate Tax.

While there is an entire lexicon of specialized terms associated with the GST, some basic terminology is essential to even a rudimentary understanding of this tax. A few of the key words are as follows:

Transferor: A person transferring property which is subject to Federal Gift or Estate Tax.

Skip Person: A person who is more than one generation below the Transferor, such as a grandchild.

Direct Skip: Any transfer subject to Federal Gift or Estate Tax which is made to a Skip Person.

Taxable Distribution: Any distribution from a trust to a Skip Person prior to a Taxable Termination. (Both terms are misnomers, since tax does not necessarily have to be paid on a Taxable Distribution or on a Taxable Termination.)

Taxable Termination: A transfer to a Skip Person which occurs when all other interests in a trust come to an end.

GST Exemption: An amount, which is indexed for inflation, which an individual may transfer free of GST. For 2000, the amount is $1,030,000. A person may allocate all or a portion of the exemption to a transfer which has GST implications in order to protect the transfer from GST, either currently or in the future. If no allocation is made, there are automatic allocation rules which will apply.

Generation Skipping

Marvin's estate plan provided for significant sums to his ten adult grandchildren. Marvin's children, the parents of the grandchildren, were all living and received the balance of his estate.

This is an example of a generation-skipping transfer at death, in this case a Direct Skip: Marvin is the Transferor, and the grandchildren are Skip Persons.

However, to the extent that Marvin's bequests to his grandchildren are protected by allocation of his remaining GST Exemption, no GST Tax will have to be paid.

Summary of GST Return Requirements

Generation-skipping transfers *made by a decedent*, during life or at death, are reported— and GST Exemption allocated— on returns which have been discussed above. Therefore, our treatment here will be brief.

Lifetime Direct Skips and other lifetime transfers with GST implications are reported on a Federal Gift Tax return.

Direct Skips at death and other transfers at death having GST implications are reported on Schedule R of the Federal Estate Tax return.

If the decedent was a beneficiary of a trust created by another, the decedent's death could result in a Taxable Termination with respect to that trust. If so, the Trustee of that trust will have to file a Generation-Skipping Transfer Tax Return for Terminations, Form 706GS(T).

If, following the death of the decedent, a Taxable Distribution is made from a trust of which the decedent is the Transferor, the Trustee of that trust must prepare a Notification of Distribution from a Generation-Skipping Trust, Form 706GS(D-1). Copy "A" of this form is filed with the IRS; Copy "B" is sent to the distributee. The distributee is then responsible for filing a Generation-Skipping Tax Return for Distributions, Form 706GS(D).

State Generation-Skipping Transfer Tax

The Internal Revenue Code allows a credit for state taxes paid with respect to a Taxable Distribution or a Taxable Termination (but not Direct Skips), if the transfer occurs at the same time as and as a result of the death of an individual. Many states have enacted statutes to take advantage of this credit, including Michigan. Worksheets for the computation of the Michigan GST Tax are contained in the instructions for the Michigan Estate Tax. Other states may have different requirements.

Tax Returns for Household Employees

If the decedent had any household employees, you should check with the decedent's accountant to make sure that Social Security, unemployment, and withholding taxes are remitted and the necessary returns are filed when due.

You may wish to consider making a special severance payment to these individuals, especially those with long service. Absent a contract, there is no legal requirement to do so. However, many families do this to express their appreciation to the employees and to help defray their expenses while they look for a new position.

Business Tax Returns

Tax returns for a business of the decedent are the responsibility of the managers of the business and are not discussed here. We will nevertheless mention one important election that is available to a partnership of which the decedent was a partner.

As a general rule, the income tax bases of partnership or limited liability company assets are not adjusted upon the death of a partner. However, a partnership may make a so-called *Section 754 election* to adjust the basis of partnership property by the difference between the basis of a new partner's interest in the partnership and his proportionate share of the basis of the partnership property.

If the decedent owned partnership interests you should raise with your accountant or attorney the possibility of making Section 754 elections. If permitted by the partnership or limited liability company, these elections could result in increased depreciation and other advantages to those who inherit the partnership or limited liability company interest.

CHAPTER 20

....

SHOULD YOU TAKE FIDUCIARY FEES?

Should You Take Fiduciary Fees?

You Are Entitled to Be Paid

If you serve as a Personal Representative, you are entitled to a Personal Representative fee from the estate. If you serve as a Trustee, you are entitled to a trustee fee from the trust. If you are acting in both capacities, you may take a fee for each.

In rare cases, the Will or trust agreement may direct that the fiduciary serve without compensation. In these situations, it may still be possible to get permission from the Probate Court to pay fees, notwithstanding this direction.

You must first decide whether or not to take a fee. If you resolve to do so, you must then decide the amount to charge, which must be reasonable. In this brief chapter, we discuss the factors to be considered in coming to the right decision.

Should You Charge?
Personal Aspects

In deciding whether or not to take a fee, you should consider your relationship to the decedent and to the beneficiaries and your personal feelings about the matter.

In many situations, if a family member is serving as fiduciary he or she will feel no fees should be taken, that the work is just part of being family, and that it would be unseemly to take a fee. This is often a first reaction, before actually doing the work.

Often, after the fiduciary realizes how much work has been involved, and that he or she was doing all the work and other family members were merely sitting back and reaping the benefits, a fiduciary fee seems appropriate.

Sometimes, the decedent will have intended that the fiduciary was to be paid and may have made that intention known. If that is the case, the decedent's intention should be taken into consideration and may tip the scale in favor of taking fees.

You must be the judge of whether it is appropriate or will cause problems with other family members if you take fiduciary fees in a family setting. If possible, the matter should be discussed with the others involved, so that they know how you feel, and you have an opportunity to discuss the basis upon which you intend to charge and why you feel the proposed fees are fair.

Ask your attorney for some suggestions as to what would be a fair fee, given the factors discussed below. Give the other family members a copy of this book to peruse so that they can see what may be involved in administering an estate. This may make it easier for them to understand why they should insist that you take a fee.

In some cases the fee issue is clearly addressed in the Will or trust instrument, and the basis of payment is sometimes mentioned.

When the fiduciary is the decedent's attorney or accountant, for example, it is sometimes indicated that the person should be paid his or her regular hourly rate for providing professional services. This is intended to address the argument that Personal Representative or Trustee services are "administrative" and not entitled to be compensated at the same rate as professional services. However, the professional is taking time which would normally be billed to other clients, and thus would probably not accept the appointment unless the time spent is adequately compensated.

What's Fair is Fair

The time involved and the effect on the fiduciary's "other" job cannot be ignored.

Steve, a litigation attorney, acted as his father's Personal Representative in handling a sticky estate with numerous issues arising on an IRS estate tax audit. However, he saw his income from his law practice drop significantly. He found himself spending as much time working on estate matters as on his own practice.

He kept track of his time, achieved a great result for the family, and ultimately Steve's estate attorney suggested that he take a reasonable fiduciary fee, to which his siblings gladly agreed. They received the benefits of his work, and felt it was only fair that he be properly compensated.

Charitable Beneficiaries

In the case of a Michigan estate, if there are charitable beneficiaries the Michigan Attorney General may be an interested person and may have something to say about what fiduciary fees are taken. This is an extra measure of protection for the charities.

Where charities are beneficiaries, make sure to ask your attorney about whether and when the Attorney General should be notified of the estate administration, and the extent to which the Attorney General will be involved in any fee issues, which varies from case to case. (See Chapter 14, "Keep the Beneficiaries Informed.")

Tax Implications

If you are a beneficiary, you must also consider the tax implications. Any fee payment you receive will be taxable income to you in the year that you receive it. However, such a payment may be deductible by the estate in determining its Federal Estate Tax or fiduciary income tax.

An analysis should be done which compares the options, taking into account the difference between your tax bracket and that of the estate or trust, and arrives at the best overall result. The estate's attorney or your own tax advisor should be able to assist you.

In some cases the estate's bracket is significantly higher than that of the fiduciary, and it makes sense to take the fees and benefit from the spread between the rates. This is clear in a taxable estate where there is only one beneficiary, who also happens to be the Personal Representative.

However, if there are several beneficiaries, then the personal aspects may come into play, and the tax saving objective may not be determinative.

Remember that, regardless of the potential tax benefits, any fiduciary fee must still be reasonable.

What is a Reasonable Fee?

In deciding how much to charge, you should evaluate the following:

① The amount of time required.

② The size and complexity of the estate.

③ The knowledge and skill needed and the results obtained.

④ Your experience and qualifications.

⑤ The fees customarily charged in the area.

No one factor is determinative. If the matter is to be submitted to the Probate Court, you should expect the Judge to be very interested in how the fees were determined, which of the above factors support the fee that is being requested, and whether all the beneficiaries agree. There is no hard and fast rule and you should ask your attorney what would be considered reasonable in the particular case.

If you decide to take a fee, you should advise the beneficiaries as soon as possible, preferably in your first letter to them. You should keep a detailed record of time spent and services performed, as you may have to present that to justify your fees several years down the road, because the other beneficiaries have challenged them, because you have decided to seek Probate Court approval, or because the IRS is questioning the fee deduction on audit of an estate tax or income tax return.

Uncle Sam Paid Part of the Fees

Larry didn't really want to take a fiduciary fee, but his attorney pointed out to him that it would save taxes.

The estate was a taxable one, with Federal Estate Tax being imposed at a marginal 40% rate. Larry's personal income tax rate was only 15%.

Larry decided to take the fees, just to save the taxes. Later he made a gift to his siblings, who were the other beneficiaries, so each got their share of the after-tax amount he took as fees.

NOTES

"The safest way to double your money
is to fold it over once
and put it in your pocket."
—Kin Hubbard

CHAPTER 21

TRANSFER REMAINING ASSETS TO BENEFICIARIES

Transfer Remaining Assets to Beneficiaries

When and How? It Depends.

When and how assets are transferred to beneficiaries depends on a number of factors, such as whether or not there is a probate estate, whether or not estate taxes must be paid, how the assets are held, and what types of assets are involved.

In this chapter, we will explain how to fulfill your duty of transferring the assets to the beneficiaries while avoiding personal liability to beneficiaries, creditors, or taxing authorities.

Beneficiaries vs. Fiduciary

Most beneficiaries want to receive what is coming to them at the earliest possible moment. Many have no idea of the administrative steps that must be completed before you will be in a position to make distributions or of the time that these steps will require.

Beneficiaries may naively believe that you can sit down and write them a check for the full amount of their inheritance within a week or two of the decedent's death, whereas the reality may be that this cannot occur for up to two years. It is imperative that you educate the beneficiaries in this regard. (See Chapter 14, "Keep the Beneficiaries Informed.")

Even if you explain all of the administrative constraints and provide a time line which indicates your best estimate of when distributions can be made, you may be pressured to make distributions sooner. If you are the fiduciary, it is your responsibility to see that distributions are not made prematurely. Depending on the type of distribution being contemplated, you may need answers to the following questions before the distribution is made:

❑   Have all property rights been finally fixed? Is there a contest of the Will or trust instrument pending? May the spouse elect against the Will? Are disclaimers being considered?

❑   Have all assets been inventoried and valued?

❑   Is Probate Court approval required for the distribution that is contemplated and, if so, has it been obtained?

❑   If a Federal or state estate tax return or a state inheritance tax return must be filed, are there any assets which should be retained for possible examination by an auditor or appraiser in connection with an audit of the return?

❑   If Federal or state estate taxes or state inheritance taxes must be paid, must any of these taxes be apportioned to or recovered from beneficiaries? If that is so, then beneficiaries of specific bequests, for example, may not be entitled to the total dollar amount provided for them in the instrument.

❑   If any assets are to be distributed in kind, are all beneficiaries in agreement as to who is to receive what and how the various assets are to be valued?

❑   Have all creditors been paid?

❑   Have closing letters been received from taxing authorities?

If you are considering making any distributions before all creditors have been paid or before tax clearances have been received, you must be extremely careful. If you are a fiduciary, you have what is known as *fiduciary liability*. If liabilities to creditors or liabilities for taxes exceed the remaining assets in the estate or trust for which you are responsible, you could be required to pay these obligations out of your own pocket to the extent of any distributions you allowed to be made.

Case Study: Fiduciary Liability After An Audit Adjustment

John was Personal Representative of his uncle's probate estate and Successor Trustee of his uncle's trust. John made sure that all creditors were paid. John had his uncle's estate planning attorney prepare Federal and state estate tax returns. The combined tax on the two returns was $950,000. John filed the returns and paid the tax.

On audit of the Federal Estate Tax return, the values of several limited partnership interests were significantly increased, which resulted in additional tax of $125,000 being assessed. John's attorney told him about the audit changes and the additional tax but John—distracted and not thinking clearly—believed that the attorney was going to "take care of it." Then, under pressure from two of his cousins, John distributed the remaining assets in the estate and trust to the beneficiaries.

When John realized the additional tax hadn't been paid, he notified the beneficiaries and asked each of them to return a portion of his or her distribution to cover the $125,000 tax assessment.

One beneficiary told John he had already spent the money on his child's college tuition. Another replied that he was referring the matter to his attorney. John never heard from the other beneficiaries.

John was held personally liable for the $125,000. Neither the IRS nor the Tax Court bought into his defense that he thought the attorney was going to take care of paying the additional tax! He was therefore found to have distributed assets to beneficiaries while he knew there was tax due. Ultimately John was forced to liquidate most of his brokerage account and take out a second mortgage on his house to satisfy the debt to the IRS.

Partial Distributions

You may be able to make one or more partial distributions pending receipt of tax clearances. In fact, for income tax purposes, you should— if possible— distribute enough in each tax year to "carry out" the income of the estate or trust to the residuary beneficiaries, since this will normally result in the income being taxed at a lower rate. (See Chapter 19, "The Tax Man Cometh.")

However, you should be conservative and take care not to distribute too much until all tax liabilities have been finalized or you have been released from personal liability. (See Chapter 22, "Going Forward: Avoiding Loose Ends.")

If the Will or trust instrument provides for pecuniary bequests (e.g., gifts of a specified sum of money) and the aggregate of these amounts is modest relative to the total size of the estate, these bequests should be paid as soon as funds are available to avoid the running of interest.

In Michigan, unless a contrary intent is indicated by the Will, a general pecuniary bequest bears interest at the legal rate, which in Michigan is currently 5%, beginning one year after the first appointment of a Personal Representative. Also, by satisfying these bequests, you will eliminate the need for these beneficiaries to contact you to ask when they can expect to be paid.

Prior to payment, however, be sure to determine if estate taxes must be recovered from these amounts, as discussed below.

What Do the Beneficiaries Get?

What a beneficiary receives is known variously as a *bequest*, a *legacy*, or a *devise*. The precise legal definitions of these terms differ, but in common everyday usage, they are treated as synonyms. We will use the term *bequest* in our discussion.

Specific Bequests

A *specific bequest* is a gift of some specific article or asset, such as "my antique desk" or "my IBM stock." If the decedent's Will (or trust instrument) leaves such an item to a beneficiary, and the decedent (or trust) owned it at the time of his death, then the beneficiary is entitled to it.

If, however, the decedent (or trust) did not own the article, the beneficiary cannot have it, but may be entitled to something of equal value. (See the discussion of *ademption* in Chapter 13, "Who Shares in the Estate?")

If estate taxes must be paid, the Will or trust instrument may direct that taxes be *apportioned*, meaning that taxes are to be allocated to all beneficiaries in proportion to their interests. If this is the case, specific and general bequests will bear their share of the tax and you must be sure to collect the tax from the specific beneficiaries.

General Bequests

A *general bequest* is a gift which is payable out of the general assets of the estate or trust. For example, "I give to my brother, Colin, the sum of $50,000." If the estate is not large enough for all general bequests to be made in full, a proportionate reduction must be made in each. (See the discussion of *abatement* in Chapter 13, "Who Shares in the Estate?")

Again, if estate taxes must be paid, the Will or trust instrument may direct that taxes be apportioned. In that event, specific and general bequests would generally pay their portion of the tax and you must either withhold the tax from the payment or collect the tax from the general beneficiaries.

Case Study: Fiduciary Liability After Distributing Without Considering Tax Allocation

Ruth was the Personal Representative of her aunt's probate estate. A business major in college, Ruth was intent on administering the estate as efficiently as possible. She quickly determined the assets of the estate and made an estimate of the Federal and state estate tax that would be due. Satisfied that there would be plenty of money to cover debts, expenses, and taxes, she then mailed checks for $25,000 to the ten beneficiaries who were to receive cash bequests in this amount.

Several weeks later, Ruth received a call from an attorney representing one of the remainder beneficiaries of the estate. The attorney told Ruth that her aunt's Will directed that estate taxes be apportioned among all beneficiaries and that the $25,000 bequests should have been reduced by the amount of tax allocable to them. Ruth consulted an estate planning attorney who confirmed what the remainder beneficiary's attorney had told her.

Ruth was unsuccessful in recovering the taxes from four of the ten beneficiaries who had received the $25,000 payments and she was forced to reimburse the remainder beneficiaries for these taxes from her own funds.

Residuary Bequests

A residuary bequest is a gift of all or a part of the property after debts, taxes, and specific and general bequests have been satisfied.

The direction in a Will or trust instrument for the distribution of residue is typically fractional in nature, such as: "My residuary estate shall be distributed one-half to my daughter, Mary, one-quarter to my son, John, and one-quarter to my son, William."

Distribution may be made pro rata, meaning that each residuary beneficiary is given his or her proportionate share of each of the assets comprising the residue. This method is unquestionably fair since it treats all residuary beneficiaries equally. In Michigan, absent a contrary provision in the Will or trust instrument, pro rata distribution is not mandatory. Disproportionate shares or different kinds of property may be distributed to different beneficiaries.

So, if Mary wants the IBM stock, John wants the municipal bonds, and William wants the house, this can be accommodated. To protect yourself, however, you should have all of the remainder beneficiaries agree to such a distribution in writing. If you have liquidated the estate and only cash remains, then the pro rata versus non-pro rata issue is moot.

Advancements

It is possible that a beneficiary may have received all or part of his or her bequest from the decedent during the decedent's life. You may hear this referred to as an *advancement* although, strictly speaking, this term should be used only in relation to an intestate share. The correct word in the context of a provision in a Will is *satisfaction*.

Whether or not lifetime gifts from a decedent to a beneficiary were in satisfaction of a bequest must be determined under state law. Michigan has a statute which addresses this question. If under the statutory guidelines a lifetime gift is determined to have been in total or partial satisfaction of a beneficiary's testamentary entitlement, then the gift must be taken into account in determining what the beneficiary is to receive.

Distributions in Cash or Kind

Many Wills and trust instruments allow the fiduciary to make distributions in cash or *in kind*, or partly in each. A distribution is made *in kind* when the distribution is of property, such as securities, real estate, or personal property, rather than in money.

It should be decided early in the administration which assets are to be distributed in kind and which will be sold and the proceeds distributed in cash. This plan will then drive how the assets are managed over the course of the administration and how much cash is raised. (See Chapter 16, "Protect and Preserve Estate Assets.") When it comes time to make a distribution, the estate should consist of cash and other assets as you had planned.

If a pecuniary bequest is satisfied in kind, Michigan law provides that the property the fiduciary selects for that purpose must be valued at its value on the distribution date, unless the governing instrument expressly provides otherwise.

Distributions Outright
or in Trust

A beneficiary's distribution may or may not be outright. The Will or trust instrument may direct that a beneficiary's share be held (or remain) in trust. The trust may continue until the beneficiary attains the age of majority, or there may be partial distributions at specified ages, or the trust may last for the beneficiary's life.

The Trustee may have discretion to make or not make certain distributions. There may be different provisions for different beneficiaries. (For example, Mary and John may receive their shares outright while the share for William is to be held in trust.)

You must read the Will or trust instrument very carefully to make sure you understand and comply with its terms. Ask your attorney to provide you a written summary of the terms of the trust so that you know you are interpreting them correctly. Provide copies of the summary to the beneficiaries or the parents or guardians of minor beneficiaries.

If the Will directs that one or more trusts be created, or if the trust instrument provides for the creation of one or more new, or *spinoff*, trusts, these trusts must be *funded*. There is more to this than meets the eye and you should have the assistance of your attorney in this process. (See Chapter 22, "Going Forward: Avoiding Loose Ends.")

Distributions to Minors

If any distribution is to be made outright to a minor, you should consult with your attorney. In Michigan, a minor is an individual under the age of eighteen years.

Wills and trust instruments often provide for amounts payable to minors to be held in trust until the individual attains majority, or sometimes give discretion to retain the amount in trust until that age.

If a distribution is to be made to a minor and no trust is provided, it may be necessary for a conservator to be appointed to receive the property for the minor. This will require a Probate Court proceeding.

Alternatively, a Personal Representative may also transfer the property to a custodian under the Michigan Uniform Transfers to Minors Act, if the Will or trust instrument authorizes such transfers.

However, even if the instrument is silent with regard to transfer of a minor's bequest to a custodian, the distribution may still be made to a custodian if (a) the Personal Representative or Trustee believes it is in the best interests of the minor, (b) the transfer to a custodian is not prohibited by or inconsistent with the provisions of the Will or trust instrument, and (c) if the transfer exceeds $10,000 in value, the transfer is authorized by the court.

How Are the Assets Held?

In the Probate Estate

Cash distributions from the probate estate are accomplished by simply writing a check on whichever of the estate's accounts has check writing privileges.

Distributions in kind are more involved. Assets in the decedent's name go into the probate estate and, eventually, to the beneficiaries. The residue of the probate estate often "pours over" to the decedent's trust and ultimately passes to the beneficiaries of the trust. In theory, the assets must be retitled at every step:

① From the decedent's name to the probate estate.

② From the probate estate to the decedent's trust.

③ From the decedent's trust to the trust beneficiaries.

In practice, it may be possible to bypass some or all of the intervening transfers. As an extreme example, assume that the decedent's probate estate, consisting of securities in a brokerage account, pours over to his trust. The trust then terminates and passes outright to the decedent's two children, Peter and Paul.

If the probate estate is ready to be closed, and if the Personal Representative of the probate estate and the Trustee of the trust are the same person or are otherwise agreeable, the brokerage firm could be requested to reregister the securities from the name of the decedent directly into the names of Peter and Paul.

This will not work in all cases. Holders of assets in the decedent's name may insist that they be retitled in the name of the probate estate. There may be a separate Trustee who would want to physically receive the assets into the trust. There may also be income tax complications.

To accomplish any transfer, contact the holder of the assets for forms and instructions.

Remember that it may be necessary or advisable to get Probate Court approval before making a distribution of probate assets.

In a Trust

Cash distributions may be made from the trust by writing a check on the trust's check writing account.

In kind distributions must be done by retitling the assets in the names of the beneficiaries. The necessary forms and instructions may be obtained from the holder of the assets.

As previously explained, you must make sure you understand the dispositive provisions of the trust or trusts with which you are dealing. (See above, "What Do the Beneficiaries Get?") A trust may terminate upon the decedent's death, but it need not. A trust may continue for any period that is within the limits of the rule against perpetuities which, in Michigan, could be as long as 90 years.

Whether or not the decedent had a trust, there may be other trusts, such as a predeceased spouse's marital trust or family trust, from which distributions are to be made as a result of the decedent's death. This depends on the terms of the trust in question.

As mentioned, a trust may provide for distributions which create yet other trusts. (See above, "What Do the Beneficiaries Get?") There could be a marital trust for a spouse, a family trust (also called a credit shelter or bypass trust), or a trust for a child, grandchild, or other individual. The funding of such trusts requires specialized knowledge and you should enlist the assistance of your attorney. (See Chapter 22, "Going Forward: Avoiding Loose Ends.")

ITF, TOD, and POD Designations

One or more bank deposits may have been made by the decedent in trust for another. These accounts are sometimes called *Totten Trusts*, *In Trust For* accounts, or *ITF* accounts. Under Michigan law, these accounts are payable to the person for whom the deposit was made.

Michigan law also provides for the ownership of securities in *Transfer on Death* (TOD) or *Pay on Death* (POD) form. If the decedent owned securities which were titled in this fashion, the securities may be reregistered in the name of the beneficiary.

Joint With Rights of Survivorship

Property which was held jointly by the decedent and one or more others with rights of survivorship passes automatically to the surviving joint tenant or joint tenants. The survivors need only retitle the property. For bank and brokerage accounts, it will generally be necessary to present only the decedent's death certificate. Ask the bank or brokerage firm if other documentation will be required.

In the case of real estate, the survivors should record a certified copy of the death certificate with the Register of Deeds for the county where the property is located. This may be done by attaching a copy of the legal description of the property to the death certificate and submitting both documents for recording together.

It may be that an asset was held jointly for convenience only and the surviving joint owner does not claim ownership. This is often done with bank accounts. In this case, the asset should be treated as belonging to the decedent and distributed as part of the probate estate. (See Chapter 11, "Inventory the Assets.")

If estate taxes must be paid and the Will directs that taxes be apportioned, the surviving joint tenants are responsible for their portion of the tax and you must collect it from them.

With Named Beneficiary

Life insurance proceeds will be paid by the insurance company to the beneficiary or beneficiaries named in the policy. If the beneficiary is the probate estate and you are the Personal Representative, you will receive the proceeds. If the beneficiary is the decedent's trust and you are the Trustee, the money will come to you. Otherwise, a fiduciary is not involved with the distribution of life insurance payments.

Other assets which pass to the beneficiary or beneficiaries are pensions, retirement plans, IRAs, and various types of annuities. The decedent may have named a trust as beneficiary. It is possible though not usual for the decedent's estate to be the beneficiary. This may be intentional or could happen if no beneficiary is named at all, or if the named beneficiary predeceases the decedent. If the estate or trust is not the beneficiary, the benefits pass without the involvement of a fiduciary.

If you are the beneficiary of a pension, retirement plan, IRA, or annuity, whether in your individual capacity or as Trustee or Personal Representative, you must be aware that these vehicles typically offer different settlement options which may have widely different tax consequences.

This is an exceptionally complicated area which is governed both by the U. S. Department of Labor under the Employee Retirement Income Security Act of 1974 (ERISA) and by the Internal Revenue Code and Treasury Regulations. You should not make any election without competent advice, as most elections are irrevocable. You should seek advice from your attorney, who will review the documents and discuss the options with you.

If estate taxes must be paid and the Will directs that taxes be apportioned, the beneficiaries are responsible for their portion of the tax and you must collect it from them.

Type of Property
Automobiles

If the decedent owned one or more cars in his or her sole name whose total value does not exceed $60,000, and there is no other sole-name property which necessitates the opening of a probate estate, the decedent's surviving spouse or heirs may, under Michigan law, transfer the title at a Michigan Secretary of State's office by presenting a certified copy of the death certificate.

Make sure that title to the vehicle is actually transferred. If an accident occurs while the vehicle is still titled in the decedent's name, there could be liability to the estate.

Other Personal Property

Personal property that is specifically bequeathed, whether by a personal property memorandum, Will, or trust instrument, should be delivered to the appropriate beneficiary.

If personal property is to be divided between or among two or more beneficiaries and the Will or trust instrument does not specifically direct how this is to be done, the Personal Representative or Trustee must see that it is done fairly.

One method is to have the beneficiaries first draw lots to determine an order of selection and then have each beneficiary choose one item. This process is repeated until all items have been taken or until no beneficiary wants any of the remaining articles. Any articles not claimed are then sold.

A refinement of this approach is to value each item and make equalizing distributions in cash so that each beneficiary receives the same total amount of property and cash.

If a Federal Estate Tax return must be filed, valuable items should not be distributed to beneficiaries until a Waiver of Inspection has been obtained from the IRS. This is especially true of valuable jewelry or artwork. Otherwise, if the estate tax return is audited, the agent could require you to make the property available for examination or appraisal by the IRS.

Real Property

Execute a Personal Representative's or Trustee's deed conveying property to the beneficiary. This type of deed is designed especially for fiduciaries and creates less liability for the fiduciary than the typical warranty deed.

In Michigan the transfer from the estate or trust to a beneficiary is exempt from State Real Estate Transfer Tax. However, the transfer will uncap the value of the property for Michigan Real Property Tax and a transfer affidavit must be filed by the beneficiary with the local tax assessor.

You should have your attorney prepare the necessary deed and transfer affidavit. The beneficiary should also be advised to consider purchasing title insurance insuring his or her title to the property. If you have located title insurance in the decedent's records you should pass it along to the beneficiary receiving the property, as a prior policy may be helpful to the title insurance company and in some cases will result in a credit against the new premium.

Other Considerations

You should make sure that you are protected with respect to any distribution which you authorize.

❑ You should ensure the distribution is regarded as proper. If a Probate Court order is required, be sure you have one. Even if a court order is not required, you may want to get one, or possibly a settlement agreement signed by all of the beneficiaries.

❑ You must be able to prove that the beneficiaries got what you say you gave them. You should get receipts. For distributions made by check, the canceled check will serve as a receipt, but if the distribution is intended to be a final distribution, then a receipt will say so and serve a purpose beyond a canceled check.

❑ Consider taking steps to facilitate the recovery of the money, if need be, to pay additional debts, expenses, and taxes. The attorney can draft a refunding agreement for the beneficiaries to sign, in which they would agree to repay what they have received in certain circumstances. This is no assurance that the money will actually be repaid, but it may be better than no agreement at all.

In addition, consider the following additional steps when making distributions:

❑ If a Federal or state estate tax return or a state inheritance tax return must be filed, make sure all property transferred to the spouse is of a type which qualifies for the estate tax marital deduction.

❑ Suggest to beneficiaries that they open a brokerage, management, or trust account to receive the assets coming to them. If the amount is large, also suggest that they obtain competent investment advice.

❑ If you are making a "final" distribution, you should hold a certain amount in escrow to cover any unexpected additional liabilities. If the amount is relatively small, these funds should be in a non-interest bearing account so no additional fiduciary income tax return will be required. When you are satisfied that there are no remaining liabilities, you may disburse the balance remaining to the beneficiaries.

❑ Do not leave assets in the decedent's name or in joint name with the decedent. This will only complicate matters upon the later sale or transfer of the assets, or upon a later death.

CHAPTER 22

. . . .

GOING
FORWARD:
AVOIDING
LOOSE ENDS

Am I Done Yet?

When you have grappled with all the tasks we have explored in the preceding chapters, you may believe that you are done. Beneficiaries are no longer calling you; your life is beginning to take on some semblance of normalcy. It has been a long time. You want to pack up all of the estate stuff in boxes and take it down to the basement.

Before you declare yourself finished, however, there are a few more matters that must be dealt with, as we explain in this chapter.

On the Business Side
Obtain All Tax Clearances

❑ If a Federal Estate Tax return was filed, the Personal Representative should receive a closing letter from the Internal Revenue Service summarizing either the information shown on the return as filed or the changes agreed to on audit or on appeal.

❑ A copy of the closing letter may be sent to the IRS with a letter requesting that the Personal Representative be released from personal liability for the estate tax. The IRS should then send a United States Estate Tax Certificate of Discharge from Personal Liability, Form 7990. (Some IRS districts have taken the position that the closing letter itself with evidence of payment of the tax serves to discharge the Personal Representative from personal liability. These districts will not issue Form 7990.)

❑ If a Michigan Estate Tax return was filed, a copy of the Federal closing letter must be sent to the Estate Tax Section, Michigan Department of Treasury. The

Department of Treasury will then issue a Receipt/Discharge of Liability, Form C-6733.

❑ If estate or inheritance tax returns were filed with other states, releases should be requested from those states.

❑ It is also possible to request to be released from personal liability for the decedent's Federal Income and Gift Tax. This is done by filing a Request for Discharge from Personal Liability Under Internal Revenue Code Section 6905, Form 5495, with the IRS Service Center where the returns were filed. We suspect, though we cannot confirm, that filing this form may precipitate an audit of the returns for which the release is requested.

❑ A release for Michigan income taxes may likewise be requested. Send a letter to:

> Income Tax Division
> Michigan Department of Treasury
> Lansing, MI 48922

Obtain Probate Court Closing Statements

❑ If there is a probate estate, and you are the Personal Representative or a Personal Co-Representative, make sure you close the estate and receive the appropriate Certificate of Completion or Settlement Order. (See Chapter 15, "To Probate or Not to Probate.")

❑ If you were the guardian or conservator of the decedent, file a final report or account and obtain a written discharge from the Probate Court.

Adjust Basis in Decedent's Assets

Each asset of the estate that is includible in the decedent's gross estate for Federal Estate Tax purposes receives a new basis equal to its value for Federal Estate Tax purposes. (See Chapter 11, "Inventory the Assets.")

If you have assets that were includible in the decedent's gross estate, make sure your records show the new basis. If the assets are reflected on a brokerage account or mutual fund statement which shows basis, verify that the basis shown on the statement agrees with your records. If not, ask the brokerage firm or mutual fund company to correct it. You should also furnish the new basis information to your accountant or tax preparer.

You must also retain documents which substantiate this new basis. If a Federal Estate Tax return was filed, you should keep a copy of the return and any audit adjustments. If no return was filed, you should keep a copy of the inventory showing the date-of-death values.

If you have any question about which assets have a new basis and what that basis is, you should ask your attorney. You should do this without delay. If you sell an asset and the gain or loss for income tax purposes is figured using the old basis, the result will be incorrect and will probably cost you additional tax.

Funding of Trusts and Bequests

If the decedent had a revocable living trust, the governing instrument may provide for the creation of one or more new *spinoff* trusts. It is also possible for *testamentary* trusts to be created under the Will. The decedent may of course also direct, in either a Will or trust agreement, that one or more outright bequests be distributed.

A transfer in trust or an outright bequest may be *pecuniary* (referring to a dollar amount) or *fractional*, and it may be *formula* or *nonformula*. This results in four possible combinations:

Nonformula Pecuniary, such as "the sum of $100,000."

Nonformula Fractional, such as "one-quarter of my residuary estate."

Formula Pecuniary, such as "that amount which reduces Federal Estate Tax payable as a result of my death to zero."

Formula Fractional, such as "a fractional share of my estate, the numerator of which equals that amount which reduces Federal Estate Tax payable as a result of my death to zero, and the denominator of which equals the entire value of my estate."

Funding refers to the satisfaction of a transfer in trust or an outright bequest with assets. Funding of small nonformula pecuniary bequests is normally done in cash and presents no special problems. All other types of funding, however, raise important questions, such as:

① Should funding be done in cash or in kind? If in kind, what assets should be selected?

② Are assets to be valued as of date of death or date of distribution?

③ In the case of a formula funding, what is the amount that results from the application of the formula?

④ Will funding trigger gain for income tax purposes? Can this be avoided?

⑤ What are the other income tax consequences of funding?

⑥ What are the consequences of a partial funding?

⑦ If funding is to be fractional, must it be *pro rata*— must each and every asset be fractionalized—or may assets be selected on a *pick-and-choose* basis as long as the required fractional amount of the estate is allocated to the trust or bequest to be funded?

As these questions suggest, this is a complicated and highly technical area. Mistakes could have serious tax and property rights consequences. You should review any funding matters with your attorney, who will advise you concerning the requirements of the Will or trust instrument, the rules imposed by the Internal Revenue Code, and possible tax savings strategies.

The funding of trusts and bequests is often deferred until the Federal Estate Tax closing letter is received. This is because formula language often refers to values "as finally determined for Federal Estate Tax purposes."

However, the creation and funding of spinoff trusts cannot be delayed indefinitely. To do so violates the terms of the instrument, which require creation of the spinoff trusts, if not at a specified time, then within a reasonable time. Long delays can result in significant adverse tax consequences.

For example, extremely long delays in creating a marital trust could jeopardize the estate tax marital deduction allowed on the decedent's Federal Estate Tax return, make the accurate allocation of assets between the marital trust and other trusts a near impossibility, and create an income tax nightmare.

Trust Administration

If the decedent's trust continues, or if one or more new spinoff trusts are created, you may be the Trustee of these entities. You may also be Trustee of other trusts, for example, trusts of the decedent's spouse. If so, you are responsible for the ongoing administration of these trusts.

You will have to manage the investments and make distributions in accordance with the governing instrument. You will have to see that fiduciary income tax returns are prepared and filed. You will have to provide accounts to the beneficiaries at least annually.

Unless you are experienced in these matters, you should seek professional assistance. Your attorney can advise you regarding your responsibilities and can either prepare the required accounts and tax returns or refer you to an accountant who is experienced in this area.

Distribute Balance of Funds Held in Escrow

When the last distribution from the estate or trust was made, you should have held an amount in escrow to cover any unexpected additional liabilities. (See Chapter 21, "Transfer Remaining Assets to Beneficiaries.") When, in your judgment, sufficient time has passed and you no longer feel the need to hold this reserve, you should disburse the funds to the beneficiaries who are entitled to them.

Continuing Investment Management

If you have not yet been able to get to it, this is the time to think about the management of the investments for which you are now responsible. These include investments in your own name (or in the name of your own revocable living trust) which you received from the decedent's probate estate or trust, or which became yours as the surviving joint tenant, as well as assets you owned prior to the decedent's death. There may also be investments in a continuing trust of which you are Trustee.

For our recommendations in this regard, see Chapter 16, "Protect and Preserve Estate Assets," under the heading "How Will Assets Be Managed Going Forward?" Also see the tips in Chapter 23, "Financial & Estate Planning for the Survivors."

Decide What to Do About Pending Litigation

If the decedent was involved in legal proceedings at the time of his death, the Personal Representative stands in the decedent's shoes and is responsible for continuing the matter in the decedent's behalf. Even if no probate estate is otherwise necessary, if litigation is going to be continued you will generally need to have a Personal Representative appointed for this purpose.

If the decedent's death was, or may have been, the result of another person's action (or inaction), there may be grounds for the Personal Representative to bring a lawsuit for wrongful death. If you are the Personal Representative, you should discuss this with your attorney.

If you are a family member who might be entitled to damages under a wrongful death claim, you should discuss the possibility of a law suit with the Personal Representative. If the Personal Representative does not want to proceed, then you should discuss your options with your own attorney.

Not all litigation needs to be pursued. Sometimes people bring suits out of frustration, or out of "principle," and after their death an objective evaluation leads to the conclusion that it is just not worth the time, effort, and expense to continue the litigation. If you are the one responsible for the decision to continue, settle, or drop pending litigation, do so objectively.

If wrongful death litigation is to be pursued, be mindful of the possible estate tax consequences. If the alleged damages are based on the decedent's conscious pain and suffering, and if as a result a significant portion of the damages will go to the estate (and not directly to family members), those monies will be includible in the gross estate for estate tax purposes. Even if the gross estate was under the amount which would be subject to estate tax (see Chapter 19, "The Tax Man Cometh"), significant damages could bring the gross estate to the taxable level. The bottom line may be that a significant portion of those damages may go to the IRS for estate taxes.

On the other hand, sometimes damages can be payable on account of the losses suffered by close family members due to the death, and payable directly to them and not to the estate. Damages payable directly to the family members would generally not be part of the gross estate, and not subject to estate taxation. This should be taken into account in deciding whether and how to pursue the litigation, and how to structure a possible settlement in a manner that will yield the most to the family.

How Long Should You Retain the Files?

There are no hard and fast rules which dictate how long you must keep files pertaining to the administration of the estate. If there is no threat of litigation, you may consider discarding most files after five or six years. We recommend that you retain some items permanently.

These include the following:

❑   A copy of the Will. (The original should have been filed with the Probate Court.)

❑ Executed (signed) copies of any trust agreements and Trustee appointment letters.

❑ All annual accounts for the probate estate or for any trust.

❑ A copy of the Federal Estate Tax return and all state estate or inheritance tax returns.

❑ Closing letters for all estate or inheritance tax returns.

❑ Certificate of Completion or Settlement Order from the Probate Court.

❑ Original of any settlement agreement signed by beneficiaries.

On the Personal Side
Memorializing the Decedent

Many families compile memory books to preserve their remembrances of the decedent. These can range from simple scrapbooks or photo albums to elaborate full color publications which are given to all family members and friends as keepsakes.

We know of one case where a family member invested many hours of time to compile a twelve-page, single-spaced biography of the decedent, which he then sent to all members of the extended family. In addition to honoring and remembering the decedent, this biography will be very valuable to those recipients who are interested in their genealogy and family tree.

Today some families might do the same thing but post it on a family Web site so it can be easily accessed by relatives around the country and around the world.

This is also the time to consider charitable giving in memory of the decedent. You may have already identified a charitable cause for memorial contributions on behalf of others at the time of the funeral. There are unlimited opportunities to create charitable funds in the decedent's honor, which can make a positive contribution to our community and society and keep the decedent's memory alive for future generations.

"What we do for ourselves dies with us. What we do for others and the world remains and is immortal."
—Albert Pine

Perpetual Care of Grave Site

You should check with the cemetery regarding arrangements for perpetual care, which consists of cutting the grass and removing any debris. In addition, you may wish to visit the grave periodically to trim grass from around the monument and footstone, remove twigs, and satisfy yourself that everything is in order.

Most cemeteries have rules governing what decorations may be placed on the grave. Many cemeteries offer to place pine branch "blankets" on the grave in winter and remove them in the spring. The cemetery may also offer to place flowers on certain holidays.

A Final Word to the Beneficiaries

When the administration of the estate is complete, you have an opportunity to deliver a final message to the beneficiaries. You should take this seriously and consider carefully the thoughts you want to leave with them. You may want to offer words of conciliation or you may feel moved to comment on some aspect of the decedent's philosophy.

One Personal Representative wrote to his brother and sisters as follows:

> With this distribution, the administration of mother's estate is complete. I now want to take off my "executor" hat and say a few words as your brother. As long as mother was alive, the four of us kept in touch through her. Now, however, if we want to have a relationship, we must communicate directly. This means making the occasional call, writing the occasional note or card, sending the occasional e-mail, and visiting whenever possible. Is this important? I think it is, because *we are a family*. We go back a long way—longer than any friend, longer than any spouse. No one else knows, as just one example, all the things that went on at the dinner table on [street name]. We have the

ability to share, from this unique perspective, one another's joys and sorrows, to provide support, to *be there* for each other. This is pretty precious and is something that I hope we will all want to preserve.

In another case, a trustee shared thoughts of what his aunt and uncle had been trying to accomplish with their gifts and bequests, as an expression of their family's philosophy with regard to wealth. He wrote the beneficiaries in the following terms:

> Since I expect this will be my last letter to you as trustee, I feel that I should share with you something of the philosophy of Robert and Elizabeth in regard to their bequests to us. Robert and Elizabeth believed that our family should improve itself financially from generation to generation; that money should be kept in the family, invested, and made to grow; that it should be passed on to the next generation "to see what they can do with it," as Elizabeth put it. This philosophy goes back at least as far as Robert [family name], Sr., the grandfather of Robert and Elizabeth. It can be seen in the enclosed agreement penned by their father, Robert [family name], Jr., as he began to deed lots from [name] Subdivision to his children in 1940. It was the hope of Robert and Elizabeth that we would be good stewards of the funds entrusted to us, that they would multiply under our care and devolve upon future generations of our family.

We sincerely hope you will take a moment to reflect on these suggestions, and then move on to consider our final message in Chapter 23, "Financial & Estate Planning for the Survivors."

NOTES

"I am of the opinion that my life belongs
to the community... and as long as I live,
it is my privilege to do for it whatever I can.
I want to be thoroughly used up when I die,
for the harder I work, the more I live.
I rejoice in life for its own sake.
Life is no brief candle to me.
It is a sort of splendid torch which I have
got hold of for a moment and I want to
make it burn as brightly as possible
before handing it on to future generations."

—George Bernard Shaw
Irish Playwright

CHAPTER 23

FINANCIAL & ESTATE PLANNING FOR THE SURVIVORS

Financial & Estate Planning for the Survivors

Now is the time for you to get your own financial and estate planning house in order. Your situation has probably changed as the result of the loss you just suffered. Your family situation may be very different if you've lost a child, parent, or spouse. Your financial situation may be very different if you've received a sizeable inheritance. This may be the largest sum of money you will ever acquire at one time.

Equally important, if you've been involved in administration of the estate, you have probably learned the importance of proper estate planning. This may be because the decedent's estate was impeccably planned, in which case you can appreciate how much it helped you. Or perhaps the decedent's estate planning was sorely neglected, and it caused a myriad of problems—financial losses, family disputes, unnecessary taxes, frustration, delays, and expense—and you have learned the real cost of poor planning or no planning at all.

In any event, there is no time like the present for you to address your own planning. Since this book is not about financial and estate planning, but rather about estate administration, we'll only touch upon a number of the most important areas for you to address. We urge you to deal with them sooner rather than later.

Financial Aspects

In recent years people in the financial services industry have talked about $10 trillion in wealth which will be transferred from the senior generation to the next generation over the coming decades.

Those numbers may be far short of the actual figure: In October, 1999, Boston College researchers updated the estimate. The figure, they say, is more in the range of $41 trillion to $136 trillion. ("A Larger Legacy May Await Generation X, Y and Z," *New York Times*, October 20, 1999, page C2.)

Whatever your share of that pie, your inheritance may be the largest amount you will ever have, perhaps aside from your own retirement nest egg.

Many people will simply take what they receive, leave it in the same form ("If that stock was good enough for Dad, it's good enough for me..."), or if it's in cash then they may put it in the bank. In many cases, that can be a terrible mistake, one you will only come to appreciate years down the road. Here are a few tips you should consider with your windfall.

X-Ray Your Securities

Whatever securities you have received, make sure you know what you have and make an affirmative decision, on a case-by-case basis, to either sell them or keep them. Don't let inertia govern.

You may have received individual stocks and bonds, mutual funds, money market accounts, certificates of deposit, or government bonds. The worst thing you can do is just sit on them.

Whether to hold onto them or sell them should be a financial decision, not an emotional one. Mom or Dad (or whoever was kind enough to leave them to you) may have bought them or held them for years for their own reasons, but your decision should be based on the here and now, and what's likely to happen tomorrow and in the years to come.

People often avoid selling appreciated securities because they do not want to trigger capital gains tax. For the moment, that's not an issue for you because you probably have a new cost basis (step-up in basis) to the date-of-death value.

A large concentration of a particular stock may have been acquired over many decades because of an employment relationship with the company, stock splits or stock dividends, or a dividend reinvestment program. Whatever the reason, we suggest you take a good, hard look at what you have and ask your-self this simple question:

If you had everything in cash, is this the portfolio you would create for yourself?

Look at each security. How has it performed over the last year, three years, and five years? If the returns are not consistent, are you comfortable with the volatility of the security?

If there are mutual funds in the basket, are they expensive to hold? How do their expenses compare with others of the same type? Are there other alternatives which you presently own or can identify which have lower expense ratios?

Are the investments themselves sound? Are the industry sectors represented those which you feel will do well in the future? Are they sufficiently diversified, taking into account other investments you already have?

If the basket of investments includes individual bonds, you have even more thinking to do. If there are tax-free municipal bonds, does your personal income tax rate merit that type of investment? Is the state of the issuer such that you are also exempt from state income tax on the bond interest?

Are the maturities acceptable to you? If they are very long term, you may be subject to more volatility in their values over time. If you can't handle that volatility, then consider selling some and investing in shorter-terms bonds or maybe stocks, depending on how they all fit in your asset allocation.

Dump the Losers

If the entire basket of securities is high quality, with great returns and even better prospects— stocks, bonds, and mutual funds you would buy today if you had the opportunity—you're in great shape. Most likely, however, there will be a few that you would rather not own.

Some may be hands-down dogs, and you should decide how quickly to sell them. Others may just not be what you would want to own. They may not be the best investments, but nothing to panic over. Put those securities on a watch list and take your time over the next year to make a decision about whether to sell those as well or continue to hold.

Evaluate What's Left, Based on Your Own Goals

Maybe the securities you've inherited would, on some sort of objective basis, be fine investments, but are they consistent with your own goals and objectives?

For example, Uncle Don was really into day trading high-tech stocks and left you a bundle of very exciting opportunities. You've looked at the charts on these stocks over the past couple of years, and the past few months, and your stomach fell as you watched the incredible volatility. You already have a fair amount in high-tech and you don't feel you can handle much more.

You may decide to diversify the inherited securities in another sector or sectors to allow you to sleep better at night.

Another example: Grandma was a great believer in U.S. Treasury bonds. "You'll never lose a penny on these," she often told you. That's correct, but if you're young and looking for appreciation, a large concentration of fixed income securities—even the best quality—just won't meet your growth objectives.

You get the point: Even if what you inherited is high quality, it may not all be right for your goals, objectives, and investment personality. Decide which ones aren't a good fit and move them out.

Rebalance Your Entire Portfolio

After you've figured out what you're going to hold and what you're going to sell, and the tax consequences of any of that, make sure to consider your own investments as well.

Do you have an asset allocation? Have your investment goals, time horizon, or personal situation changed much since you originally set it up? At this time you'll need to reset the overall allocation for stock, bonds, and cash.

If you don't relate to this discussion—which is entirely possible since your inheritance may well be the first sum you've ever had to invest—then we strongly suggest you start learning about investments, from the ground up.

Every stock brokerage firm and online brokerage service will provide you brochures about the basics, and bookstores and public libraries are filled with books on investing as well. Take the time to read about investing and within a few weeks you'll be ready to move forward.

Consider Professional Investment Help

Not everyone who receives an inheritance, whether relatively small or very large, has the time or inclination to invest and manage it themselves. Many of those who might be so inclined still prefer to hire professionals to do the job for them.

A professional investment advisor can help you evaluate the portfolio, identify your goals and objectives, decide what to hold and what to sell, and help you set up the right portfolio for yourself and your family to give you a good chance to achieve financial success and security in the future. Revisit the discussion on financial advisors in Chapter 10, "Where to Turn for Help."

Services for Senior Citizens

If the survivors include senior citizens, a whole host of other issues will arise:

How long can the senior citizen stay in the family home, and what are the other options?

What charitable and volunteer organizations exist within the community to provide services to seniors?

What services are available for those with various disabilities? What should be done if the senior citizen is or may be suffering from Alzheimer's disease?

What organizations provide information on other specific health conditions?

See Appendix D for a partial listing of further resources on services for senior citizens.

Estate Planning
Review Your Estate Plan

A death in the family is the typical trigger for a complete review of your estate planning. This is a major change in your family situation, and may also involve receipt of a substantial inheritance.

Many people believe that once they have signed their estate planning documents, they can put them in the vault and forget about them. Not so. They should be reviewed whenever there are significant changes in your family (which would include marriages, divorces, births, and deaths), changes in your assets, or changes in the tax law.

Your attitudes toward family and charity may also change over the years. Planning techniques also evolve. It's a good idea to have your plan reviewed every five years in any event, just to see if you still like it or want to make changes.

Certainly a death can cause you to rethink many aspects of your estate plan, and also to consider your plan more seriously, since death is no longer merely a theoretical possibility.

Who should receive what, how should they receive it, who has already passed away, and are relationships the same as they were the last time you reviewed your documents? Who should now serve under your Power of Attorney and Health Care Designation? These are but a few of the questions that will come up when you look at your existing estate planning documents.

If you have never addressed your estate planning, then now is the time. Remember, you do have an estate plan. It's either the one that you set up for yourself, or the one that the law provides for you. It's your choice.

Coordinate Your Estate Plan

Some people still forget that many arrangements "outside" their estate planning documents will override those documents, and need to be coordinated with the overall plan.

Joint ownership, beneficiary designations on life insurance, annuities, IRAs and retirement plans, and Payable on Death designations on government bonds, for example, all need to be reviewed. If the assets will pass in a way which is inconsistent with your Will or trust, then changes may have to be made in the form of ownership or beneficiary designations.

Now is the time to check joint ownership and beneficiary designations. You may have been the surviving joint owner on property owned jointly with the decedent, and now have a decision to make as to how to deal with that property.

You may have been the primary beneficiary on IRAs or annuities, and now have to designate your own beneficiaries. If you have inherited some large IRAs you have some serious planning to do to maximize the tax benefits of those accounts and defer the income to the extent possible, if that's your game plan.

If the accounts were yours in the first place, and the decedent was your beneficiary, then you have to rethink your beneficiary designations also.

Whatever you do, you must make sure that you've covered all the bases and that your estate plan, which you took pains to have drafted, will work in the context of all the assets which make up your estate.

Share Information with Your Family

As you've just been involved in administering an estate, you know how important it can be to have complete information. Make sure that your family doesn't have to search for information when handling *your* estate.

Prepare a detailed checklist describing every asset and liability, locations of accounts, computer passwords, locations of safe deposit boxes and keys, and full life insurance and other insurance information.

Suffering the loss of a family member is traumatic enough without having to worry about how to pay bills, where accounts are located, how to access password-protected computerized records, whether there is a safe deposit box, and where the keys might be.

Insurance companies won't seek out your beneficiaries to pay them benefits. To make a claim your beneficiaries will ei-

Estate Planning Checklist

The authors have prepared a detailed Estate Planning Checklist, which may be downloaded from the publisher's Web site:

http://www.
carobtreepress.com

ther have to know that there is insurance and with which company, or they will have to do an investigation to locate that information.

Plan Beyond Your Will or Trust

Many people often view their estate plan as what is found within their Will or trust. A review of the documents may, in fact, reveal that the plan is fine, as far as it goes.

But many planning opportunities appear only after careful consideration of all of your assets and objectives with regard to those assets. Tremendous long-range tax benefits can be achieved by lifetime planning, annual gift programs, moving investments, business assets, personal residences, and other assets down one or more generations, at the least tax cost possible.

If you focus only on your Will or trust, you may be overlooking tremendous planning possibilities. If your estate is a modest one, then this may not be a concern. But if your estate has grown over the years to the point where it may be taxable, then you really should begin to consider other options to minimize estate taxes.

Plan for Several Generations

If you have children or grandchildren, and a large estate, you ought to think about planning for more than one generation.

Most parents feel that if their children have reached a certain age, whether that be 35, 40, or even 45, they are comfortable leaving them their share of the estate outright, not in trust. This decision reflects a degree of confidence in the children—which is fine—but it overlooks estate tax problems your children may have in their own estates.

The tax law allows you to leave a certain amount of your estate—which could be up to about $2 million for a married couple—in such a way that it can pass to your *grandchildren*, or even lower generations, free from estate tax in your *children's* estates.

"I'm proud of
paying taxes.
The only thing is—
I could be
just as proud
for half the money."
—Arthur Godfrey

This type of planning is obviously only for those with a large estate, and it won't save you any estate tax in your estate. But it will allow your *children's* estates to eventually avoid significant taxes, and your grandchildren may ultimately receive many millions more when your children pass on.

It can even be done in a way that allows your children use of the funds if they need them during their lifetimes. So you don't really have to bypass your children to provide them these potential benefits.

Consider Life Insurance

Not everyone needs life insurance. However, life insurance can be particularly useful in large estates to create additional tax-free wealth, outside the taxable estate, to replace all or part of the estate taxes.

A policy which pays on the last death (so called *survivorship* or *second-to-die*) insurance can be obtained even where one spouse has a poor health history. These types of policies are generally less expensive than insurance on the healthier spouse alone.

If you're single, don't rule out life insurance, even at an advanced age. Competition between insurance companies is such that a policy may be available for less than you think, though your health will obviously be a critical factor.

The insurance lobby is one of the most powerful in this country. The special tax-free treatment of life insurance proceeds—achieved through the efforts of that lobby—should not be overlooked.

The premiums on a large policy may appear to be high, and certainly the agent will earn a sizeable commission. But the ultimate benefit to your family could be even greater, in dollars, and also in terms of investment return for your premium dollar. If properly structured, it can also be totally free from income and estate taxes.

Start Planning Early

If your estate is now at the taxable level—$675,000 in the year 2000, gradually increasing to $1 million by 2006, and double that for married couples—you should be thinking about ways to limit the estate tax burden. Most planning techniques will benefit from an early start. So it's really not in your interest to procrastinate.

For example, you can give away $10,000 each year ($20,000 per year for married couples), to as many people as you choose, without incurring gift tax and without using up any of your lifetime estate and gift tax exemption. This is your annual gift tax exclusion, and it expires on December 31 of each year. It's a "use it or lose it" proposition.

Other techniques involve transferring assets out of your estate, which also moves the future growth or appreciation on those assets out of your estate. Starting earlier removes more of the future appreciation.

Yet other techniques, keyed to your life expectancy, benefit from your being younger at the time you implement them. In the case of life insurance, premiums are generally lower the younger you are. If you wait until "later" to take out the insurance, future health problems could increase the premiums or you could even become uninsurable.

So it's really in your interest to develop a plan and begin to implement it as soon as you can reasonably do so.

Communicate Your Love and Ethical Values

While actions certainly speak louder than words, many of us take for granted that our children and grandchildren appreciate how much we love them, and know and understand our ethical values.

But verbalizing all of this in what is called an *Ethical Will* can be a fulfilling experience for you, and will give your family something to cherish and remember. It may also clearly express your feelings on a number of issues which are important to you, and on which you hope they will follow your lead. The not-yet born children of your children's children will thank you and bless you for it!

Most attorneys—and most clients—are not familiar with Ethical Wills. However, you will find valuable insights into this concept, and numerous real life examples from the past and from current times, in *So That Our Values Live On— Ethical Wills and How to Prepare Them*, edited by Jack Riemer and Nathaniel Stampfer (Jewish Lights Publishing, 1991).

This book will be most helpful to you in developing your own Ethical Will. It is available in bookstores or direct from the publisher at 802-457-4000, credit card orders 800-962-4544, 9:00 a.m.- 5:00 p.m. Eastern time, Monday through Friday. For more information on the publisher see their Web site at http://www.jewishlights.com.

According to a review in the *Los Angeles Times:* "While the book is written from a Jewish viewpoint, its principles can easily be adapted by people of other faiths."

Be Charitable

In the overall context of time, we are here for but a moment, mere grains of sand on an infinitely large beach. In the words of Hillel, a sage who lived in the first century:

<blockquote>

If I am not for myself, who will be for me?

If I am only for myself, what am I?

If not now, when?

</blockquote>

There is so much work to be done to better mankind in so many ways, charitable giving is not really an option but an important obligation of each of us, to whatever extent and in whatever way we can.

We say to our clients, "Give until it feels good." Work closely with the charities you favor so that you can see and feel first hand the good that you are doing and how much it is appreciated.

Consider leaving something for charity in your Will or trust, and also look into various ways of benefiting charity during your lifetime.

The numerous tax benefits to be derived from the various forms of charitable giving are merely icing on the cake. Your contributions do so much to uplift the minds, bodies, spirits, and souls of those you help! And you will also be leaving a legacy for your children and grandchildren to follow!

APPENDIX

. . . .

Appendix A: General Resources

Government Agencies
Veterans Affairs
Banks and Trust Companies
Valuation and Appraisal Services
Life Insurance Search
Unclaimed Property (Escheated or Abandoned Property)
Pension Benefits Search
Missing Heir Search Firms
Handwriting Experts and Document Examiners
Translation Services

Appendix B: Michigan Probate Courts

Appendix C: Grief Support Services

Appendix D: Services for Senior Citizens

Internet Links
To Sources Cited
www.carobtreepress.com

NOTES

"It's a good thing to have money and
the things money can buy,
and it's a good thing to check up and
make sure you haven't lost
the things that money can't buy."
—Proverb

Appendix A
General Resources

The following resources may be useful in administering an estate and are provided for your information.

Some resources are listed for the Detroit area only, or for Wayne, Oakland, Macomb, and Washtenaw counties only, and we apologize to those located in other parts of the state and outside of Michigan. However, by its nature this list is necessarily incomplete. Check the publisher's Web site, http://www.carobtreepress.com, for periodic updated versions of the Appendix.

The individuals and companies listed below which provide services advertise the described services to the public. No endorsements or recommendations are made with regard to any company, organization, or individual listed. It is the responsibility of the person engaging any service provider to confirm their competency and the reasonableness of their fee structure.

Government Agencies
Internal Revenue Service
Web site: http://www.irs.gov
This Web site permits you to print most IRS forms that you might require in connection with administering an estate, including individual and fiduciary income tax returns (Form 1040 and Form 1041), Federal Estate Tax return (Form 706), as well as Application for Employer Identification Number (Form SS-4).

To order IRS forms or publications by telephone for delivery via the U.S. Postal Service, call 1-800-TAX-FORM (1-800-829-3676).
Braille material is available for those with visual impairments by writing to:
> National Library Service
> 1291 Taylor Street, NW
> Washington, DC 20542

IRS forms and publications may also be ordered for delivery via fax-on-demand, by calling 703-368-9694.
Live IRS telephone assistance: 1-800-829-1040; for persons with hearing impairments: 1-800-829-4059 (TDD).

Michigan Department of Treasury
Lansing, Michigan 48922
Web site: http://www.treas.state.mi.us/
General Treasury information: 517-373-3200; TDD 517-373-9419
Income Tax information: 1-800-487-4700
Tax Forms: 1-800-FORM-2-ME (367-6263)
Estate Tax: 517-373-3163
Fiduciary Tax: 517-373-1426
Sales, Use & Withholding Taxes: 517-373-3190
A complete Michigan Treasury telephone and fax list may be found on the Web at http://www. treas. state. mi. us/contacts/treacont.htm

Michigan Attorney General
Charitable Trust Section
P.O. Box 30214
Lansing, MI 48909
517-373-1152

Social Security Administration
Web site: http://www.ssa.gov
1-800-772-1213. See Chapter 7, "Social Security Benefits," for further Social Security contact information.
A copy of the booklet "Social Security Survivors Benefits" (Publication No. 05-10084) is available at http://www.ssa.gov/pubs/10084.html

Veterans Administration (see Veterans Affairs section below)

Bureau of the Public Debt
Savings bond information is available at Bureau of the Public Debt Online: http://www.savingsbonds.gov. This site provides comprehensive savings bond value tables and extensive information on what to do with bonds on the death of a bond owner (search the site for the word "death").

Veterans Affairs

Veterans Benefits Administration
Web site: www.vba.va.gov
Links to general descriptions of all veterans benefits, including life insurance and burial benefits, survivors benefits, and contacts for further information, are provided at:
http://www.vba.va.gov/benindex.htm
For downloadable forms to claim benefits:
http://www.vba.va.gov/pubs/forms1.htm

Department of Veterans Affairs,
National Cemetery Association
Web site: http://www.cem.va.gov
Information on burial and memorial benefits is available from the Department of Veterans Affairs, National Cemetery Administration, including links to information on national cemeteries, headstones and markers, Presidential Memorial Certificates, military funeral honors, state cemetery grants programs, how to locate veterans, and how to obtain military records and medals.

United States Department of
Veterans Affairs
Detroit, Michigan Regional Office
Patrick V. McNamara Building
477 Michigan Avenue
Detroit, MI 48226
Web page, with links to benefits descriptions and related sites: http://www.vba.va.gov/ro/central/detr/default.htm
A copy of the 95-page booklet "Federal Benefits for Veterans and Dependents" may be downloaded at http://www.vba.va.gov/ro/central/detr/Forms.htm or obtained from the VA Office.
Contact your local VA Regional office for assistance in determining available benefits and applying for benefits by calling 1-800-827-1000. You may also e-mail the Regional Office that serves your area.
E-mail address for the Detroit Regional Office: detroit.query@vba.va.gov. E-mail addresses of other Regional Offices may be found at http://www.vba.va.gov/benefits/address.htm

County Veterans Services Offices

These offices provide free assistance in obtaining veterans' benefits from the Federal, State and County governments, and in appealing adverse decisions.

Macomb County Veterans' Affairs

21855 Dunham Road, Room 3
Mount Clemens, MI 48036
810-469-5315
Web site: http://www.libcoop.net/macomb/graphicpages/departments/veterans.html

Oakland County, Michigan Veterans Affairs

Web site: http://www.co.oakland.mi.us/c_serv/ocvs/index.htm.
Office Hours: Monday-Friday, 8:30 a.m.-12:00 noon and 1:00-5:00 p.m. No appointment necessary. Field visits are available for the housebound.

Pontiac Office:
North Office Building, 26B
1200 N. Telegraph Road
Pontiac, MI 48341-0468
248-858-0785

Southeast Oakland Office
1151 Crooks Road
Troy, MI 48084-7136
248-655-1250

West Oakland Office
West Oakland Office Building
1010 E. West Maple
Walled Lake, MI 48390-3588
248-926-3368

Washtenaw County Veteran Services

2140 E. Ellsworth Road
P.O. Box 8645
Ann Arbor, MI 48107-8645
734-971-2195; Fax 734-971-2276
Hours: 8:30 a.m. - 5:00 p.m., Monday-Friday

Wayne County Veterans Affairs Department

Book Tower Building
1249 Washington Boulevard, Suite 510
Detroit, MI 48226
313-224-5045; Fax: 313-224-8179
Web site: http://www.waynecounty.com/veterans/veterans_homepage.htm

The Wayne County Veterans Affairs Department provides assistance with funeral expenses. Those veterans and spouses with assets less than $25,000, excluding the family residence, are eligible. The veteran must have received an Honorable Discharge from the United States Armed Forces, with at least 90 days of recognized wartime service. Spouses of veterans are not eligible for government marker.

The County of Wayne will provide up to $300 toward burial benefits and $50 toward the cost of installing a Government Marker. The following documentation is required at time of application: Military Discharge (DD-214); certified death certificate; itemized funeral bill; proof of marriage; complete information regarding assets. The application must be completed by the claimant within two years from the date of death. To expedite your meeting you should call in advance and schedule an appointment. No mail-in applications are accepted.

Banks and Trust Companies

Following are the major banks and trust companies doing business in the Metropolitan Detroit area, in alphabetical order. Other smaller banks and trust companies located throughout the area and the state also handle trust and estate administration and should not be overlooked.

Bank One
Comerica Bank
Huntington Bank
National City Bank
Northern Trust Company
Old Kent

Many banks have integrated their trust administration services into groups which provide banking, trust, investment, and other services, sometimes called *Private Banking and Investment*. We recommend that you call the bank branch manager concerning your needs, and ask him or her to arrange an appointment at a convenient location with the person best able to assist you.

Valuation and Appraisal Services

Your attorney or accountant should be able to refer you to a valuation expert or appraiser who can value the particular assets in question. You may also want to refer to associations of valuation professionals for a guide to their members, such as the following:

American Society of Appraisers
P.O. Box 17265
Washington, D.C. 20041-0265
703-478-2228; Referral Line: 1-800-ASA-VALU (1-800-272-8258)
Web site: http://www.appraisers.org

National Association of Certified Valuation Analysts (NACVA)
1245 E. Brickyard Road, Suite 110
Salt Lake City, Utah 84106
801-486-0600; Fax 801-486-7500
Web site: http://www.nacva.com

Life Insurance Search

Life Benefits Search, Inc.
P.O. Box 6132
Lakeland, Florida 33807
1-800-770-2485
Web site: http://www.lifesearch.net
This company offers to send inquiries to over 1,700 life insurance companies at over 1,200 addresses for a flat fee of $150.

It inquires whether the company had a life insurance, annuity, or pension benefit in effect for a given individual at the date of death. The insurance company generally responds to it via e-mail with "no" answers, which Life Benefits Search, Inc. forwards to person who requested the search. However, if the answer is "yes" the insurance company generally responds directly to the family member or attorney. The beneficiary must then make a formal claim for benefits.

Unclaimed Property (Escheated or Abandoned Property)

The State Treasuries of many states, including Michigan, have millions of dollars in lost or forgotten assets from dormant bank accounts, uncashed checks, valuables left in safe deposit boxes, and stock certificates. Because these properties were considered abandoned and unclaimed by the bank or company entrusted with them, they are turned over to the state, as required by law. The respective state is the custodian of these assets and returns them to their owners (or the owners' heirs) when they are rightfully claimed.

MissingMoney.com is a database that is searchable on the Web and contains unclaimed property records from participating states and corporations. It is sponsored by the states and the National Association of Unclaimed Property Administrators, and permits searching for unclaimed assets at no charge. Web site:
http://www.missingmoney.com

The **National Association of Unclaimed Property Administrators (NAUPA)** consists of state officials charged with the responsibility of collecting and reuniting lost owners with their unclaimed property. NAUPA has a Web site, which was developed by state unclaimed property experts to assist the public, free of charge, in efforts to search for funds that may belong to you or your relatives. Their web site also answers questions about what is unclaimed property, how it becomes abandoned, information about finders, addresses of state unclaimed property offices, and links to the Web sites of various states which provide online searches for unclaimed property.
NAUPA Web site:
http://www.unclaimed.org

State of Michigan
Unclaimed Property Office
Mailing address:
Unclaimed Property Division
Michigan Department of Treasury
Lansing, Michigan 48922
Office Location:
Unclaimed Property Division
Michigan Department of Treasury
101 E. Hillsdale St.
Lansing, Michigan 48933
517-335-4327; Fax: 517- 335-4400
Web site: http://www. treas.state.mi.us. unclprop/unclindx.ht.
Web site to search the Michigan Unclaimed Property Division database ("Money Quest"):
http://www. treas. state.mi. us/unclprop/searchunclaimedproperty.htm

Pension Benefits Search
The **Pension Benefit Guaranty Corporation (PBGC)** protects the retirement incomes of about 43 million American workers—one of every three working persons—in nearly 40,000 defined benefit pension plans. PBGC is a federal government corporation established by Title IV of the Employee Retirement Income Security Act (ERISA) in 1974 to encourage the growth of defined benefit plans, provide timely and uninterrupted payment of benefits, and maintain pension insurance premiums at the lowest level necessary to carry out the Corporation's obligations.

PBGC

1200 K Street N.W.

Washington, DC 20005-4026

202-326-4000; 1-800-400-7242

For TTY/TDD users, call the federal relay service toll-free at 800-877-8339 and ask to be connected to the number you want.

Web site: http://www.pbgc.gov

PBGC maintains the **Pension Search Directory**, which helps PBGC find people who are owed pensions they earned from private defined benefit pension plans that have been closed. These are traditional pensions that promise a specified monthly benefit at retirement. The Pension Search Directory may be accessed through the PBGC Web address above, or directly at http://search.pbgc.gov/srchname.cfm

PBGC has included among the names of unlocatable people some who, based on the records currently available to PBGC, are not entitled to a benefit under the provisions of their insured pension plan. This provides unlocatable people who have no benefit entitlement an opportunity to contact PBGC and provide additional documentation that may establish their entitlement to a benefit. Additional search tips may be found in PBGC's guidebook "Finding A Lost Pension," which is available at http://www.pbgc.gov/pubs.htm

Missing Heir Search Firms

Some missing heir search firms will locate heirs at no charge to the estate, but a percentage fee is charged to the heir. Other firms will charge the estate or the heir a flat fee or an hourly fee unrelated to the amount of assets involved. It is the responsibility of the person engaging the search firm to inquire as to how fees will be charged and compare services offered by various firms. No recommendation is made as to any firm listed.

International Genealogical Search, Inc.

P.O. Box 34000

Seattle, WA 98124-1000

1-800-ONE-CALL (1-800-663-2255);

Fax: 1-800-663-3299

Web site: http://www.heirsearch.com

Harvey E. Morse, P.A.

2435 South Ridgewood Avenue

South Daytona, FL 32119

904-760-5000; 1-888-2INHERIT

Fax: 904-760-6400; 1-800-410-5665

Web site: http://www.probate.com

Handwriting Experts and Document Examiners

Individuals and companies listed in this section advertise services in detection of forgery, handwriting and printing identification, ink analysis, and other document-related problems. No recommendation is made as to any person listed.

John P. Ricci, Forensic Document Examiner

1230 W. Church Road

Morris, Michigan 48857-9759

517-625-7319; Fax 517-625-3732

Riley & Welch Associates
Forensic Document Examinations, Inc.
920 Trowbridge Road, Suite 352
East Lansing, Michigan 48823
517-394-1512

Speckin Forensic Laboratories
2105 University Park Drive, Suite A
Okemos, Michigan 48864
517-349-3528; Detroit 313-965-8086;
1-888-999-1009; Fax 517-349-5538
Web site: http://www.4n6.com
E-mail: speckin@4n6.com

Translation Services
Inter-Lingua
65 Cadillac Square, Suite 2200
Detroit, Michigan 48226
313-965-5898; Fax 313-961-6769
E-mail: ralou@aol.com

Windsor Translation Bureau
545 Ouellette Avenue, Suite 201
Windsor, ON N9A 4J3, Canada
519-256-8897; 1-877-742-5982
Fax: 519-256-0243
Web site: http://www.wintranslation.com

By its nature, this listing is incomplete, and we apologize for any omissions.

Remember that all web sites referred to in this book may be accessed directly from the publisher's Web site:

http://www.carobtreepress.com

Listings are provided as a convenience to the reader, and no recommendation or endorsement is made of any organization, company, or individual listed.

Any organization not listed which wishes to be listed in a future edition should forward its information to the publisher at the address provided at the beginning of this book. All listings are in the discretion of the publisher.

Appendix B
Michigan Probate Courts
(By County, in Alphabetical Order)

Alcona
County Building
P. O. Box 3328
106 Fifth St.
Harrisville 48740
517-724-6880

Alger
Courthouse Complex
101 Court St.
Munising 49862
906-387-2080

Allegan
Probate Court
2243 33rd St.
Allegan 49010
616-673-0250; Fax: 616-673-2200
E-mail: p03@voyager.net

Alpena
Alpena County Annex Building
719 W. Chisholm St.
Alpena 49707
517-354-8785; Fax: 517-356-3665

Antrim
County Building
205 Cayuga
P. O. Box 130
Bellaire 49615
231-533-6681; Fax: 231-533-6600

Arenac
120 N. Grove St.
Box 666
Standish 48658
517-846-6941

Baraga
Courthouse
16 N. Third St.
L'Anse 49946
906-524-6390; Fax: 906-524-6186

Barry
Suite 302
220 W. Court St.
Hastings 49058
616-948-4842; Fax: 616-948-3322

Bay
1230 Washington Avenue
Bay City 48708
517-895-4205; Fax: 517-895-4194

Benzie
Government Center
P. O. Box 398
Beulah 49617
231-882-9675; Fax: 231-882-5987

Berrien
Courthouse
811 Port St.
St. Joseph 49085
616-983-8365

Branch
Courthouse
31 Division St.
Coldwater 49036
517-279-4318

Calhoun
Calhoun County Justice Center
161 E. Michigan Avenue
Battle Creek 49014-4066
616-969-6794; Fax: 616-969-6797
E-mail: p13@voyager.net

Cass
Courthouse
110 N. Broadway
Cassapolis 49031
616-445-4452
Fax: 616-445-4453

Charlevoix
County Building
301 State St.
Charlevoix 49720
231-547-7214; Fax: 231-547-7256

Cheboygan
Courthouse
P. O. Box 70
Cheboygan 49721
231-627-8823; Fax: 231-627-8868

Chippewa
Courthouse
319 Court St.
Sault Ste. Marie 49783
906-635-6314; Fax: 906-635-6852
E-mail: p17@voyager.net

Clare
Clare County Bldg.
P. O. Box 96
Harrison 48625
517-539-7109

Clinton
Courthouse
100 State St.
St. Johns 48879
517-224-5190; Fax: 517-224-5102

Crawford
Courthouse
200 W. Michigan Ave.
Grayling 49738
517-344-3237; Fax: 517-348-8529

Delta
County Building
310 Ludington St.
Escanaba 49829
906-789-5112

Dickinson
Courthouse
P. O. Box 609
Iron Mountain 49801
906-774-1555

Eaton
Courthouse
1045 Independence Blvd.
Charlotte 48813
517-543-7500 or 517-485-6444

Emmet
Courthouse
200 Division St.
Petoskey 49770
616-348-1764; Fax: 616-348-0672

Genesee
919 Beach St.
Flint 48502
810-257-3528

Gladwin
Courthouse
401 W. Cedar Ave.
Gladwin 48624
517-426-7451

Gogebic
Courthouse
200 N. Moore St.
Bessemer 49911
906-667-0421; Fax: 906-663-4660

Grand Traverse
400 Boardman Ave.
Traverse City 48684
231-922-4640

Gratiot
Courthouse
214 E. Center St.
P. O. Box 217
Ithaca 48847
517-875-5231; Fax: 517-875-5331

Hillsdale
Courthouse
29 N. Howell
Hillsdale 49242
517-437-4643

Houghton
Courthouse
401 E. Houghton Ave.
Houghton 49931
906-482-3120

Huron
County Building
250 E. Huron Ave.
Bad Axe 48413
517-269-9944

Ingham
300 Grady J. Porter Bldg.
303 W. Kalamazoo St.
Room 400
Lansing 48933
517-483-6300; Fax: 517-483-6150

Ionia
Courthouse
100 Main St.
Ionia 48846
616-527-5326; Fax: 616-527-5321
E-mail: p34@voyager.net

Iosco
County Bldg.
P. O. Box 421
422 Lake
Tawas City 48764-0421
517-362-3991; Fax: 517-362-1459

Iron
Courthouse
2 S. Sixth St.
Ste. 10
Crystal Falls 49920-1413
906-875-3121; Fax: 906-875-6775

Isabella
County Bldg.
200 N. Main St.
Mt. Pleasant 48858
517-772-0911; Fax: 517-775-2068

Jackson
312 S. Jackson St.
Jackson 49201
517-788-4290; Fax: 517-788-4291

Kalamazoo
County Building
227 W. Michigan Ave.
Kalamazoo 49007
616-383-8666; Fax: 616-383-8685

Kalkaska
County Government Center
P. O. Box 780
605 N. Birch St.
Kalkaska 49646
616-258-3314; Fax: 616-258-3329

Kent
320 Ottawa Ave., NW
Grand Rapids 49503
616-336-3630

Keweenaw
Courthouse
HC1 Box 607
Fourth St.
Eagle River 49924-9700
906-337-1927

Lake
Courthouse
1094 N. Michigan Ave.
P.O. Box 1330
Baldwin 49304
231-745-4614

Lapeer
255 Clay St.
Lapeer 48446
810-667-0261; Fax: 810-667-0271

Leelanau
Courthouse
301 E. Cedar St.
P. O. Box 595
Leland 49654
231-256-9803; Fax: 231-256-9845

Lenawee
Rex B. Martin Judicial Bldg.
425 N. Main St.
Adrian 49221
517-264-4610; Fax: 517-264-4616

Livingston
Courthouse
2nd Floor
200 E. Grand River
Howell 48843
517-546-3750; Fax: 517-546-3731

Luce
County Government Bldg.
407 W. Harrie St.
Newberry 49868
906-293-5601; Fax: 906-293-3581

Mackinac
Courthouse
100 Marley
St. Ignace 49781
906-643-7303

Macomb
Wills & Estates Division
21850 Dunham Rd.
Mt. Clemens 48043
810-469-5290; Fax: 810-783-0971

Manistee
Courthouse
415 Third St.
Manistee 49660
231-723-3261

Marquette
Courthouse Annex
234 W. Baraga
Marquette 49855
906-225-8300; Fax: 906-225-8293

Mason
Courthouse
P. O. Box 186
E. Ludington Ave.
Ludington 49431-0186
231-843-8666

Mecosta
Courthouse
400 Elm St.
P. O. Box 820
Big Rapids 49307
616-592-0136

Menominee
Courthouse
839 Tenth Avenue
Menominee 49858
906-863-2634; Fax: 906-863-8839

Midland
301 W. Main St.
Midland 48640-5183
517-832-6880; Fax: 517-832-6607

Missaukee
111 S. Canal
P. O. Box 800
Lake City 49651
231-839-2266; Fax: 231-839-5856

Monroe
106 E. First St.
Monroe 48161
Probate Register 734-240-7353

Montcalm
Courthouse
211 W. Main
P. O. Box 309
Stanton 48888-0309
517-831-7316; Fax: 517-831-7314

Montmorency
Courthouse
P. O. Box 789
12265-M32
Atlanta 49709
517-785-4403

Muskegon
County Building
990 Terrace St.
Muskegon 49442
616-724-6241; Fax: 616-724-6232

Newaygo
1092 Newell
P. O. Box 885
White Cloud 49349
231-689-7270

Oakland
1200 N. Telegraph Rd.
Pontiac 48341
248-858-0260

Oceana
Oceana County Bldg.
100 S. State St.
Ste. M-34
Hart 49420
231-873-3666; Fax: 231-873-4177

Ogemaw
Ogemaw County Bldg.
806 W. Houghton Ave.
West Branch 48661
517-345-0145; Fax: 517-345-5901

Ontonagon
Courthouse
725 Greenland Rd.
Ontonagon 49953
906-884-4117

Osceola
410 W. Upton
Reed City 49677
Register 231-832-6124

Oscoda
Courthouse Annex
P. O. Box 399
Court Street
Mio 48647
517-826-1107; Fax: 517-826-1126

Otsego
225 W. Main
Rm. 213
Gaylord 49735
517-732-6484

Ottawa
12120 Fillmore St.
West Olive 49460-9672
616-786-4110; Fax: 616-786-4154

Presque Isle
151 E. Huron Ave.
Rogers City 49779
517-734-3268

Roscommon
County Bldg.
P. O. Box 607
Roscommon 48653
517-275-6513

Saginaw
County Building
111 S. Michigan
Saginaw 48602
517-790-5320; Fax: 517-790-5328

St. Clair
201 McMorran Blvd.
Rm. 216
Port Huron 48060
810-985-2066; Fax: 810-985-2179

St. Joseph
Courthouse
P. O. Box 190
125 Main
Centreville 49032
616-467-5538; Fax: 616-467-5560

Sanilac
Courthouse
60 W. Sanilac Ave.
Rm. 106
Sandusky 48471-1096
810-648-3221; Fax: 810-648-2900

Schoolcraft
Schoolcraft County Courthouse
Rm. 129
Manistique 49854
906-341-3641

Shiawassee
County Courts Bldg.
110 E. Mack St.
Corunna 44817
517-743-2211

Tuscola
Courthouse
440 N. State St.
Caro 48723
517-672-3850

Van Buren
Courthouse Annex
212 Paw Paw St.
Paw Paw 49079-1495
616-657-8225; Fax: 616-657-7573

Washtenaw
Courthouse
101 East Huron Street
P. O. Box 8645
Ann Arbor 48107
734-994-2476; Fax: 734-996-3033

Wayne
1305 City-County Building
Two Woodward Ave
Detroit 48226
313-224-5708

Wexford
Courthouse
503 S. Garfield St.
Cadillac 49601
231-779-9510

Appendix C
Grief Support Services

Referrals to sources of grief support services can be obtained from churches, synagogues and temples, hospice organizations, funeral homes, hospitals, and community health centers.

The following is a partial list of sources of grief support services of which the authors are aware in our community and nationally. Services vary considerably from place to place. While most are free, some organizations may charge dues or fees for services. We recommend that you inquire about services and fees when you call a particular program. No listing of this type could be complete, and some of these groups may have changed. Therefore, neither the authors nor the publisher assume responsibility for the accuracy of the information below or level of service provided by these organizations.

Any organization not listed which wishes to be included in a future edition of this book or on the publisher's Web site should forward its information to the publisher at the address listed at the beginning of this book. All listings are in the discretion of the publisher.

Hospice of Michigan
16250 Northland Drive
Southfield, MI 48075
1-888-HOM-5656 (1-888-466-5656)
Web site: http://www.hom.org
Hospice of Michigan offers a wide range of grief support services from its clinics throughout Michigan. Those services include grief support counseling, grief recovery seminars, children and youth services, and mailings to families at regular intervals during the year following the death of a loved one. You may find a schedule of its grief activities in Southeastern Michigan, Western Michigan, and Northern Michigan, at http://www.hom.org/griefschedule.html, or call their toll-free number for information.

Beaumont Hospital
Royal Oak, Michigan
248-551-0775 or 1-800-328-2291

Barbara Ann Karmanos Cancer Institute
313-966-9761 or 1-800-527-6266
Web site: www.karmanos.org

St. John's Hospital (Oakland)
248-967-7323

SPACE: For Changing Families
Drop-in discussion groups for those men and women who are divorced, separated, or widowed. Educational programs. Nondenominational, nonsectarian. Southfield, Michigan.
248-355-9936

AARP Grief and Loss Programs

601 E Street, NW
Washington, DC 20049
202-434-2260; Fax: 202-434-6474
Web site: http://www.aarp.org

AARP provides information, services, and referrals regarding grief support and coping with a loss. AARP Grief and Loss Programs, with local sponsors, offers a variety of program formats to serve bereaved adults of all ages. AARP's programs include: AARP Widowed Persons Service, an outreach program in which trained widowed volunteers reach out to newly widowed persons; AARP Bereavement Outreach Service, an outreach program in which trained volunteers reach out to give peer support to all newly bereaved persons; AARP Widowed Persons Support Groups for newly widowed persons; and AARP Bereavement Support Groups for all bereaved persons. The AARP web site also provides referrals and links to other organizations.

Bereavement and Hospice Support Netline

An online directory of bereavement support groups and services and hospice bereavement programs from across the United States that provides information to help people find appropriate assistance and support in coping with issues of loss and grief. Due to funding cuts in 1997, minimal updates and maintenance have been done to this site; however, it is still a good source of information.
Web site: http://www.ubalt.edu/bereavement/

Grief support where death occurred from a suspicious nature, deaths due to trauma, homicide, deaths of person who have not seen a doctor and have no doctor assigned to them:

Oakland County Medical Examiner
248-858-5097

Support groups for those affected by suicide-homicide:

Survivors of Suicide (S.O.S.)

313-224-7000

Suicide Support Group

For any person affected in any way by a suicide. Birmingham, 248-646-5224

Survivors of Homicide

248-456-0909 or 1-800-231-1127

Groups for widowed men and women:

Rochester: "A New Beginning"
William R. Potere Funeral Home
248-651-8137

Rochester: "You Are Not Alone"
Pixley Memorial Chapel
248-651-9641

Birmingham: "Welcome to Widow"
St. Columban
248-646-5246

Troy: "Personal Approach to Loss"
Desmond Funeral Home
248-362-2500

Royal Oak: Shrine Widowed Group
248-541-5860

Appendix D
Services for Senior Citizens

The following is a partial list of organizations providing services for senior citizens in Michigan and in the Detroit Metropolitan area in particular. Many of these are located in Oakland County, because the source of much of the information was the Oakland County Probate Court Directory of Human Resources, Alpha Agency Listing, which is available at the Oakland County Probate Court's web site link: http://www.co.oakland.mi.usc_serv/ pcourt/guide/contents.html. That Directory has additional information on many of these agencies and others, including location, description of services, eligibility for services, and fees.

If the named agency does not serve your area, a similar agency may do so. The agencies listed below may be able to provide a referral.

This list is not exhaustive and we regret any omissions. If you would like your group considered for inclusion in our next edition, or listing on the publisher's Web site, please contact the publisher at the address at the front of this book. Listing does not imply endorsement by the authors or the publisher, and readers should evaluate organizations, programs, and services before relying upon them.

Information and Referral

Area Agency on Aging 1B
248-948-1640; 1-800-852-7795
Serves Livingston, Macomb, Monroe, Oakland, St. Clair, and Washtenaw counties.

Area Agency on Aging
313-222-5330 (serves Detroit area) and 1-800-815-1112 (serves Western Wayne county)

Birmingham Area Senior Coordinating Council (BASCC)
248-642-1040

Catholic Social Services
Older Adult Services
248-333-3700

Community Services of Oakland
248-542-5860

Cottage Hospital (Henry Ford)
810-779-7900

Deaf and Hearing Impaired Services, Inc.
248-473-1888

Detroit Medical Center
313-886-1600

ElderCare Locater Service
1-800-677-1116

Harper Hospital
Senior Health Center
313-745-1741
(In process of forming support services)

**Henry Ford Hospital
Senior Services Center**
313-874-7200

Jewish Home and Aging Services
248-661-2999

Jewish Information Service
248-967-4357

Lutheran Social Services of Michigan
313-823-7700

Michigan Assisted Living Association
734-525-0831

Michigan Office of Services to the Aging
517-373-8230

**Mt. Clemens General Hospital
Senior Health Services**
810-493-8500

**Oakland Livingston
Human Services Agency**
248-209-2600

Oakwood Hospital
1-800-543-9355 (referral line)

Senior Resource Line
1-800-328-2241

Senior Support Services
248-647-9010

St. John's Hospital - Macomb
248-948-1640; 810-469-6313

St. Joseph Mercy - Oakland
1-800-957-4383

St. Joseph's Hospital - Clinton Township
810-263-2411

United Way of Pontiac - North Oakland
First Call for Help
248-456-8800

**University of Michigan Hospital
Geriatric Center (Ann Arbor)**
734-764-6831

Well Being for Aged Parents
(coping with aged parents)
Madison Heights: 248-967-7700
Southfield: 248-355-9936
Rochester Hills: 248-651-6950

**William Beaumont Hospital
Older Adult Services (OAS)**
248-551-0777

Case Management/ Care Management
Agency Area on Aging
248-52-7795

Counseling
Catholic Social Services
Farmington: 248-471-4140
Pontiac: 248-334-3595
Royal Oak: 248-548-4044
Waterford: 248-559-1500

Jewish Family Services
248-544-4004

Oakland Family Services
Berkley: 248-544-4004
Pontiac: 248-858-7766
Walled Lake: 248-624-3811
Waterford: 248-673-7710

Macomb County Department of Senior Citizen Services
810-469-6313

Elder Care
Citizens for Better Care
1-800-833-9548

OLSHA Senior Services
248-858-5164

Senior Strides Program
248-857-6948

Home Delivered Meals
Emerald Kitchens
248-546-2700

Kosher Mobile Meals
248-967-0967

Mercy Service for Aging
248-473-1812

Oakland County Mobile Meals
248-398-0990

National Health Organizations
Call the National Health Information Center for a complete listing of health organizations dealing with specific health conditions
1-800-336-4797

Medical Care Assistance
North Oakland Medical Center Family Practice (sliding fee scale)
248-857-7432

St. Joseph Outpatient Clinic (sliding fee scale)
248-858-3069

United Way First Call for Help (Prescriptions)
248-456-8800

Volunteer Organizations Providing Services to Seniors
Macomb Family Services, Inc.
Senior Volunteer Program
810-254-5660
Provides services to link homebound Seniors, who are medically at risk, with health care services in the community.

Interfaith Volunteer Caregivers
Interfaith Volunteer Caregivers Projects (IVCPs) are groups of congregations, community agencies, and health care providers working together to develop projects that recruit, train, and mobilize volunteers who provide in-home assistance to those in need. Through the efforts of churches, synagogues, temples, and agencies across the nation, more than 400 IVCPs are now in operation in 45 states.

National Federation of Interfaith Volunteer Caregivers, Inc.
368 Broadway, Suite 103
P. O. Box 1939
Kingston, New York 12401
914-331-1358 or 1-800-350-7438

Flint Area (Interfaith-Interlink)
810-733-7250

Grosse Pointes & Harper Woods (Interfaith Caregivers at S.O.C.)
313-882-9600

Ingham County
(Catholic Charities-Diocese of Lansing)
517-342-2467

Livingston County
(Livingston County Catholic
Social Services)
810-227-2151

Macomb County Interfaith
Volunteer Caregivers
31654 Mound Road
Warren, Michigan 48092
810-983-3633
Provides transportation and help with errands; minor home repairs, maintenance, chores, and yard work; light housekeeping and meal preparation; friendly visits and supportive phone calls; respite care (relief breaks for full-time family caregivers); and other assistance that can help someone remain safely at home.

Monroe County
(Monroe County Interfaith
Volunteer Caregivers)
313-243-2233

Oakland County
(Pontiac Area Lighthouse Caregivers)
248-335-2462

Shiawasee County
(Respite Volunteers of Shiawasee)
517-725-1127

St. Clair County
(St. Clair County Interfaith Volunteer
Caregivers)
810-984-2357

Washtenaw County
(Catholic Social Services of
Washtenaw County)
313-712-2211

Wayne County
(Caring Together)
313-831-7263

Other areas of the state and country:
1-800-350-7438
(National Federation of Interfaith Volunteer
Caregivers)

Other Services
Detroit Radio Information Service
313-577-4146
A radio reading and information service for the blind and print-impaired.

Kenny Foundation
1-800-237-3422
Statewide information and referral service connects people with disabilities, family members, and professionals with resources concerning barrier free design, education, employment, equipment, legislation, recreation and hobbies, support groups, transportation, travel, and more.

Alzheimer's Association
Detroit Area
248-557-8277

Allegan/Ottawa
616-392-8365

East Central Michigan
(Genesee, Lapeer and Shiawassee)
810-767-3737

Marquette/Alger
906-228-3910

Mid-Michigan
(Clare, Tuscola, Gladwin, Arenac, Isabella,
Midland, Bay, Gratiot, and Saginaw)
517-839-4179

Northeastern Michigan
(Alcona, Cheyboygan, Iosco, Montmorency,
Oscoda, Roscommon, Alpena, Crawford,
Ogemaw, Otsego, and Presque Isle)
517-356-4087

Northwest Michigan
(Antrim, Leelanau, Emmet, Wexford,
Kalkaska, and Charlevoix)
1-800-337-3827

South Central Michigan
(Clinton, Eaton, Ingham, Jackson,
Washtenaw, Lenawee, Livingston, Monroe,
and Hillsdale)
1-800-782-6110

West Central Michigan
(Kent, Barry, Ionia, Mecosta, Montcalm, and
Newaygo)
616-949-7890

West Shore
(Muskegon, Oceana, and Mason)
616-726-4456

Southwestern Michigan
(Berrien, Branch, Calhoun, Cass, Kalamazoo,
St. Joseph, and Van Buren)
616-372-3290

NOTES

"Old age is not for sissies."
—Robert Cook

INDEX

. . . .

"The trick of it is to stop thinking of it as *your* money."
—IRS Auditor

This page intentionally left blank.

How to Order Additional Copies of this Book

Additional copies of this book may be ordered by mailing a check to the order of Carob Tree Press, LLC, in the amount of $24.95 per book, plus 6% Michigan sales tax for orders to Michigan addresses, plus $5.00 shipping and handling per book (via U.S. Post Office Priority Mail), with your name and address, to:

Carob Tree Press, LLC
211 West Fort Street, 15th Floor
Detroit, Michigan 48226-3281

You may also order on our Web site: http://www.carobtreepress.com, where arrangements have been made for credit card charges.

This book is also available at special quantity discounts when purchased in bulk by corporations, organizations, or groups. For more information please contact Carob Tree Press at 1-877-537-4178 (toll-free), via fax at 313-983-3325, or via E-mail: inquiries@carobtreepress.com.